War on Terror

Unfolding Bible Prophecy

Dr. Grant R. Jeffrey

Frontier Research Publications, Inc.
P.O. Box 129, Station "U", Toronto, Ontario M8Z 5M4

War on Terror

ISBN 0-7394-2441-6

Unless otherwise indicated, Scripture quotations are from the Authorized King James Version.

Cover design: The Riordon Design Group

Comments on Grant Jeffrey's
best-selling books

ARMAGEDDON	•	MESSIAH
APOCALYPSE	•	THE PRINCE OF DARKNESS
FINAL WARNING	•	THE SIGNATURE OF GOD
HEAVEN	•	THE HANDWRITING OF GOD
MILLENNIUM MELTDOWN	•	PROPHECY STUDY BIBLE
FLEE THE DARKNESS	•	BY DAWN'S EARLY LIGHT
MYSTERIOUS BIBLE CODES	•	JESUS: THE GREAT DEBATE
SPEAR OF TYRANNY	•	JOURNEY INTO ETERNITY
SURVEILLANCE SOCIETY	•	TRIUMPHANT RETURN

"Grant Jeffrey has written an extraordinary new book, *The Signature of God*, that provides astonishing proof that the Bible was inspired by God. Grant is recognized as the leading researcher in Bible Prophecy today."
Hal Lindsey, Hal Lindsey Ministries

"The *Prophecy Study Bible* is a phenomenal publishing effort by one of America's premier prophecy experts. Comprehensive, understandable, and powerful. A great work!"   *Dr. Ed Hindsen, Editor – Jesus Study Bible*

"The *Prophecy Study Bible* is the most comprehensive, contemporary, and in-depth study of the most relevant prophecies in the Bible — A must addition to every serious student of the Word of God."
Dr. Chuck Missler – Koinonia House Ministries

"*Prince of Darkness* was written by acclaimed Bible Prophecy teacher Grant R. Jeffrey. This unequaled masterpiece is the result of 30 years of intense research. It will stir you and inspire you as few books have. . . . It is extremely well written — extraordinarily researched and fascinatingly presented . . . this is the best book I have ever read on this subject."   *Jack Van Impe, Jack Van Impe Ministries*

"*Armageddon: Appointment With Destiny* has been our hottest single religious title. . . . We took it on with tremendous enthusiasm because there was something very exciting about the way Grant wrote, and it was something that we thought might go beyond the traditional religious audience."   *Lou Arnonica, Vice President,*
Bantam Books, New York Times, October 22, 1990

"We are excited about Grant Jeffrey's new book. . . . Now the book with the latest information on prophetic fulfilment, the book of the nineties, is *Armageddon: Appointment With Destiny*. It will show that God is in control and, most importantly, it will also prove to be a powerful witnessing tool to those who need Christ."   *David Mainse: Host, 100 Huntley Street*

Table of Contents

Acknowledgments

War on Terror: Unfolding Bible Prophecy explores the motives and plans of the Islamic terrorists whose goal is the destruction of our way of life. This book also documents the evidence that Iraq and other Middle East nations have supported the al Qaeda terrorist attacks against America as well as other targets including Israel.

This book will demonstrate that we are now engaged in an unprecedented war against global Islamic terrorists who are powerfully backed by eight nations in the Middle East that have demonstrated repeatedly that they desire the destruction of America, Israel, and the rest of the nations of the West that support democracy, religious and political choice, and the freedom to live your life as you desire.

The tragedy of September 11, 2001 awakened everyone to the evil goals of the Islamic terrorists led by Osama bin Laden and his numerous allies. Fortunately, the United States and her allies are absolutely committed in their determination to destroy those who seek to destroy their nation and their freedom. We will win this unprecedented war against Islamic terror because there is no other option. Fortunately, America is now led by President George W. Bush, a man who believes in Jesus Christ as his Savior, and who understands the true nature of the evil threat posed by thousands of terrorists, as well as the nations who provided them

7

with funds, intelligence, communications, and support. The only way to defeat global Islamic terrorism is to "drain the swamp" by defeating those nations who provide them with support in their deadly attacks on both Israel and the West. Rather that succumb to fear, those who have faith in God should realize that we are rapidly approaching the time when Jesus Christ as our Messiah will return to set up His holy Kingdom on earth forever.

Jesus Christ declared: "And when these things begin to come to pass, then look up, and lift up your heads; for your redemption draweth nigh" (Luke 21:28).

My parents, Lyle and Florence Jeffrey, inspired me by their lifelong commitment to the prophecies of His Second Coming and a profound love for Jesus. Special thanks to my editorial assistant, Adrienne Jeffrey Tigchelaar, and Rick Blanchette for his excellent editorial services.

I dedicate *War on Terror* to my loving wife Kaye. She continues to inspire my research and writing as well as being my faithful partner in the publishing ministry of Frontier Research Publications, Inc. Without her encouragement and constant assistance this book would never have been completed.

I trust that my research will inform, inspire, and encourage you to personally study the Bible's prophecies about the remarkable prophetic events in these last days that set the stage for the return of Christ.

Dr. Grant R. Jeffrey
Toronto, Ontario
January, 2002

Introduction

The world changed forever on September 11, 2001. All of us who love freedom and religious liberty should realize that we are now involved in a worldwide war against terror. Islamic terrorists are committed to the destruction of our freedom and our way of life. Their openly declared goal is to replace our democratic governments with an unprecedented extremist Islamic regime similar to the Taliban government in Afghanistan from 1996 until their defeat in December, 2001. All who love religious freedom and democracy are now "in harm's way." Tens of thousands of fanatic Islamic terrorists who now hide in over sixty nations across the globe have declared war on our democratic nations, our citizens, and our western values of freedom and choice. We can and will win this war against terror. However, it will take years for the nations involved in the alliance against terror to defeat the tens of thousands of Islamic terrorists as well as the eight Middle Eastern nations that support terror attacks against the West. It is vital that we stay the course until we defeat these extremist Islamic terrorists.

The West has been governed for several centuries by Judeo-Christian values derived from the Bible and the philosophy of spiritual and intellectual freedom introduced since the Reformation. The Islamic terrorists violently reject our modern western values of religious, intellectual, and political freedom, free enterprise, democracy, and respect for human rights. They have openly committed themselves to destroy western culture and civilization.

This book will explore the origin and progress of the continuing "War against Terror" that the western nations and their allies have launched against the terror groups who cravenly killed more than three thousand innocent men, women, and children on September 11, 2001. The only "crime" of these thousands of people in the sight of the terrorists was that they were citizens of the United States of America. However, the three thousand plus innocent victims included hundreds of citizens from over seventy nations including Christians, Jews, Muslims, and those of other faiths. The nineteen fundamentalist Islamic assassins did not care about their victims' beliefs, politics, religion, or race. The terrorists' goal was simply to kill the largest possible number of innocent Americans to create fear, terror, and confusion within the population as well as in the political leadership of the West.

The ultimate goal of the Islamic terrorists is clearly spelled out in the 1996 "Declaration of War" against the West issued by the al Qaeda terrorist leader Osama bin Laden. Their goal is the complete physical and moral destruction of the western nations as well as of the non-fundamentalist Arab governments such as Jordan, Saudi Arabia, and Egypt. The terrorist groups Islamic Jihad and al Qaeda, united under the leadership of Osama bin Laden, are determined to overthrow all governments in the world and replace them with extreme fundamentalist Islamic governments similar to the fanatic Taliban regime that ruled in Afghanistan. Their ultimate goal is the forced conversion—accept Islam or die—of all the people on earth to their extremist Islamic faith.

These extremist goals and methods of the terrorist Islamic fundamentalists are rejected by an overwhelming majority of over a billion Muslims who follow the faith of Islam throughout the world. The Taliban in Afghanistan killed other Muslims that reject their more extreme views. However, the unrelenting hate-filled Islamic propaganda against Americans and Jews has motivated a whole generation of Muslims throughout the world to express a certain degree of sympathy for these outrageous and evil attacks on September 11, 2001. It is essential that moderate Muslim governments join in the effort to suppress the despicable and evil attacks on the West and upon the Jewish people. They need to teach their populations to accept the right of other nations and other faiths to exist in freedom as well as their own citizens' right to experience the religious freedom to worship as they choose.

For the last two decades, the fundamentalist Islamic terrorists and the nations that support them have enjoyed many victories against the western nations without paying the price for their outrageous terrorist attacks. Beginning with the terrible bombing of the U.S. Marine barracks in Beirut in 1983, killing 241 marines, Islamic terrorists experienced an unbroken series of victories because the West had not yet awakened to the true nature and reality of this war to the death between extremist Islamic terrorists and western nations. The list of major attacks by the terrorists also include: the brutal massacre of 18 U.S. soldiers in Mogadishu, Somalia, in 1993; the 1993 bombing of the World Trade Center; the 1996 attacks on U.S. troop barracks in Saudi Arabia; the 1998 bombings of two American embassies in Africa; the terrorist attack on the destroyer U.S.S. Cole in 2000, and the unprecedented destruction of the twin towers of the World Trade Center causing over three thousand deaths and the attack on the Pentagon on September 11, 2001. Only the incredibly heroic actions of the passengers on United Flight 93 saved us from another flying bomb hitting another important target, such as the five nuclear power plants 150 miles northwest of Washington.

Our war against international Islamic terrorism is a campaign directed at the tens of thousands of extremist Islamic terrorists who have already launched hundreds of terrorist attacks against western and Israeli interests in the last three decades. This is not a war against Islam. The evidence suggests that less than one tenth of one percent of those who are Muslims are part of the fanatical and extremist terror groups who support and dedicate their lives to Osama bin Laden and his numerous associated groups including Hamas, Egypt's Islamic Jihad, Hezbollah, and other terrorist groups. The vast majority of the hundreds of millions who follow Mohammed do not support the fanatical terrorists and their determination to destroy the West. Many Islamic clergy have publicly rejected the terrorists' beliefs and have stated that the fanatics are in violation of the genuine teachings of Islam. Millions of innocent Islamic people have freely chosen to migrate to the western nations to enjoy our political and religious freedom as well as our economic opportunities.

The truth is that these Islamic Jihad fundamentalist terrorists pose an even greater and more violent immediate threat to the Arab governments of the Middle East (Egypt, Jordan, Saudi Arabia, Algeria, et cetera) than they do to Israel, Europe, or America. Osama bin Laden has also declared war against all Arab and Islamic governments that refuse to embrace his extreme and diabolical hatred of the West and the Jewish state of Israel.

The terrorist cells of Osama bin Laden attempted to assassinate Egypt's president Mubarak in 1995 and tried to assassinate the Muslim president of Tajikistan (just north of Afghanistan) in 1999. Several days before the devastating attacks on the World Trade Center in New York and the Pentagon in Washington on September 11, 2001, bin Laden provided a service to his Afghanistan Taliban hosts by sending two of his suicide bombers to assassinate the popular Muslim leader of the anti-Taliban forces, General Ahmed Shah Massoud, the head of the Northern Alliance. Pretending to be Algerian journalists desiring to interview Massoud, these terrorists triggered a bomb hidden in their TV camera, which killed themselves and the Northern Alliance leader. Yasser el-Sirri, a well-known Egyptian Islamic activist in England, was arrested in London on October 30, 2001, and charged under Britain's new Terrorism Act in connection with this assassination of Massoud. The prosecution charged Yasser el-Sirri with providing the suicide bombers with a letter of accreditation allowing them to interview Massoud and thereby kill him according to an October 31, 2001 article in the *Toronto Star*.

War against Terror: Unfolding Bible Prophecy will explore the nature and history of the terror supporting nations and the terrorist groups that have now declared war against America, Israel, and the nations of the West who defend religious freedom and democracy for their citizens. We will examine the history and activities of these terrorist groups. Then we will analyze the powerful alliance against terror that will now bring the financial, diplomatic, police, and military forces of the civilized world against these groups of fanatical Islamic terrorists that seek to destroy our way of life.

This book will also explore the numerous prophecies found in both the Old and New Testaments that predict a time of unparalleled fear and terror that will prevail in the days leading up to the triumphant return of Jesus Christ to establish His Kingdom of God. The Lord specifically warned Christians that humanity would experience an unprecedented time of trouble in the last days. Jesus prophesied that this would be a very frightening time: "Men's hearts failing them for fear, and for looking after those things which are coming on the earth: for the powers of heaven shall be shaken" (Luke 21:26).

Fortunately, Christ concluded His prophecy with the positive prediction that these troubled times would be an unmistakable sign of His approaching Second Coming. The Lord promised His followers, "And when these things begin to come to pass, then look up, and lift up your heads; for your redemption draweth nigh" (Luke 21:28). The message of prophecy is not one of "doom and gloom" as some have suggested, but rather prophecy promises "redemption" at the return of Christ to establish the kingdom of God.

In other words, instead of being filled with fear, those who follow Jesus Christ should recognize these remarkable prophetic events as unmistakable signs of the soon coming of our Messiah to set up His kingdom of righteousness on earth. While we are naturally concerned for the safety of our family and our nations, we need to realize that a time of unparalleled troubles was prophesied to occur throughout the globe during the generation preceding the triumphant return of Christ as King of Kings and Lord of Hosts. We should recognize the clear teaching of Christ through the inspired words of the apostle Paul: "Wherefore I put thee in remembrance that thou stir up the gift of God, which is in thee by the putting on of my hands. For God hath not given us the spirit of fear; but of power, and of love, and of a sound mind" (II Timothy 1:6–7).

When we are confronted by dangers to both our nation and

our loved ones, we need to realize that our lives as Christians are under the supernatural protection of Jesus Christ. Nothing can happen to those who love Christ unless He permits it to occur because it is part of His divine will. In the book of Hebrews we find this encouraging message: "The Lord is my helper, and I will not fear what man shall do unto me" (Hebrews 13:6).

In the book of Psalms King David recorded some of the most profound thoughts ever set to pen. In Psalm 120 David spoke of the terrible terror and hatred of the surrounding enemy tribes. David declared: "My soul hath long dwelt with him that hateth peace. I am for peace: but when I speak, they are for war" (Psalm 120:6–7).

King David then wrote his inspired psalm, Psalm 121, that reminds those who trust in God that our real protection and help comes from the Lord in heaven:

I will lift up mine eyes unto the hills, from whence cometh my help. My help cometh from the Lord, which made heaven and earth. He will not suffer thy foot to be moved: he that keepeth thee will not slumber. Behold, he that keepeth Israel shall neither slumber nor sleep. The Lord is thy keeper: the Lord is thy shade upon thy right hand. The sun shall not smite thee by day, nor the moon by night. The Lord shall preserve thee from all evil: he shall preserve thy soul. The Lord shall preserve thy going out and thy coming in from this time forth, and even for evermore. (Psalm 121:1–8)

1

The September 11 Terrorist Attack on America Mobilizing Democracy for the War against Terror

We are now involved in a life and death war against Islamic terrorism that will take several years to successfully eradicate the tens of thousands of Muslim terrorists who have dedicated themselves to the destruction of Christianity, Judaism, Israel, and the West. However, with the resolve that democracies have historically demonstrated when attacked by their foes, we will marshal the military, intelligence, and political forces of the West to utterly destroy those terrorists who have declared war on our freedoms, our right to religious choice, and our modern democratic values.

The Islamic terrorists who despise our western way of life have learned that democracies are very soft and reluctant to respond initially to obvious dangers that threaten their way of life. However, once awakened to the true dangers, democracies are a much more formidable opponent to their enemies than any totalitarian dictatorship. Historically, democracies that have been attacked unjustly by their enemies awaken to defend their territory and rights with a vigorous and relentless defense that demands nothing less than the total military destruction of the enemy that first attacked it.

Following December 7, 1941, Admiral Yamamoto of the Imperial Japanese Fleet acknowledged that Japan had succeeded in inflicting a massive military blow against America at Pearl Harbor. However, he wisely warned his enthusiastic colleagues that their initial success would be followed within months by an enormous and sustained military response by the American nation that would never relent until they had utterly destroyed the Japanese Empire. Admiral Yamamoto had spent many years during the 1920s and 1930s inspecting the vast industrial strength of America, long before U.S. industry had been mobilized for modern warfare. He realized that America, once motivated to engage in total war, would wreck devastating vengeance against its Japanese attackers. When the vast American industrial machine mobilized for wartime production it began to produce rifles, tanks, ships, and airplanes on a scale that no one had ever imagined. For example, in August 1945, the last month of World War II, the U.S. armaments industry manufactured over 9,000 C-47 military cargo planes. Once the U.S. armaments industry mobilized for total war, it was capable of producing astonishing levels of armaments that overwhelmed both Germany and Japan's industrial production and their military forces.

The world now faces the prospect of a protracted, violent, and costly multi-year war to eradicate the deadly threat from the Islamic extremists who have declared war on the very freedoms and values that make our western world unique and precious. While this unprecedented war on terror will test the political resolve, the military capabilities, and the moral resources of the population and leadership of the western nations, we will succeed in defeating the terrorist-supporting nations as well as the thousands of deadly terrorists. These Islamic terrorists will discover a terrible truth: America can be a wonderful friend, but it can also be a ruthless and deadly enemy to those who attack her.

For the last three decades eight Arab nations have provided massive financial, intelligence, weapons, training camps and protective support for thousands of terrorists who have dedicated their lives to the destruction of Israel and the western nations. These eight terrorist supporting states include: Afghanistan, Iraq, Sudan, Yemen, Syria, Iran, Somalia, and Libya. When our coalition against terror destroys their terrorist support bases, their vast financial resources, and the powerful intelligence resources of the eight nation states that support terrorism, thousands of individual terrorists will gradually lose their ability to stage massive attacks against our citizens and cities. Eventually, the scourge of international terrorism will be reduced to the status of a continuing police and justice problem.

This is a war that we must win. It is a war that we will win if we maintain the same unyielding resolve that our fathers' generation maintained when faced with the tremendous World War II challenge from the Nazi and Japanese assault on our nations.

The September 11 Attacks: Was There No Warning?

America and the western world were shocked when thousands of innocent lives were destroyed by the four terrorist hijacking attacks on September 11 together with the unprecedented destruction of the multiple towers of the World Trade Center complex, the four planes, and the Pentagon. Hundreds of billions of dollars were lost in the widespread economic devastation from the physical destruction of the WTC, the lost jobs, landsliding stock market losses, massive retail and manufacturing losses, failed businesses, and the impact on the general economic recession.

Evidence from captured videos reveals that the terrorists, including Osama bin Laden, were astonished at the massive physical damage they accomplished with the four hijacked airplanes together with the enormous economic losses that have reverberated throughout the economies of the western world in the months following the attacks. However, I also believe that bin Laden never, in his worst nightmare, dreamed that his evil terrorist attacks would awaken the sleeping giant of America and unleash the overwhelming military power of the United States and its western coalition against terror.

Was there no warning to alert our intelligence and police about a terrorist attack such as the September 11 simultaneous hijackings and attacks on major buildings? Tragically, the answer is that there were multiple warnings about a coming Islamic terrorist terror attack against major American targets. The problem is that these warnings were ignored. In 1995, two captured al Qaeda Islamic terrorists revealed detailed plans to hijack and bomb up to twelve American passenger jets over Asia as well as another plan to hijack several jets and fly them into the White House, the Pentagon, and the CIA headquarters in Langley, Virginia. Evidence was gathered that al Qaeda was using flight simulators to train their terrorist pilots to attack very high office towers.

Thirty years ago, in September 1970, four terrorist teams from the Popular Front for the Liberation of Palestine hijacked four airplanes simultaneously (Pan American, BOAC, TWA, and Swiss Air). The four planes were blown up after they were forced by the terrorists to fly to an airport in Jordan. Finally, in August 2001, an Arab named Musseff who requested training in flying at a flight school in Illinois was arrested by the FBI after they were alerted by the manager that Musseff insisted that he be trained to steer a Boeing 747 in flight but did not want to learn to take off or land the passenger jet. When arrested, the man refused to talk and remains in custody. He has now been indicted in the terrorist plot. When you consider the cumulative evidence, it is simply not true that our police and intelligence agencies had no warning of the September 11 attacks.

Many people are asking why the $31 billion spent annually on counterterrorism utterly failed to warn American intelligence authorities of the devastating terror attacks on the World Trade Center and the Pentagon. The answer is complicated. First, the powerful intelligence capabilities of the Central Intelligence Agency, the National Security Agency, and the Federal Bureau of Investigation were intentionally gutted years ago by the U.S. Congress following the 1978 Senator Church Intelligence

Committee hearings held under the authority of President Jimmy Carter. Following disturbing revelations of a variety of poorly planned spying missions and failed assassination attempts against Fidel Castro and other enemies, the U.S. Congress passed laws and the president issued executive orders that effectively eliminated the ability of U.S. intelligence agencies to develop human intelligence sources in enemy nations.

Following the 1978 Senate intelligence hearings, over eight hundred of America's most experienced CIA intelligence case officers were fired or resigned. This eliminated our ability to acquire meaningful information from people willing to risk their lives to betray their dictatorial and communist governments. Experienced case officers like these are the core of an effective intelligence agency's human intelligence resource. It takes decades to train them, and they cannot be quickly replaced. In addition, American national security agencies had very few Arab-speaking officers capable of analyzing the thousands of messages intercepted by our surveillance systems.

A presidential executive order prohibited U.S. intelligence agencies from becoming involved in assassination attempts against foreign heads of governments. Incredibly, in the mid-1990s, an executive presidential order was given by President Clinton that prevented American intelligence agencies from hiring anyone as an agent or informant who had a criminal record or had been accused of human rights abuse. This insane law made it virtually impossible for our national security agencies to penetrate the Islamic terrorist cells or to effectively spy upon our other enemies in nations such as Russia, China, and the Middle East. This restriction was the equivalent of asking the FBI to penetrate the Mafia but forbidding them to use any informers who have a criminal or unsavory background. You cannot penetrate a criminal organization or an Islamic terror cell with a group of Sunday school teachers. Criminal investigations would simply dry up if our police were forbidden to employ criminal informers and make plea bargain deals with lower level criminals to develop valuable information to enable them to convict drug lords and organized crime figures.

Similarly, the previous restrictions on our intelligence agencies and the elimination of eight hundred of our most experienced spy handling case officers following the 1978 Church Senate committee hearings tied the hands of those remaining U.S. security people trained to develop the necessary information to protect our national interests. The virtual elimination of our human intelligence resources throughout the world since 1978 forced American intelligence agencies to depend almost entirely upon the electronic intelligence information developed from our sophisticated spy satellites, intercepted electronic communications, and incredibly detailed photographs from spy planes and space-based satellite systems that can photograph the name of a manufacturer printed on a golf ball from ten miles in space. Unfortunately, while such electronic surveillance systems work very well against sophisticated industrial societies such as Russia, China, or Serbia, they are almost useless against a terrorist cell of the al Qaeda group hiding in caves in very primitive terror supporting states such as Iraq, Somalia, Yemen, or the mountains of Afghanistan.

Finally, after the horror of watching thousands of innocent Americans die because of the intelligence failure of the FBI and CIA, the U.S. Congress and president have now passed new laws letting intelligence and counterterrorism agencies "off the leash" so they can do their job effectively. Unfortunately, it will take years to rebuild our critical human intelligence operations and "deep cover" sources around the globe.

Israel's Mossad Warned of the Terror Attacks

The British *Sunday Telegraph* newspaper reported on September 16, 2001, that Israel's Mossad intelligence agency officials flew to Washington in August 2001 to warn the CIA and the FBI that an Islamic terrorist cell of as many as two hundred agents was planning a major terrorist attack on America in the immediate future. The paper reported that the Israeli officials specifically warned their intelligence counterparts in Washington, D.C., that "large-scale terrorist attacks on highly visible targets on the American mainland were imminent."

While there was no information identifying specific targets, Israeli intelligence actually linked the terrorist plot to Afghanistan-based terrorist Osama bin Laden. They also revealed that their sources provided "strong grounds" for suspecting the involvement of Iraq as the nation supporting this threatened bin Laden attack. Incredibly, an American administration official admitted to the *Sunday Telegraph* paper that it was "quite credible" that the CIA and FBI failed to pay serious attention to the Israeli warning: "It [the CIA and FBI] has a history of being overcautious about Israeli information." However, the U.S. official admitted that "if this is true, then the refusal to take it seriously will mean heads will roll."[1]

Unfortunately, no amount of after-the-fact analysis of Iraq's attack will change the situation that allowed a devastating terrorist attack to destroy the lives of more than three thousand innocent Americans.

Terrorism Warnings Before the September 11 Bombings

On September 17, 2001, FBI Director Robert Mueller insisted his agency had "no warning signs" prior to the terrorist attacks.[2] As the above information on the warnings given to the FBI by Israeli intelligence confirms, Mueller's comment is not exactly true.

In 1995 an al Qaeda Islamic terrorist named Abdul Hakim Murad was arrested by Philippines' investigators after a fire occurred on January 6, 1995, in the Manila apartment hideout of Ramzi Yousef. He had been building a large bomb. In the confusion, Ramzi Yousef escaped, but he was eventually captured in Pakistan and was finally extradited to New York, where he was sentenced to life in prison for his role in the 1993 bombing of the World Trade Center with several other bin Laden terrorists. Abdul Hakim Murad confessed that he was a partner of Ramzi Yousef, who was planning the simultaneous hijacking of several passenger planes that would be flown into the CIA headquarters in Langley, Virginia, the Pentagon, and the White House. Murad was convicted of terrorism and is now serving a life sentence.

Rodolfo Mendoza, a Philippine intelligence investigator stated, "Murad narrated to us about a plan by the Ramzi cell in the continental U.S. to hijack a commercial plane and ram it into the CIA headquarters in Langley, Virginia, and also the Pentagon." Significantly, Murad was a pilot with a U.S. commercial pilot's license obtained on June 8, 1992. Philippine intelligence investigators declared that they told the FBI that they had found evidence from Murad for plans to target commercial towers in San Francisco, Chicago, and New York City. The FBI has evidence that both Yousef and Murad are members of Osama bin Laden's al Qaeda.[3]

Another bin Laden terror plot against U.S. aviation was confirmed in 1995 when intelligence investigators in the Philippines found detailed terrorist plans encrypted in Ramzi Yousef's laptop computer. The information on Yousef's laptop was encrypted; however, the investigators were successful in obtaining the secret password to enable them to unlock the hidden messages on his hard drive. They were stunned to realize that the laptop contained extensive plans for the simultaneous hijacking and bombing of twelve U.S. airlines flying overseas in the Pacific within a forty-eight-hour period.[4]

In light of the growing chorus of intelligence warnings from European and Middle Eastern nations, including very specific warning from Israel's Mossad, it is almost incomprehensible that no specific airline security precautions were taken in the months before the four tragic hijackings on September 11, 2001.

Suspicious Insider Trading by al Qaeda Terrorists

Most investors follow an investment strategy of "buying low and selling high." However, a small number of sophisticated investors counter this trend by purposely buying options known as "puts." They also sell stocks short today at a high price with the expectation that the stock will fall in price in the near future. Then they can complete the transaction by buying the stock at the lower price to complete the transaction and make a huge profit on the difference in price. Put options are purchased by investors who are convinced that a stock will soon fall in price. When the stock does fall, the purchaser of the put option or the short seller of stocks is able to make a great deal of money. Naturally, securities investigators closely watch the behavior of such adventurous investors to make certain that they are not making their investments or speculations on the basis of some illicit insider knowledge about the stock that the general investing public does not know about.

In the days following the devastating September 11, 2001

World Trade Center bombings, securities regulators were alerted to a number of very suspicious stock transactions in companies that suffered major price falls due to their connection with the terrorist attacks. Counterterrorism investigators have traced bin Laden's vast investments of al Qaeda and Taliban heroin profits for several years. According to a study by Don Radlauer, a futures investment expert, the evidence clearly points to al Qaeda's advance knowledge of the September 11th attack.[5]

It is already clear that some trades were made with illicit advance knowledge of the September 11 terror attacks. The Chicago Board Options Exchange noted that several investors made the unusual decision to purchase 4,744 put options of United Airlines stock on September 6 and 7, although no publicly available information justified this speculative investment. However, immediately following the September 11 terrorist attack, United Airlines stock dropped 42 percent, from $30.82 per share to $17.50. If the securities investigators are correct, those investors who purchased these "puts" on United Airlines stock made almost $5 million in illegal profits due to their assumed advance knowledge of the coming attacks.

According to the Chicago Board Options Exchange, only one day before the aircraft terror attacks someone purchased 4,516 put options on American Airlines even though there was no news to justify an expectation that America Airline's stock would fall. However, when the market reopened, American Airlines stock immediately fell 39 percent, from $29.70 to $18.00 per share. This would provide a potential illicit gain of $4 million to investors who may have known about the coming attack. It is significant that no other U.S. airline was subject to these unusual investment strategies just prior to the attacks using United and American Airlines flights. Investigators noted that similar unusual speculation in the shares of Morgan Stanley Dean Witter & Co., an investment company that occupied twenty-two floors of the World Trade Center, took place during the three days prior to the attack. When Morgan Stanley's share price immediately fell from $48.90 to $42.50 following the attacks, investigators calculated that the inside traders who probably knew about the coming terrorist bombing were able to make approximately $1.2 million.[6]

American and international finance ministers as well as banking and stock exchange officials throughout the world are now trying to identify, track, and seize the hundreds of millions of dollars in the bank accounts, investments, and assets of Osama bin Laden's al Qaeda terrorist network. This is just one new method that we must use to fight the new war on terrorism.

Airline Security

The damage done to North America's economy, including more than $100 billion in physical damage to New York City, is far greater than any counterterrorism expert would ever have estimated prior to the bombings. Over a $1 trillion of stock market and bond losses in North America alone have re-emphasized the dangers to our way of life from Islamic terrorists who are dedicated to the destruction of America and her allies.

One of the greatest tragedies about September 11 is that relatively simple and inexpensive changes in our airline security procedures that could have been easily implemented would have made the simultaneous hijacking attack with four planes almost impossible. Over the last few years, my wife Kaye and I have been appalled by the totally inadequate and incompetent airline security procedures throughout North America. It was common to see the cockpit door left wide open for hours during a flight. Even if the cockpit door was closed, it was purposely designed to be so weak that it could be kicked down from either side. The pilots' association refused to agree to strengthening security by replacing the fragile doors with stronger steel doors with powerful locks. They claimed that a totally secure door might cause danger to the pilots if there was a decompression of the passenger area. They suggested that the difference in air pressure might cause severe damage to the cockpit team. However, a small opening allowing air pressure to equalize in such a crisis would solve that problem without compromising airline security by utilizing fragile cockpit doors.

While airport security screening in Europe and many other nations is performed by well-trained police or military personnel, most airport security screening staff in America and Canada are poorly paid, minimally trained, unmotivated, and very inexperienced due to more than 100 percent turnover of staff every year. Most airport security personnel are contracted out to international security companies who win contracts from the airlines by offering the lowest possible bid. The North American practice of placing airport security screening under the control and expense of individual airlines places them in a direct and inevitable conflict of interest that adds to the problem of protecting passengers. The airlines are desperate to keep their planes on time and to move their passengers as quickly as possible into their seats. In the years before September 11, 2001, North American airlines repeatedly refused to introduce consistent and effective security procedures because of the inevitable costs, possible delays, and occasional inconvenience to their passengers.

A few months before the World Trade Center bombing, I followed a male passenger through airport security who was carrying a hunting knife on his belt with at least a six-inch blade. When I questioned the security supervisor about this obvious danger to other passengers, he shrugged and told me to mind my own business. Over the past decade, both FBI and FAA inspectors have repeatedly tested airport security by sending investigators dressed as civilians through the screening equipment carrying handguns, knives, grenades, stun guns, explosives, and mace. Despite the sophisticated X-ray technology, the airport security personnel missed the majority of the test weapons even when the investigator purposely acted in an aggressive, guilty, or fearful manner.

Changes are only now beginning to be made to the airplanes, airports, and passenger security systems. Cockpit doors are now being reinforced to protect pilots from attack. The U.S. government will now play a more active role in airline security, with baggage checkers ultimately falling under federal jurisdiction. Specially trained air marshals dressed in civilian clothes and armed with low-powered but accurate pistols will now be flying on all U.S. flights. Airlines have now restricted the amount of carry-on luggage we may carry on board. I hope this is only the beginning and that all aspects of airline safety will be scrutinized and improved. Much more needs to be done to assure proper security against future terrorist attacks.

Endnotes

1. *Sunday Telegraph*, 16 Sept. 2001.
2. *Washington Post*, 17 Sept. 2001.
3. Maria Ressa. CNN. 18 Sept. 2001.
4. Maria Ressa. CNN. 18 Sept. 2001.
5. Don Radlauer. "Black Tuesday: The World's Largest Insider Trading Scam?" 19 Sept. 2001. http://www.ict.org.il/articles/articledet.cfm?articleid=386.
6. Don Radlauer. "Black Tuesday: The World's Largest Insider Trading Scam?" 19 Sept. 2001. http://www.ict.org.il/articles/articledet.cfm?articleid=386.

2

Who Are the Terrorists?

Many people are confused about the identity and purpose of the Islamic terrorists who have declared war on America. Despite months of watching CNN commentators and reading countless newspapers, the average citizen is still unable to determine the agenda of the enemy. This chapter will attempt to explain who the terrorists are, and what they hope to achieve.

Who Is Osama bin Laden?

Osama bin Laden was born in 1957 in Riyad, Saudi Arabia. His full name is Osama bin Mohammed bin Laden. He is one of fifty children born to a man named Mohammed bin Laden who became extremely wealthy by building an enormous construction company in Saudi Arabia. Bin Laden's father, Mohammed bin Laden, became a close friend of several royal princes of Saudi Arabia. He rapidly built his construction company and was given the important and very lucrative contract to rebuild the enormous Muslim holy places in Mecca and Medina, the two most holy sites in Islam.

In 1973, after several years of living as a wealthy Arab playboy, enjoying the fleshpots of Beirut, et cetera, Osama became seriously interested in Islam and entered into religious studies with several extremist Muslim teachers. These Islamic scholars instilled within Osama a fanatical hatred of Jews, Christians, and the western world. One Arab journalist who had the opportunity to spend some time with bin Laden has reported that he "wants to die a martyr and believes he will go to heaven."[1]

Osama travelled to Afghanistan in the late 1980s to join the Afghan fighters to resist the brutal Soviet occupation of that country. He provided millions of dollars from his inheritance and fought side by side with the Afghan fighters. The CIA assisted the Afghans with money, ammunition, and especially Stinger surface-to-air missiles that shot down hundreds of Russian helicopters until the USSR gave up and retreated in 1989.

When Iraq invaded Kuwait in August 1990, the United States responded by assembling a massive western military force including 700,000 U.S. soldiers in the deserts of Saudi Arabia in preparation for a devastating invasion of Iraq. In the spring of 1991, the American air force succeeded in destroying the Iraqi air force in six weeks and then rapidly overwhelming Saddam Hussein's Republican Guard, the fourth largest army in the world. While most Saudi citizens rejoiced in the United States' protection of their nation from the ravenous attack of the brutal Iraqi army, Osama bin Laden was outraged by the presence of Christian and Jewish American soldiers in the deserts of his country, "the birthplace of Islam," even though U.S. soldiers were protecting Saudi Arabia from Iraq.

When bin Laden openly engaged in anti-government political activities that severely criticized the Saudi royal family, he was expelled to Sudan in 1994. Subsequently, the Saudi government canceled his passport and citizenship, as well as freezing all of his financial assets in Saudi Arabia. Osama ran the family construction business in Sudan for several years and continued to build up his army of al Qaeda terrorists from his new headquarters in Khartoum, Sudan. His forces launched several terrorist attacks against American troops in Somalia.

Following the devastating bombings of two American embassies in Nairobi, Kenya, and Dar-es-Salam, Somalia, on August 7, 1998 (killing several hundred and wounding over five thousand), the Sudanese government responded to powerful pressure from the United States and expelled all al Qaeda terrorists from the country. Osama traveled to Afghanistan in 1996 and set up his secret bases in a series of huge caverns hidden deep within the rugged mountains of that desolate nation. He solidified his alliance with the fanatical Taliban government and its leader Mohammed Omar, who Osama had befriended. Osama actually became the de facto finance minister of the extremist Taliban government, charged with handling its hundreds of millions of annual earnings from the cultivation and export of over 80 percent of the world's illegal heroin and its many secret international bank accounts.

Osama bin Laden Declared War on America

Bin Laden issued a public Declaration of War against America in 1996, encouraging Muslims everywhere in the world to kill U.S. soldiers. In 1998, he issued another fatwa (a religious decree) in which he now commanded his followers to kill all Americans, soldiers or civilians, anywhere on earth wherever they could be attacked. Bin Laden declared that any Muslims who refused to heed his call to terrorism are "apostates." (Muslims who have forsaken the faith of their fathers.)

The overwhelming fundamental and strategic goal of the Islamic terrorists headed by bin Laden and his numerous al Qaeda allies is this: to expel all Americans, military and civilian, from Saudi Arabia and the entire Middle East. This non-negotiable demand is repeated in every one of bin Laden's public declarations, including his August 1996 Declaration of War against U.S. soldiers and his two fatwas in February 1998 against all American citizens. Bin Laden's "Declaration of War against the Americans Occupying the Land of the Two Holy Places" declares: "The latest and the greatest of [the] aggressions, incurred by the Muslims since the death of the Prophet . . . is the occupation of the land of the two Holy Places—the foundation of the house of Islam, the place of the revelation, the source of the message and the place of the noble Ka'ba, the Qiblah of all Muslims—by the armies of the American Crusaders and their allies."[2]

Bin Laden also founded the International Islamic Front for Jihad against the Jews and the Crusaders. This group has now published a fatwa that proclaimed a Jihad against the Christians who conquer Muslim lands. This applies to nations such as Spain that were conquered centuries ago by Muslim armies. In February 1998, bin Laden announced that many key terrorist groups had joined an alliance between al Qaeda and the International Islamic Front for Jihad Against the Jews and Crusaders including the Egyptian Islamic Jihad, the Egyptian al-Gama'at al-Islamiyya, and the Harakat ul-Ansar.

In May 1998, John Miller of ABC News was granted an unprecedented interview with Osama bin Laden in which he revealed his diabolical hatred of the Jews and the Christians of the West. He claimed that "Jihad," holy war, is essential to allow the Islamic nations to defeat the world of the Christian and Jewish "heretics." Bin Laden declared that terrorism against western men, women, and children is justified because he denies that any are innocent. He claims that the degraded moral standards of his Christian and Jewish enemies justify any Islamic terrorist atrocities. This obscene justification of evil is delivered by a man who has repeatedly attacked and destroyed the lives and bodies of men, women, and children representing many different faiths, including Islam, in numerous nations throughout the world. Bin Laden claims that the United States should be held responsible for what he calls acts of world "terrorism," including the WWII nuclear attacks on the Japanese cities of Hiroshima and Nagasaki, as well as the allies' bombing of Iraq. In addition, he displays a deep hatred for the Jews and the state of Israel. He has used pejorative and hate-filled antisemitic language in his many attacks on the Jewish people.

Bin Laden justified terrorist attacks against Israel because of his claims that the Jews were responsible for attacks on Arab villagers at Dir Yassin during the 1948 War of Independence and the brutal attack by Lebanese militias against Palestinians in the Sabra and Shatila refugee camps in 1982 when Israel drove the PLO out of Lebanon.[3]

Bin Laden in Hiding from U.S. Retaliation

The former Saudi Arabian diplomat, Abdullah bin Saad al-Otaibi, stated that al Qaeda had built, "well-constructed and well-equipped" deep subterranean chambers to protect bin Laden's terrorist groups. Hundreds of deep bunkers and extensive caverns were built to withstand sophisticated smart bombs and deep-penetration cruise missiles. These bunkers are equipped with food supplies, ample batteries, sophisticated Internet communication networks, oxygen supplies, comfortable housing, air conditioning, and water tanks. Al-Otaibi revealed that bin Laden does not trust anyone except possibly his top aide, the leader of the Egyptian Islamic Jihad, Ayman al-Zawahiri, who is known to be the technical genius who plans many of the most sophisticated terrorist attacks including the September 11 attack on the WTC. Every three days, bin Laden changes his bodyguards to make it virtually impossible for enemies to trace his movements or his current location.[4]

There are reports from intelligence sources that Osama bin Laden arranged for a Russian plastic surgeon to surgically alter his facial features to enable him to escape the growing surveillance of the western intelligence agencies. A report from Al Watan Al Arabi in Paris, France, in August 13, 1999, described an elaborate attempt to disguise the face of Osama bin Laden, the world's most hunted terrorist, and to also change the features of his favorite wife as well as several key assistants and trusted bodyguards that travel with him everywhere.[5] Bin Laden never sleeps in the same place twice. Just as his equally unpopular and hunted associates Saddam Hussein and PLO leader Yasser Arafat, Osama bin Laden knows that his many enemies are now closing in upon him. Therefore, he constantly changes his plans, his routes of travel, and the cave headquarters he occupies. His constantly changing itinerary makes it very difficult for his enemies to target him for assassination.

Bin Laden's Power in Afghanistan

A former Saudi diplomat to Afghanistan recently claimed that Osama bin Laden was the true power in Afghanistan until the American victory in December 2001, not the Taliban. Bin Laden had become the true finance minister of the Afghan Taliban regime and had arranged to hide their many secret bank accounts and assets throughout the world derived from the hundreds of millions of profits from illegal heroin grown annually throughout the country under the direction of the Taliban soldiers. The former charge d'affaires of Saudi Arabia to Afghanistan, Abdullah bin Saad al-Otaibi, revealed that the Taliban rulers were themselves unaware of the exact location of bin Laden's secret terrorist camps in Afghanistan, according to the published interview. Saudi diplomat Al-Otaibi stated that bin Laden actually exercised greater power than the Taliban. He suggested, "That's why the movement cannot hand him to the United States."

Not everything ran smoothly for Osama in Afghanistan though. Various sources revealed a serious conflict between his terrorists from Egypt and his fighters from Iran. In addition, many Afghanistan people strongly rejected the foreign dominance over their nation by the thousands of Arab terrorists of bin Laden's al Qaeda. Many of bin Laden's al Qaeda fighters came from Pakistan, Sudan, Yemen, Chechnya, or Bosnia, and were deeply resented by the Afghan people as well as some Taliban fighters.

The Taliban rulers of Afghanistan hired expert foreign marksmen who were intended to target American military aircraft with anti-aircraft weapons during U.S. attacks against their military bases. The Taliban acquired a number of Russian SA-2 surface-to-air missiles together with hundreds of SA-7 and SA-14 shoulder-fired anti-aircraft missiles. However, U.S. planes flew so high over Afghanistan that Taliban and al Qaeda soldiers were unable to target American bombers.

Bin Laden's Terrorist Army: al Qaeda

While al Qaeda ("the base") was organized by bin Laden, it includes a number of additional terror groups including the violent Egyptian Islamic Jihad and other major terrorist groups. Initially bin Laden focused on his mission during the late 1980s of assisting the Afghanistan mujahideen (Afghan guerilla fighters) who were fighting a desperate battle to drive the Soviet Union's invading army from their nation. Bin Laden recruited thousands of young Muslim men throughout the Middle East and other Islamic nations to join in a Jihad ("holy war") against the Soviet "infidels."

In recognition of the danger to western security posed by Russia's occupation of Afghanistan and its centuries-long ambition to obtain direct access to the Indian Ocean, America joined with Saudi Arabia and Pakistan in an unusual anti-Soviet alliance. The alliance armed the mujahideen with sophisticated communications and modern armament including hundreds of advanced shoulder-held U.S. surface-to-air Stinger missiles. These Stinger missiles were of tremendous significance in turning the tide of war against the Soviet Union's forces. The mujahideen quickly became adept at shooting down both Russian planes as well as their powerful HIND helicopters that previously allowed the Russian Spesnez special forces the mobility needed to effectively attack the elusive Afghan guerilla forces.

When the Russian army finally abandoned their futile decade-long effort to occupy Afghanistan in 1989, the victorious mujahideen forces quickly captured the capital Kabul but proved unable to build a strong government with support from the many different tribes and ambitious warlords. The country descended into a confused but deadly civil war as various generals used the captured Soviet military equipment in attempts to defeat their rivals. Finally, after four years of brutal civil war and general chaos, a group of Islamic extremists known as the Taliban ("teachers of religion") gathered weapons and seized control of significant parts of the ruined nation. They quickly imposed a brutal Islamic law and killed anyone who rejected their extreme Islamic agenda.

Bin Laden's al Qaeda immediately set up dozens of terrorist training camps throughout Afghanistan in 1996 under the protection of the Taliban. Despite repeated demands by the United States and the United Nations to the Taliban government to surrender the al Qaeda terrorists known to have been involved in numerous terrorist attacks—including the 1998 American embassy bombings in Africa—the Taliban absolutely refused to surrender bin Laden or any other terrorists within its territory.

Over the years, Osama bin Laden used his estimated $250 million inheritance from his father's estate and his brilliant financial investments to provide enormous funds to build his Islamic terrorist army and support the financially destitute Taliban government. In addition, numerous Saudi millionaire businessmen and some Saudi princes contributed millions to his al Qaeda group as willing support or as protection money to assure that their companies and families would not become the targets of terrorist attacks.

Al Qaeda recruited tens of thousands of Islamic fundamentalists from the Muslim southern republics of the former Soviet Union and the Middle East to be trained to join forces with the Taliban troops. Until America's victory in December, 2001, the Taliban, powerfully supported by both Saudi Arabia and Pakistan's Interagency Security Service (ISS), succeeded from 1996 to 1999 in driving the remnants of the former Afghan government's army into the far north of the country, an area comprising less than 20 percent of the nation (the Northern Alliance).

The war against terrorism will differ considerably from our past conflicts. Bin Laden's al Qaeda and his extremist Islamic terrorist allies operate globally. They are decentralized, operating in virtually independent cells of ruthless terrorists who do not personally know other terrorists in different cells or the leaders who are directing their activities. Thus, they cannot betray their leaders, even if they wanted to. Al Qaeda supports numerous terrorist groups and independent terror organizations including groups in Afghanistan, Pakistan, the Philippines, Algeria, Eritrea, Tajikistan, Chechnya, Somalia, Yemen, Sudan, and Kashmir. The evidence accumulated over the last decade by the CIA, the FBI, Israel's Mossad, France's Surete, and the British MI6 reveal that the new face of international Islamic terrorism, al Qaeda, is dedicated to meticulous long-term strategic planning, virtually untraceable financial transfers, incredibly secure communications, rigorous training of terrorist agents, and utterly ruthless and suicidal commitment to the destruction of its enemies: the State of Israel, the Christian and modern democratic nations of the West, as well as the various Arab and Islamic governments who reject their extremist Islamic views.

Al Qaeda's True Goals

Osama bin Laden declared that the ultimate goals of al Qaeda are the following:

- To force all American soldiers and civilians as well as all western influence out of every single Muslim nation, especially Saudi Arabia.

- To destroy Israel militarily and through terrorist means.
- To destroy every single pro-western Arab government in the Middle East.
- To unite all Muslims throughout the world and set up, by force, a global Islamic nation adhering to the extreme Islamic fundamentalist rule of the first caliphs.[6]

It is important that the citizens and leaders of the West as well as all non-extremist Islamic governments realize that if al Qaeda ever achieves its goals, every western democratic and Arab non-Taliban government in the world would be overthrown and replaced by an extremist Islamic government such as the woman-hating Taliban regime in Afghanistan. All people (Christians, Jews, Muslims, Hindus, Buddists, and atheists) would be forced to submit to the extremist faith and dictatorial rule of the most extreme fundamentalist Islamic regime, or die. Even the vast majority of Muslims, who reject the fanatical interpretation of Islam taught by the Taliban and al Qaeda, would be forced to submit to their extremist rules or suffer persecution and death. Humanity would enter a nightmare of living and dying in a global religious concentration camp.

The extremist al Qaeda Islamic theology is based on the ancient Muslim concept of Jihad, a "holy war" declared against all who reject their extreme Muslim views. Al Qaeda repeatedly calls for the killing of any "apostate" Muslims and the destruction of Arab governments who reject their demands to force the world to accept their beliefs. Virtually all Islamic religious scholars throughout the world have rejected the extremist religious views of the Taliban and al Qaeda. However, this extreme Taliban view is based on the writings of two modern Sunni Muslim scholars—Mohammed ibn Abd al-Wahhab and Sayyid Qutb.

Mohammad ibn Abd al-Wahhab, who lived in Saudi Arabia in the late 1700s, declared that the Islamic religion had become corrupted in the centuries following the death of their prophet Mohammed in A.D. 632. Al-Wahhab rejected all Muslim theological teachings and customs developed during the following thousand years of Islamic scholarship. His extreme puritanical group succeeded in conquering the whole Saudi Peninsula around 1800 and his sect, known as Wahhabism, became the dominant Islamic teaching in Saudi Arabia ever since. During the last century, another radical Islamic religious scholar in Egypt, Sayyid Qutb, announced that western civilization was the deadly enemy of Islam. Qutb attacked all of the leaders of various Muslim nations because they did not submit fully to his demands for Islamic purity. Sayyid Qutb taught that all Muslims must engage in Jihad to defend Islam and to purify it from western influences.

It is essential that all governments and every citizen throughout the world understand that there is no room to negotiate with the supporters of this extremist al Qaeda group of fundamentalist Islamic terrorism. They demand that every person on earth submit totally to their extremist Islamic regime or die. Therefore, we must awaken to the hard truth that we are now engaged in a bitter, long-term but essential war against ruthless and implacable terrorist enemies to preserve our political and religious freedom, our democratic government, as well as our western and modern way of life.

When our parents' generation faced the relentless forces of Hitler's Nazi armies that had conquered virtually all of the nations of Europe and North Africa in 1942, they realized that there was no possibility of negotiation with the Nazis because Hitler wanted their death. The only thing we can do when confronted by the implacable, evil hatred of Hitler or bin Laden is to recognize we face a desperate, implacable enemy who is committed to our destruction, as well as our families, and everything we love and hold dear. Our only logical and moral response is to marshal all of the spiritual, economic, and military forces at our command and attack this enemy until we utterly destroy him. Make no mistake—the West and its many friends throughout the world are now involved in an unprecedented war against Islamic terrorism to preserve our values, our freedom, and our very way of life. It is time for every citizen and all government leaders to recognize that this terrorist attack on the West is an attempt to destroy everything that makes life worthwhile. There is no room to negotiate or compromise. They desire our complete destruction. Therefore, we must marshal the courage, faith, and resolve "to stay the course" until we defeat the scourge of Islamic terrorism and free our society from its threat to all we hold dear.

How Do the Terrorists Communicate?

The police and intelligence agencies throughout the world have launched an unprecedented war against the terrorist networks since September 11. They are desperately attempting to break through the new secret encryption techniques used by the terrorist networks to send their deadly messages and plans to destroy countless lives throughout the world. *USA Today* reported on February 7, 2001, that bin Laden and others "are hiding maps and photographs of terrorist targets and posting instructions for terrorist activities on sports chat rooms, pornographic bulletin boards and other Web sites, U.S. and foreign officials say."

A new, sophisticated computer espionage communication technique, steganography, is an ancient art of embedding a secret message within another open message. Advanced steganographic computer technology prevents American intelligence agencies from discovering the hidden message secretly embedded within a seemingly innocent photograph on the internet. While traditional encryption techniques involve the attempt to create an unbreakable code relying on ciphers to scramble a particular message, steganography has a distinguished and devious history of misleading enemies about the very existence of secret messages hidden in "plain sight."

Herodotus, the ancient Greek historian living centuries before Jesus Christ, described the Greek technique of disguising a secret communication warning of a coming invasion that was written on the bottom interior slot of a wooden tray that held a clay tablet containing the official message. During the last century filled with numerous wars, countless messages were secretly transmitted to military headquarters using secret invisible ink that were only revealed when the ink was heated.

Today, Islamic terrorists can send secret messages using the ancient technology of steganography utilizing modern computer software such as S-Tools, White Noise Storm, or Steghide. These sophisticated computer programs allow the user to secretly embed hidden messages within computerized digital information such as audio, video, or photographic image files that are then transmitted through the Internet to someone on the other side of the world. The steganographic software secretly stores vital digital messages within seemingly insignificant parts of digitized graphic files, such as innocent photos of family outings.

For example, the program Steghide secretly embeds your digital message within .bmp, .wav, and .au computer files, while MP3 Stego hides messages within mp3 files. An especially devious computer program, known as Snow, actually embeds its secret message within additional white space added to the end of every line within a text file or normal e-mail message. Another steganography program, Spam Mimic from Disappearing Cryptography, secretly encodes your hidden message into what appears to be a typical innocent but easily ignored spam e-mail message. The FBI is deeply concerned that al Qaeda and other Islamic terrorist groups may be sending secret messages to its terrorist cells in America and Europe through the technique of embedding steganographic instructions within the video transmission by Osama bin Laden that proclaims his latest Declaration of War against the West. This is the reason the White House has wisely requested western TV networks to refrain from re-broadcasting Osama bin Laden's TV messages to the world, in case they might contain hidden steganographic messages to his sleeper terrorist cells in the West thereby enabling them to launch future terrorist attacks against us.

Bin Laden's Plans to Use Biological and Chemical Weapons

Since 1993, the intelligence agencies of the western nations discovered compelling evidence that al Qaeda has spent enormous resources to acquire nuclear, biological, and chemical weapons. The multiple anthrax attacks that have occurred since September 11, 2001, include several letter attacks using lethal airborne anthrax. Only a nation state capable of building sophisticated biological laboratories could create this type of deadly airborne anthrax. This can only be produced with expensive milling machines that break down the microscopic spores into tiny particles capable of floating in the air and entering a victim's lungs. Only three nations are capable of producing weapons-grade airborne anthrax: Russia, the United States, and Iraq. The evidence for Iraq's long term intelligence involvement with bin Laden's al Qaeda terrorist group is overwhelming, as will be demonstrated in a later chapter.

Dr. Michael Osterholm, the chief of Disease Epidemiology at the Minnesota Department of Public Health, recently warned the National Foundation for Infectious Disease about the danger of biological weapons in the hands of terrorists. Dr. Osterholm warned, "The United States is ripe for a terrorist attack using biological weapons and is nowhere near ready for it. . . . There are a growing number of extremist terrorist groups and religious fanatics who believe it is now time for our 'decadent capitalist society' to come to an end, and they are actively pursuing ways to bring that about. Germ warfare is their method of choice."[7]

On ABC's PrimeTime, U.S. Army colonel David Franz admitted to Diane Sawyer and Sam Donaldson that "the likelihood of a biological attack in the U.S. is now extremely high." General Jack Singlaub was the former commander of all U.S. military forces in South Korea, in addition to being a qualified expert in counterterrorism. Singlaub warns that we face a very real threat of major terrorist attacks against America and other western nations that might occur during the following months. Unfortunately these future terrorist attacks may include nuclear, chemical, and biological weapons of mass destruction.

U.S. Attorney General John Ashcroft, who directs the Justice Department and the FBI, declared that the government is preparing Federal Emergency Management Agency officials in 120 major U.S. cities for the possibility of coming terrorist attacks on their cities. Ashcroft warned, "It is clear that American citizens are the target of choice of international terrorists. Americans comprise only about 5 percent of the world's population. However, according to State Department statistics, during the decade of the 1990s, 36 percent of all worldwide terrorist acts were directed against U.S. interests." The Attorney General told the recent U.S. Senate hearings on terrorism and weapons of mass destruction: "We are now in the process of completing training and exercises for the nation's largest 120 cities under the Domestic Preparedness Program."[8]

Tragically, despite numerous government plans and resources to protect people after a terrorist chemical or biological attack, there are presently no plans to inform U.S. citizens as to how they might personally prepare themselves and protect their families against the possibility of a future terrorist biological or chemical weapons attack on American cities. Obviously, the government has the ability to provide the ultimate protection and medical assistance if a terrorist attack does occur in your city or country. However, until government assistance arrives, there are a number of significant steps you can take personally to protect your loved ones. In chapter 10, you will discover several steps you can take that will assist you in providing a level of protection until the government emergency medical authorities can assist your family.

Al Qaeda's Attempts to Acquire Nuclear Weapons

Intelligence reports confirm that a senior representative of Osama bin Laden's group, Jamal al-Fadi, met with a Sudanese army commander in Khartoum to arrange for the purchase of a lead cylindrical container holding enriched South African uranium for $1.7 million. Another attempt by al Qaeda to buy several pounds of weapons-grade enriched nuclear materials from the Russian mafia was discovered by western intelligence agencies and successfully intercepted in Prague, the Czech Republic, in 2001, as reported by German TV news in the fall of 2001. The *Times* newspaper in London reported in late October 2001 that a secret intelligence source in England reported that al Qaeda did not yet possess tactical nuclear weapons but that they would definitely use them against western and Israeli targets if they ever obtained weapons of mass destruction. British prime minister, Tony Blair, has stated several times that bin Laden would launch weapons of mass destruction against western nations if he could obtain them.

The director of the CIA, George Tenet, warned the U.S. Senate Intelligence Committee in 2000 that Osama bin Laden was definitely trying to acquire nuclear materials. One of the biggest worries for the CIA and the FBI is that, while building a nuclear fission bomb is clearly beyond Osama bin Laden's capacity, the acquisition or development by the terrorists of a nuclear radiation "dirty atomic bomb" is both practical and quite probable. This type of nuclear device utilizes radioactive nuclear material (from a reactor) packed around conventional explosives. It could kill thousands of victims immediately, with thousands more dying due to radiation exposure in the period following the attack. The area impacted by a "dirty atomic weapon" might leave enough nuclear radiation to make an area of ten city blocks uninhabitable for a century or more. Western intelligence sources reported that bin Laden and his al Qaeda network have recently acquired nuclear materials to use against western targets.[9]

The CBS television program "60 Minutes," broadcast on September 7, 1997, featured an interview with the former Russian National Security Adviser, Aleksandr Lebed, who claimed that the Russian KGB had manufactured hundreds of suitcase-sized nuclear weapons during the late 1970s to be used by USSR Spesnez special forces soldiers against the West. These deadly weapons were designed to appear as normal suitcases and to be carried into a European or North American city and detonated by a Russian military spy in only thirty minutes. Lebed announced that more than one hundred of the suitcase-sized one-kiloton nuclear bombs (equal to one thousand tons of TNT, that could destroy a city center and kill up to 100,000 people), were still unaccounted for. "I'm saying that more than a hundred weapons out of the supposed number of 250 are not under the control of the armed forces of Russia. I don't know their location. I don't know whether they have been destroyed or whether they are stored or whether they've been sold or stolen, I don't know" (CBS "60 Minutes," September 7, 1997).

While some senior Russian defense officials have denied the existence of these deadly terrorist weapons, on October 2, 1997, Aleksey Yablokov, a senior advisor to former Russian president Boris Yeltsin, confirmed Lebed's warnings when he told a U.S. Congressional subcommittee that he was "absolutely sure" that hundreds of suitcase nuclear bombs were developed by the KGB during the 1970s.[10]

General Lebed, the former secretary of the Russian Security Council, indicated that the suitcase devices were compact nuclear weapons (24 by 16 by 8 inches) and were distributed to special

Soviet army intelligence units, known as the Main Intelligence Directorate, the GRU. The available information suggests that the smallest likely nuclear explosive device would be a critical mass of uranium 235 or plutonium approximately four inches across and weighing at least twenty-three pounds. In May 1997, Lebed told a delegation of U.S. congressmen that his research indicated that eighty-four of the one-kiloton bombs were still missing. While some commentators have speculated that these decades-old nuclear weapons may no longer be reliable or even functional, other nuclear weapons experts such as Carey Sublette of MILNET report that it is very unlikely that these nuclear devices would be degraded to the point that they would not function.

Reports appeared in Russia during October 1997 that Dzhokhar Dudayev, the leader of the Russian Chechen separatist forces, may have purchased or stolen several Russian tactical nuclear weapons. Lebed indicated to the U.S. that reports that Chechen terrorists had acquired several "suitcase nuclear weapons" had motivated the Russian Security Council to begin its investigation of the whereabouts of these deadly weapons.[11] A book by Andrew and Leslie Cockburn, *One Point Safe*, claims that the Chechen rebels warned the American government in mid 1994 that it had acquired two tactical nuclear weapons. Furthermore, the Chechen terrorist leaders warned they would transfer these weapons of mass destruction to Arab governments if the United States refused to recognize the independence of Chechnya from Russia.

There are reports that the Chechen rebels gave U.S. intelligence enough technical information to convince them that they truly possessed these deadly weapons. Apparently the Chechen rebels realized that Russia would massively retaliate if they ever dared to use the KGB suitcase nuclear devices. Therefore, they decided to sell the devices to al Qaeda; a terrorist group that could use these weapons because they do not represent a nation state that could be subject to political or military pressure. A secret intelligence group visited the rebel Chechnya republic but failed to verify this information. However, this report confirms that American intelligence agencies are very concerned about a "terrorist nuclear bomb."[12]

Al Qaeda's agents have attempted to purchase or steal nuclear materials to attack western targets. Osama bin Laden declared it was his "religious duty" to acquire chemical, biological, and nuclear weapons of mass destruction. In *Bin Laden: The Man Who Declared War on America*, counterterrorism expert Yossef Bodansky reported that Chechen rebels arranged to sell "suitcase nuclear bombs" acquired from Russia and the former Soviet republics of Ukraine, Kazakhstan, and Turkmenistan to bin Laden's al Qaeda during the last three years. Bodansky claims that, according to his substantial Russian and Arab intelligence sources, the Chechens were paid $30 million plus two tons of pure Afghani heroin (worth $700 million in street prices) to purchase several nuclear suitcase weapons.[13] The London newspaper *The Times* reported that al Qaeda' s group has amassed a "terrifying" range of deadly weapons even though the terrorism expert insisted that bin Laden could still not launch a nuclear attack on the West. In 1998 bin Laden wrote his declaration, "The Nuclear Bomb of Islam," which stated, "It is the duty of Muslims to prepare as much force as possible to terrorize the enemies of God."[14]

A bin Laden Suitcase Radioactive Bomb

In fact, Osama bin Laden actually possessed at least one of the Russian suitcase nuclear weapons. Israeli security forces arrested a Pakistani terrorist linked to bin Laden's al Qaeda group as he attempted to enter Israel from the Palestinian Authority territory at the border checkpoint at Ramallah during the last week of September 2001. U.S. government officials acknowledged that the terrorist was armed with a radiological nuclear backpack explosive and that he was arrested while traveling toward an Israeli target (probably Tel Aviv, Israel's largest city).[15]

This disturbing report was placed on the Internet by Richard Sale, a United Press International (UPI) reporter on October 14, 2001. Several additional intelligence sources in England and Israel personally confirmed the arrest of the terrorist with this device to me. The U.S. government official told Richard Sale that the terrorist probably entered Israel from Lebanon. Israeli intelligence authorities immediately sent this explosive information regarding the arrest and the nuclear device to President Bush and his close circle of advisors. A top-secret report about the bin Laden terrorist's possession of a suitcase nuclear device, a "dirty atomic bomb," that used radioactive material surrounding a conventional explosive, was circulated among U.S. Cabinet members.

Some of the Russian portable suitcase-sized nuclear devices were designed as true tactical nuclear bombs, while others were created as radioactive devices designed to poison a ten-block area with radioactive material (from spent nuclear reactor rods) for up to one hundred years. The American and Israeli government decided against widely releasing this disturbing report because of the fear that it would cause panic if the public knew about the dangers of radioactive suitcase bombs at the time there was widespread fear due to the continuing anthrax attacks.

The U.S. government expert who spoke to UPI's reporter Richard Sale indicated that the weapon carried by the terrorist was a backpack device that Russian intelligence agents warned the CIA about in 1995. Arab intelligence officials reported in October 1998 that Osama bin Laden purchased several Russian-made nuclear suitcase weapons from Chechen criminals who acquired them from a former republic of the USSR. The price was $30 million plus two tons of heroin worth $700 million.[16]

The implications of this captured suitcase radioactive bomb are extraordinary. The warnings that bin Laden's terrorists might have nuclear devices are no longer unsubstantiated rumors. Although there is no hard evidence that they have acquired true tactical nuclear weapons yet, his possession of a radioactive "dirty atomic" suitcase device demonstrates al Qaeda's resolve to attack the West and Israel with every weapon they can get their hands on. The December 2001 issue of *The Jerusalem Report* magazine included an article by Yael Haran on the threat from al Qaeda's possession of suitcase bombs.

On October 14, United Press International reported from Washington that Israeli security forces had arrested a Pakistani linked to bin Laden near Ramallah, who was trying to sneak into Israel a 'radioactive backpack bomb' with a 'small core of conventional explosives encased in radioactive material.' Such a device would not produce a nuclear explosion, but would spread a great deal of radioactivity if detonated, Peter Probst, a former Pentagon terror specialist, told UPI. Other rumors say the backpack contained 'components of a nuclear suitcase.' The Army Spokesman's Office would say only that it was 'studying' the report.[17]

The fact that the western nations have known about this terrorist radioactive bomb helps explain the tremendous resolve that the U.S.A. and her allies have recently demonstrated in their "war against terror." It also explains why this war against terror cannot stop with the destruction of the Taliban and al Qaeda's terror training camps in Afghanistan. We must "stay the course." We must continue this war until every one of the terrorist-supporting nations abandons their support for those terrorists who are committed to the destruction of our western religious and political freedom as well as the moderate Arab governments throughout the Middle East.

Terrorist Suicide Attacks

Most citizens in the West are very confused by the motivation of the young Arab men who participate in suicide bombing attacks against western or Israeli citizens. One of the keys to understanding the motivation of the suicide bombers, such as the nineteen Arab hijackers who commandeered the four U.S. passenger airlines on September 11, 2001, is to examine their training and philosophy.

A suicide bombing is a terrorist attack in which the planned destruction of the western or Jewish enemy depends upon the death of the terrorist. The suicide bomber understands that the attack depends on his personal destruction. He is the "human missile." The attack is normally implemented through the activation of deadly explosives hidden in the clothing of the terrorist as a portable explosive charge or contained in a vehicle he drives to the ultimate target. Unfortunately, radical fundamentalist Islamic terror groups have resorted to the use of suicide bombers in the last decade against both Israeli and, now, American targets.

Suicide terrorist attacks are now used by Islamic extremist religious as well as nationalistic fanatics who regard the use of this weapon as part of their Jihad, or holy war, against the West and Israel. The terrorist suicide bomber is not considered to have committed suicide by his religious community. Rather, he is called a "shahid," a martyr who dies as a hero in their holy war. Many of the suicide bombers come from families that are from the lower socio-economic class. While the nineteen hijackers were middle class, Osama bin Laden's video tape revealed that most did not realize, until they boarded the plane, that they were destined to die. Once the suicide bomber has completed his mission, his family usually receives praise, honor, and a substantial pension, as well as other financial rewards from the Arab authorities and his community.

The personal motivation of the suicide terrorist bomber includes the teaching that he will receive tremendous rewards in the afterlife for his sacrifice in the cause of destroying Christians and Jews. The promises to the suicide bomber include the following: an eternal life in paradise with the loving attentions of seventy-two young virgins who will sexually serve him forever in heaven, unlimited indulgence in wine, and permission to see the face of Allah, as well as the privilege to give life in paradise to seventy of his relatives. However, many non-fundamentalist Islamic teachers condemn suicide bombers as violating the Koran's rules against suicide.

A suicide terrorist attack is a favorite form of attack against their Jewish and western enemies because they produce many civilian casualties and cause extensive damage. In addition, suicide attacks provide the terrorists with global media coverage. Most international media consider a suicide attack to be very newsworthy because it indicates to them that the terrorist has displayed great determination and self-sacrifice for his cause. In addition, the global media openly follow this cynical rule about the prominence paid to any particular news story: "If it bleeds, it leads." The use of a terrorist suicide bomber results in much larger civilian casualties compared to other techniques such as remotely detonated or timed car bombs because the bomber can position himself to inflict the maximum possible damage in a crowd of innocent civilians.

The majority of suicide bombers are between eighteen and twenty-seven years old, unmarried, unemployed, and poor. Most of the September 11 bombers had studied in the Islamic fundamentalist education centers in Gaza and the West Bank that were controlled by the Hamas terrorist network. A significant number of the suicide terrorists had the desire to avenge the death of a relative or associate by Israeli authorities. It is interesting to note that some of the terrorists who were trained as "shahids" admitted they were taken to a graveyard and placed inside a grave for several hours to overcome any fear of death.[18]

It is essential that these attacks be stopped before the suicide bomber embarks on his terrorist mission. Often the family and the friends of the fanatic terrorist are the first to recognize that he is preparing to sacrifice his life to destroy his perceived enemies. But the best defense against these suicide bombers are deep penetration agents who observe the signs that a young man is being groomed by his Hamas handlers to prepare him for a suicide bombing mission. In addition, the development of extremely sophisticated technologies that can detect explosives at a distance are now providing Israeli and American security agents with the means to detect the approach of a terrorist explosive weapon that might destroy the lives of many innocent civilians.

Suicide bombing is rarely the act of a single mad terrorist who decides to create a revenge attack. Instead, it is the result of a meticulously planned terrorist attack by a terrorist group that chooses the young man, extensively trains and motivates him, and provides him with the bomb and the chosen target. To counter this wave of Arab suicide bombing will require professional intelligence, surveillance activity, active security, and the application of psychological warfare measures combined with international cooperation against the terrorist organizations that plan such attacks on both American and Israeli targets.

Endnotes

1. Ely Karmon. The Washington Institute for Near East Policy, *Policywatch* No. 347. 29 Oct. 1998.
2. http://www.kimsoft.com/2001/binladenwar.htm.
3. Yoram Schweitzer. "Osama Bin Laden: Wealth plus Extremism Equals Terrorism." 27 July, 1998. http://www.ict.org.il/articles/bin-ladin.htm.
4. "Saudi Diplomat: Osama Bin Laden, Not Taliban, Real Power in Afghanistan." 5 Oct. 2001. http://205.180.85.40/orbitz3/TampaTribune.html.
5. Where's Osama?"http://geocities.com/zincisrael/features/f74Wheres_Osama.htm.
6. Osama bin Laden's Declaration of War: http://www.ict.org.il/articles/fatwah.htm.
7. The Bio-terrorism Manual: http://www.rense.com/bioter/bioterror.htm.
8. Hearing on U.S. Federal Efforts to Combat Terrorism, 9 May, 2001, http://www.usdoj.gov/ag/testimony/2001/ag_statement_05_09_01.htm.
9. Philip Webster and Roland Watson. "Bin Laden's Nuclear Threat." *Times* Newspapers Ltd. 26 Oct. 2001.
10. William Potter. "'The Peacemaker' Is a Warning to All." The *Los Angeles Times*. 29 Sept. 1997.
11. "Is Lebed Russia's Loosest Cannon?." 2 Oct. 1997. http://www.msnbc.com.
12. Andrew and Leslie Cockburn. *One Point Safe*. Washington, DC: Doubleday, 1997, pp. 101–103.
13. Yossef Bodansky, *Bin Laden: The Man Who Declared War on America*. New York: Random House, 2001.
14. Philip Webster and Roland Watson. "Bin Laden's Nuclear Threat." *The Times*, London, 26 Oct. 2001.
15. Richard Sale. "Israel Finds Radiological Backpack Bomb." *United Press International* via COMTEX. 14 Oct. 2001. http://csf.colorado.edu/mail/isafp/2001/msg00202.html.
16. Richard Sale. "Israel Finds Radiological Backpack Bomb." *United Press International* via COMTEX. 14 Oct. 2001. http://csf.colorado.edu/mail/isafp/2001/msg00202.html.
17. Yael Haran, *The Jerusalem Report*, 3 Dec. 2001.
18. *Yediot*, 3 Sept. 1995.

3

The Key Terrorist-
Supporting Nations

For three decades, the nations of the West have cautiously responded to international Islamic terrorist attacks by using intelligence, criminal, and judicial resources to arrest, convict, and imprison individual terrorists. This approach has failed to stop Islamic terror attacks. Often the nature of a terrorist attack purposely leaves little forensic evidence to enable our American courts to obtain a legal conviction. In addition, many of the most wanted terrorists simply disappear into several dozen anti-western nations such as Sudan, Yemen, or Iraq–nations that will never cooperate in arresting or extraditing these terrorists to stand trial in the West.

Until the terrorist attacks on September 11, 2001, western governments responded to terrorism by using the criminal justice system. Unfortunately, history has demonstrated that this criminal justice response will not work against the wealthy, well-trained groups of thousands of Islamic terrorists. This approach has been as useless as if President Roosevelt had instructed the

FBI to hunt down, arrest, and bring to trial the Japanese pilots, sailors, and admirals who attacked Pearl Harbor on December 7, 1941. Criminal justice can never deal adequately with global Islamic terrorism.

When faced with malaria, you don't swat mosquitoes; you must drain the swamp. The only response to terrorists that will eradicate their huge threat to our population and way of life is to "drain the swamp" by eliminating the many terrorist-supporting states in the Middle East who support and protect the Islamic terror groups. A terror-supporting state has a government that can respond to military threats or armed invasion by stopping its support of terrorists in their midst, close the terror training camps, and cease its provision of intelligence, funds, and safe harbor to the terrorists.

This chapter will examine the overwhelming evidence that

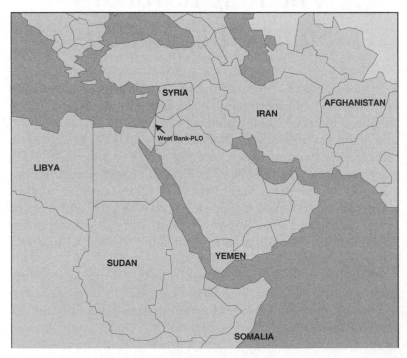

The Islamic Terrorist-supporting Nations.

a group of eight Islamic nations from Africa to Afghanistan has joined in a loose terrorist-supporting alliance that is committed to the destruction of Israel and the western nations through their support of Islamic terrorism. While the al Qaeda terrorist network of Osama bin Laden is the largest terror group and was headquartered in the mountains of Afghanistan under the protection of the Taliban Islamic regime until December 2001, several other nations have given their full financial, diplomatic, intelligence, and training support to Islamic terrorists who plan to destroy western targets. Overwhelming evidence from western intelligence agencies points to Iraq as the primary nation behind the terrorist attacks against America by bin Laden's al Qaeda group. Iraq is the most powerful and ambitious of the terrorist supporting nations that are fully at war with Israel and America. The compelling evidence that implicates Iraq in its support of bin Laden's al Qaeda terror attacks against America is fully documented in chapter 5. The remarkable prophecies about Iraq's fascinating role in the critical events of the last days are discussed in chapter 6.

In the balance of this chapter we will examine the evidence that several Middle Eastern nations have joined in a terrorist alliance against Israel and the West. The final chapters of this book will detail how the terrorists and the Islamic extremist states that support them will soon be defeated by the armed forces of the West.

Afghanistan

Immediately following the devastating September 11, 2001, bombing, America's military leadership and intelligence agencies turned their attention to the Taliban extremist Islamic government of Afghanistan. The Taliban provided security, refuge, and financial support, as well as unwavering political and religious support for bin Laden's terrorist group al Qaeda and his allies. They share a common extremist Islamic theology that is historically unprecedented in its repressive religious rule, its terrorism, and its brutal treatment of women and any political opponents. Even the extreme fundamentalist Muslim clergy ruling Iran are appalled at the actions and teaching of the Taliban. Despite the fact of continuous CNN TV, radio, and newspaper coverage of the ongoing war against terror, most people have never had an opportunity to learn the origin, nature, and goals of the Taliban.

Who Were the Taliban?

Following the retreat of the Soviet army from Afghanistan in 1989, the Russian-backed communist Afghan government repeatedly lost battles with the anti-Soviet mujahideen (freedom fighters). In 1992, the mujahideen captured the capital, Kabul, and an alliance of anti-communist guerilla warlords established their tentative new government in 1994, with Burhanuddin Rabbani as president. Tragically, the numerous Afghan ethnic groups failed to support the new central government and began a deadly civil war. Competing warlords fought to defend their ethnic tribal parts of Afghanistan.

Beginning in 1994, a group of Muslim religious extremists, known as Taliban (Arabic for: teachers of religion), began to attack these rival warlords and, with popular support, quickly established a brutal religious and military authority in various areas. By 1996, the Taliban, under Mullah Muhammad Omar, (a close friend of Osama bin Laden) seized power in Kandahar from the weak Afghan government and rapidly imposed an extremist, totalitarian dictatorship upon the Afghan population. In September 1996, they captured the Afghanistan capital, Kabul, and rapidly expanded their rule to over 80 percent of Afghanistan over the next few years.

Tens of thousands of Islamic Taliban were trained and indoctrinated in hundreds of "madrassas" religious schools and mosques in Pakistan that were well-funded by Saudi Arabia and strongly supported by the Pakistan Intelligence Service. To escape the growing danger of opposition to the corrupt royal family from their own Islamic extremists, the Saudi government exiled these religious fanatics to far-away Afghanistan and Pakistan. They provided both funds and arms to support their Jihad, or holy war, against the existing government of Afghanistan. Initially the Taliban proved to be surprisingly popular with the Afghan people because the people were so discouraged with the continuing civil war and constant attacks by rival warlords. A lot of Afghans were initially happy to see the Taliban eliminate the widespread corruption, stop the random rapes, theft, and military attacks, as well as to allow the resumption of normal business.

The Taliban established "law and order" through their imposition of an extremely strict interpretation of Islamic law (Sharia). They demonstrated their new rule of law with weekly public executions, including beheading and stoning, together with amputations and brutal floggings witnessed by thousands of citizens at local soccer stadiums. When the Taliban entered Kabul, amputated limbs as well as the heads of enemies and assumed violators of their strict laws were hung from hundreds of trees in the parks and lamp posts throughout the capital. Normal human activities such as listening to the radio or music, watching television, flying kites, or using the Internet were made illegal and were now subject to brutal punishment. Public floggings, amputations without anesthesia, and beheadings with swords were performed every third Friday in the local soccer stadium before thousands of citizens.

According to the U.S. Department of State, the Taliban were responsible for numerous atrocities and massacres of innocent civilians in Yakaolang, Mazar-e-Sharif, Bamiyan, Qezelabad, and other Afghan cities. In August 1998, the Taliban captured the northern city of Mazar-e-Sharif. Experts reported that up to five thousand men, women, and children from the northern ethnic Muslim Hazara tribe were massacred by Taliban soldiers. "Human Rights Watch estimates that scores, perhaps hundreds, of Hazara men and boys were summarily executed. There were also reports that women and girls were raped and abducted during the Taliban takeover of the city."[1]

Incredibly, if men did not wear beards, the Taliban police beat them severely. They even had beard measurers, whose job it was to make sure the men's beards were at least four inches in length. The Taliban forbade girls to attend school or women to work outside the home, thereby destroying Afghan medical care and education. Most hospitals were closed to prevent men from coming into contact with women. Incredibly, women were forbidden from leaving their homes unless accompanied by a male relative. There are 30,000 widows in Kabul who had no way of supporting their children under the Taliban. If a woman was caught using makeup or fingernail polish, her fingers were cut off. Any woman walking alone was beaten or killed by Taliban officers working for the hated Ministry for the Protection of Virtue and Prevention of Vice. The Taliban proclaimed that these extreme Islamic regulations were necessary to safeguard the "honor" of Afghan women.

The Taliban's brutal treatment of women and their political opponents together with their total support of Osama bin Laden's terrorist army caused almost every nation across the globe to ostracize them from the world community. Due to the Taliban's open support of bin Laden's terrorism against the West, only three nations—Saudi Arabia, Pakistan, and the United Arab Emirates—recognized the Taliban as the legitimate Afghan government. In the weeks following the Taliban's open endorsement of al Qaeda's terrorist attacks on September 11, 2001, both Saudi Arabia and the United Arab Emirates cut diplomatic relations with the Taliban. In addition, Pakistan, despite a large Muslim anti-American movement, joined the global anti-terrorist alliance and provided America with substantial intelligence cooperation together with permission to overfly its territory in military attacks on terrorist bases in Afghanistan. The United Nations Security Council passed Resolution UNSCR 1267 (1999) and 1333 (2000) that demanded the Taliban stop supporting terrorism and surrender Osama bin Laden to be tried for his crimes.

These "holy" Taliban leaders also financially supported their brutal totalitarian government and bin Laden's terrorist groups primarily through the cultivation, smuggling, and sale of 80 percent of the world's opium, which produces the heroin that destroys the lives of millions around the world.

Many of the Taliban belonged to the ethnic Pashtun tribe, which comprises the majority of southern Afghanistan's population. Pashtuns also live in Pakistan, including the province of Kashmir that is in dispute between Pakistan and India. Pashtuns form a large minority tribe within Pakistan and practically dominate the army of Pakistan. There is strong public support for the Taliban in the Pashtun North-West Frontier province of Pakistan.

The Taliban supporters represented only a small portion of the population of Afghanistan. While only a small percentage of the vast Pashtun tribe had joined the Taliban, there is a remarkable mystery concerning the ancient origin of the Pashtun race.

The Ten Lost Tribes and the Pashtun Tribe

One of the most fascinating details concerning America's war against the Taliban of Afghanistan is that the southern Pashtun tribes that provided most of the military manpower and political support to the Taliban government may actually be the remnants of the ten Lost Tribes of Israel. As unlikely as this appears, serious scholars have examined the historical and sociological evidence, and several have concluded that the eighteen million Pashtun (Pathan) tribesmen that extend throughout southern Afghanistan and northern Pakistan may be descended from the ten tribes of ancient Israel that were exiled to that exact territory twenty-seven centuries ago by the Assyrian Empire in 721 B.C.

A remarkable article by Dr. Shalva Weil, an Israeli anthropologist, entitled "Ten Lost Tribes" appeared in the October 22, 2001 issue of the Israeli magazine *The Jerusalem Report*. Dr. Shalva Weil wrote, "The Pathan tribesmen who constitute the Taliban majority have a strong claim of descent from the Lost Tribes. . . . Indeed they appear to be the best candidates among the diverse groups claiming Lost Tribe status. The location is right (2 Kings 17:6), and the Pashtuns have shown exceptional tenacity in adhering to their story through the centuries. They have sallow skins and dark hair and eyes, are of medium stature, wear Jewish side curls and have a typically Jewish profile. They also 'act' Jewish. There have been reports that they circumcise their boys on the eighth day; the women observe purification laws prescribed in the Torah; and they wear amulets, some of which contain the words of the Shema 'Hear O Israel. . .' ." Shalva Weil also wrote, "They had mezuzot on their doorposts, wrapped themselves in tallitot (prayer shawls), and lit candles on Friday night."

Dr. Weil wrote, "They are divided into distinct local sub-tribes reminiscent of the Lost Ten Tribes: Rabbani may be Reuben,

Shinwari may be Shimon; Daftani may be a corruption of Naftali, Jajani–Gad, Afridi–Ephraim. And the tribe I encountered during my research in the eighties, Yusuf-Zai, which straddles the Pakistani-Kashmiri border, may be the sons of Joseph." When Dr. Weil visited Pathan tribes in Kashmir, she met Muhammad Wali, a Pathan member of the Yusuf-Zai sub-tribe ("Children of Joseph"), who explained that "Yusuf" was "Ibn Yaacob" (the "Son of Jacob"). He confirmed that "Yaacob was Israel. And we are Bani Israel, the Children of Israel."[2]

It would be one of the greatest historical ironies if it turns out that the Taliban, a Jewish-hating group and supporter of terrorism against Israel, who belong to the Pashtun tribe are actually descendents of the ancient ten Lost Tribes of Israel. While this certainly presents a very curious situation, the ancient history of the Promised Land reveals nearly three centuries of bitter hatred and constant warfare between the ten tribes of northern Israel and the two tribes of the southern nation of Judah until the destruction of the ten tribes by the armies of the Assyrian Empire.

What actually happened to the Lost Tribes of Israel? Do they still exist in some forgotten part of the world? Do they have a

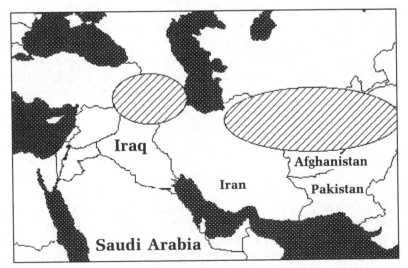

The Exile of the Ten Tribes to Assyria.

role to play in the last days? The prophecies declare that each of the twelve tribes will finally be restored to the Promised Land. The Lord promised Abraham that He would create a great nation out of his offspring through Isaac, his miraculously conceived son. Isaac, the "seed of promise," fathered a son named Jacob. Ultimately Jacob fathered twelve sons: Reuben, Simeon, Levi, Judah, Issachar, Zebulun, Gad, Asher, Joseph, Benjamin, Dan, and Naphtali. They became the leaders of the twelve tribes. But because Levi was the priestly tribe that did not receive an inheritance, Joseph's sons, Ephraim and Manasseh, headed the other two tribes to make up the twelve. When King Solomon died after building the beautiful temple in Jerusalem, the glorious united kingdom of Israel died with him. The nation of Israel was violently split into two nations, the ten tribes of northern Israel and the two tribes of southern Judah; they were never reconciled. The two southern tribes, Judah and Benjamin, retained Jerusalem as the capital of their southern kingdom. The ten northern tribes called themselves Israel and made Samaria their capital. A series of wars continued during the next three centuries. When God's prophets warned Israel to repent, the ten tribes persisted in open idolatry and rebellion against God.

The powerful armies of Assyria took King Hosea and the ten tribes of northern Israel captive. "Shalmaneser king of Assyria came up against Samaria, and besieged it. . . . And the king of Assyria did carry away Israel unto Assyria, and put them in Halah and in Habor by the river of Gozan, and in the cities of the Medes" (2 Kings 18:9, 11). They exiled 90 percent of the population of Israel to northern Assyria as captives. The Assyrian national policy was to replace the native population of Israel with the Samaritans, another captive race exiled from the northern regions of the vast Assyrian empire. These Israelite captives were settled in the regions to the north of Iraq, Afghanistan, and Iran. Over the centuries, these Israelites settled as colonists throughout present day Afghanistan and northern Pakistan. The territory mentioned in 2 Kings lies northeast of ancient Nineveh in present-day southern Afghanistan.

The River Gozan lies in northern Afghanistan. Flavius Josephus' *Antiquities of the Jews* described the location of the ten tribes as follows: "The entire body of the people of Israel remained in that country (Persia); wherefore there are but two tribes in Asia and Europe subject to the Romans, while the ten tribes are beyond Euphrates till now, and are an immense multitude, and not to be estimated by numbers."[3]

But the question remains: What happened to the ten tribes of Israel that never returned from Central Asia? Do these tribes still exist? Do they still have a role to play in the biblical prophecies that will be fulfilled in the last days?

The Bible clearly prophesies that all twelve tribes will play a significant role in the prophetic events of the last days. Ezekiel prophesied the ultimate restoration of the ten tribes of Israel to join the two tribes of Judah.

> Thus saith the Lord God; Behold, I will take the children of Israel from among the heathen, whither they be gone, and will gather them on every side, and bring them into their own land: And I will make them one nation in the land upon the mountains of Israel; and one king shall be king to them all: and they shall be no more two nations, neither shall they be divided into two kingdoms any more at all. (Ezekiel 37:21–22)

For twenty-five centuries this prophecy has remained unfulfilled.

Jeremiah prophesied about the coming kingdom of the Messiah, "In those days the house of Judah shall walk with the house of Israel, and they shall come together out of the land of the north to the land that I have given for an inheritance unto your fathers" (Jeremiah 3:18).

Isaiah revealed his prophetic vision about the restoration of all twelve tribes to the Holy Land, "And it shall come to pass in that day, that the great trumpet shall be blown, and they shall come which were ready to perish in the land of Assyria, and the outcasts in the land of Egypt, and shall worship the Lord in the holy mount at Jerusalem" (Isaiah 27:13).

The apostle James began his epistle with these words, "James, a servant of God and of the Lord Jesus Christ, to the twelve tribes which are scattered abroad, greeting" (James 1:1). The Holy

Spirit inspired this remarkable salutation by James. Therefore, the ten tribes still existed during the first century following the resurrection of our Lord. In addition, the prophet John, in his book of Revelation, prophesied that God would seal 144,000 Jews for divine protection during the terrible period of the Great Tribulation in the future. He specifically named the twelve tribes of Israel, including the ten Lost Tribes. John declared, "And I heard the number of them which were sealed: and there were sealed an hundred and forty and four thousand of all the tribes of the children of Israel. Of the tribe of Juda were sealed twelve thousand. Of the tribe of Reuben were sealed twelve thousand. . . ."

The prophet specifically named each of the twelve tribes including: Judah, Reuben, Gad, Asher, Naphtali, Manasseh, Simeon, Levi, Issachar, Zebulun, Joseph, Benjamin (Revelation 7:4–8).

Ezekiel also declared that, when the Messiah comes to establish His Millennial Kingdom, God will allocate the land of Israel among the twelve tribes:

> Now these are the names of the tribes. From the north end to the coast of the way of Hethlon, as one goeth to Hamath, Hazarenan, the border of Damascus northward, to the coast of Hamath; for these are his sides east and west; a portion for Dan. . . . A portion for Asher. . . . A portion for Naphtali. . . . A portion for Manasseh. . . . A portion for Ephraim. . . . A portion for Reuben. . . . A portion for Judah. . . . Benjamin shall have a portion. . . . Simeon shall have a portion. . . . Issachar a portion. . . . Zebulun a portion. . . . Gad a portion. (Ezekiel 48:1–27)

Since God's promises are unbreakable, we must conclude that He has preserved the ten tribes until He will restore them to the Holy Land in the final days. The prophecies in Revelation and Ezekiel confirm that the ten tribes must still exist. Somehow, God will supernaturally identify the tribal identities of these Israelites at the appropriate time.

The Ben-Zvi Institute was founded by the late Yitzhak Ben-Zvi, the second president of Israel, and focuses its research on the history of the Jewish captives in the Diaspora (among the nations). President Ben-Zvi wrote a book, *The Exiled and the Redeemed*, where he reported:

> The tribes of Afghanistan, among whom dwelt the Jews of Afghanistan for many generations, are Moslem tribes which kept, and still keep, the wondrous tradition regarding their origin from the Ten Lost Tribes. This tradition, which circulates amongst people of the Afghan tribes, is an ancient one and has historical backing. Some researchers and travellers, Jews and non-Jews, who visited these places, dealt with it, as did researchers of Afghanistan and its population from literary sources alone. Only a few facts have been published on this matter in books and encyclopedias either in the European language or in Hebrew.

In another passage of his book, *The Exiled and the Redeemed*, Ben-Zvi wrote, "There is no reason to doubt the existence of a continuous Jewish settlement in both the north and south of Caucasia, whose roots were laid in very ancient times, perhaps as early as the days of the Second Temple, perhaps even earlier."[4]

There is a curious similarity between the characteristics of these Pashtun and the ancient tribes of Israel including: circumcision of the male child on the eighth day; marriage customs including a marriage canopy and a marriage contract, the ketubbah; Levitical-type food laws; tallit, or prayer shawls; the mikvah; Sabbath customs; the fast of Yom Kippur; and the use of mezuzot on the sides of doors. Remarkably, many Pashtun pray toward Jerusalem rather than Mecca, and some wear amulets depicting the Shema prayer, "Behold O Israel, the Lord your God is One." (Deuteronomy 6:1). During plagues, Pashtun may slaughter a sheep and sprinkle its blood on the lintel and doorposts, exactly as the ancient Jews did during their ancient Exodus from Egypt.

Ultimately, only God knows the true identity and location of the ten Lost Tribes of Israel that disappeared into the vast depths of Central Asia almost twenty-seven centuries ago. However, the Bible's ancient prophecy about the restoration of the Lost Tribes of the House of Israel must be fulfilled one day. The promise of God concerning the restoration of the tribes to rejoin Judah and Benjamin cannot be broken. The Lord will someday return the ten tribes of His inheritance to their ancient Promised Land. Wherever they are, the Good Shepherd knows the sheep of His pasture and will fulfill the words of His prophecy.

The Palestinian Authority

For more than three decades, Palestinian Authority president Yasser Arafat has been the leading terrorist in the world. He introduced the technique of suicide bombing against Jewish civilian targets. Arafat pioneered terrorism such as his Black September attack on the embassy in Kartoum, Sudan, where his terrorists held the American ambassador Noel and his aide hostage for the release of Sirhan Sirhan, the Palestinian assassin of Robert F. Kennedy. When President Nixon refused to release Kennedy's imprisoned assassin, Yasser Arafat, from his hideout in Beirut, gave orders by radio to assassinate the U.S. diplomats with a machine gun. These radio messages of Arafat were intercepted by America's Echelon surveillance system as well as Israel's Mossad. Tape recordings of these messages have been shared with senior government officials for many years. Yet, strangely, Arafat has been a guest in the White House thirteen times, more than any other leader in the world.

CNN and other media constantly report the latest declaration by Yasser Arafat or his media spokespersons that he totally condemns the latest terrorist suicide bombings, and the recent attack on innocent women and children riding in a bus. However, his tactic of publicly denouncing Palestinian terrorism to western media is followed immediately by speeches in Arabic to his followers to continue the Intifada until the Jews are driven from Palestine. There are no maps showing the nation of Israel in the textbooks of the schools of the Palestinian Authority. They repeatedly deny that Israel has any right to exist in the Middle East. A report by Israel Radio Territories correspondent Avi Yisachar reported on November 9, 2000, that Yasser Arafat told Marwan Barghouti, the general secretary of Fatah and the PLO Tanzim terrorist group, that he wants Israeli blood to motivate the

Arab regimes to send the PLO more money. Marwan Barghouti bragged to his Fatah friends that Arafat told him how to interpret his public announcements about terrorism. Arafat is reported to have declared,

> Every time that you hear me declare a cease fire and a halt to the violence, ignore these declarations. You know that I am under heavy pressure from the United States and Europe. You should ignore this and continue. You should know that we are in difficult financial situation because of the Intifada. We will not receive any more money from the United States and Israel will stop the monthly transfer of funds. Our only hope for getting money is from the Arab states. But the Arab states will not give money if there is not blood. Therefore, press, press, press [*idhas, idhas, idhas*].[5]

The Areas Under The Palestinian Authority.

The *Jerusalem Post* newspaper reported on October 19, 2000, that Arafat's Palestinian Authority released its most notorious Hamas and Islamic Jihad terrorist killers from jail. Israeli security officials warned that a new wave of terror attacks would commence in Israel because the terrorists released by Arafat include technically proficient bomb-makers, operators of sophisticated terror cells, and those trained to commit suicide bombings. This release of the "worst of the worst" of known Palestinian terrorist killers is a blatant violation of peace agreements signed between Israel and the Palestinian Authority, which demand that the PA retain terrorists in prison. However, this revolving door policy of arresting known terrorists when Israel or America insist and then, a few days later, releasing them to house arrest or allowing "prison breaks" makes it impossible to obtain a true peace with the Palestinian Authority.

The terrorists released included Adnan Jaber Ghul and Mahmoud Rajeb Zatma, a master bomb-maker who made bombs that killed seventy-eight Israelis. Hashem Malek Dib helped bomb the Dizengoff Center, killing thirteen people, while Salah Talachma murdered eleven Israelis. Arafat also released the most dangerous killer of the Hamas group, Mohammed Deif, who was responsible for numerous civilian deaths.[6]

This release of deadly terrorists was designed to coincide with the beginning of the Al-Aqsa Intifada that was planned to be launched with the murder of an Israeli soldier two days before Prime Minister Sharon visited the Temple Mount in his legal exercise of the right to visit holy places that is granted by Israeli law to every citizen regardless of religion. Those who condemn the prime minister's visit as provocative should realize that this visit was discussed and approved in advance by the Palestinian Authority's security chief. It simply served as a PLO pretext to launch a violent Intifada by those Palestinians who illegally deny the right of the Jews to visit their ancient holy places.

The evidence is overwhelming that the Palestinian Authority is not a true "partner for peace" with Israel because its leadership, including Yasser Arafat, totally rejects the prospect of real peace with the Jewish state. The fundamental reason is that the Arabs and the Palestinians totally refuse to acknowledge the right of the Jews to live in the Middle East in a state with secure borders. Although they have repeatedly signed peace agreements with Israel and cosigned with America's presidents, they simply see this as a tactic to gain time, territory, funds, and strategic positioning to allow them to destroy the Jewish population when the final, decisive war takes place in the future. The proof of this discouraging truth about Arafat's commitment to terrorism rather than peace is found in the speeches he makes to Arab audiences and the textbooks that he has approved for use in Palestinian Authority schools. The evidence is overwhelming that Palestinian youth are being trained for hatred and terror attacks against Jews, not to reach out to the Israelis as partners in peace.

For example, an eleventh grade PA textbook teaches about the inevitable victory of Islam over the West with these chilling words in a section entitled "Some Outstanding Examples of Our Civilization." The text declares: "We do not claim that the collapse of western civilization, and the transfer of the center of civilization to us [Islam] will happen in the next decade. Nevertheless [western civilization] has begun to collapse and to become a pile of rubble."

A seventh grade text has a section that contains this statement: "Islam, The True Religion: The Victory of Islam. This religion [Islam] will defeat all other religions and it will be disseminated, by Allah's will, through the Muslim Jihad fighters."[7]

Yemen

Yemen expanded its security cooperation with other Arab countries during the final years of the 1990s and agreed to a number of international antiterrorist conventions. The government agreed to provide stronger border controls, territorial surveillance, and better travel documents. In addition, it authorized a new counter terrorist unit within Yemen's Ministry of the Interior. However, poor security procedures and the government's inability to exercise security authority over remote desert areas of Yemen allowed the nation to become a base for many terrorist groups, including al Qaeda. Osama bin Laden's father was a Yemeni, as are many of the most fanatical terrorists who joined al Qaeda. A wide variety of terrorist groups make their home in Yemen, including Hamas, the Egyptian Islamic Jihad, and the al-Gama' at al-Islamiyya.

On December 18, 2001 special forces of the United States supported elite units of the Yemen armed forces to attack several al Qaeda terrorist training camps in the mountains far from the capital. After President Bush put great pressure on Yemen's president to join the hunt for al Qaeda terrorists living in his country, the government reluctantly joined in the alliance's hunt to root out the terrorists who are hiding in over seventy nations.

Sudan

Sudan has been a home for several international terrorist groups during the 1990s, especially al Qaeda. The U.S. government claims that Sudan allowed Iran to provide assistance to terrorist and radical Islamic groups in Sudan. Sudan refused to comply with the 1996 UN Security Council Resolutions 1044, 1054, and 1070, which demand that Sudan end all support to terrorists. The UN resolutions also required Sudan to surrender several Egyptian Gama'at terrorists who were involved in the 1995 assassination attempt against Egyptian president Hosni Mubarak during his trip to Ethiopia. Sudan is still a safe meeting place and training facility for terrorists from the Lebanese Hezbollah, Egyptian Gama' at al-Islamiyya, al-Jihad, the Palestinian Islamic Jihad, Hamas, and the Palestinian Abu Nidal organization. Sudan's security agency provides terrorists with travel documents, weapons, and refuge. These terror groups maintained offices in the capital until quite recently.

Somalia

For many years the Islamic government of Somalia in East Africa has openly supported Islamic terrorist groups including al Qaeda. Osama bin Laden publicly boasted about his al Qaeda terrorist's involvement in the attacks upon U.S. forces sent into Somalia to protect aid workers and assist in their desperate humanitarian crisis in the early 1990s. Eighteen U.S. Rangers were wiped out in a military ambush by the terrorists working for the Somalia war lords in their capital, Mogadishu, on October 3, 1993. The American government refused to provide the U.S. forces with tanks and heavy equipment despite urgent requests by their commanders on the ground. Rather than respond with overwhelming military force to this brutal attack on America's soldiers, President Clinton withdrew American armed forces from Somalia. This tragic decision created an abiding popular belief in the Arab world that the U.S. did not have the resolve (the "guts") to engage in military action against them that would result in severe American military casualties.

It is important to note that throughout history Arabs have responded to the perceived military weakness of their enemies with massively increased aggression. The Islamic terrorists have a proven contempt for the value of life, both their own lives as well as their enemies. It is not surprising that America's unwillingness to risk U.S. soldiers' lives in military actions against them during the 1990s Clinton administration gave the terrorists the false impression that the United States was unwilling to fight a serious "war to the death" against them. Osama bin Laden often refers to America's "defeat" in Somalia, the bombings of U.S. troops in Lebanon, Saudi Arabia, and the September 11, 2001 attack in New York and Washington as proof that America lacks the resolve and, therefore, cannot win against the growing militant forces of Islam.

However, the dramatic and overwhelming American-led victory of the alliance against terror over the terrorist forces of the Taliban and al Qaeda in Afghanistan will help reverse this incorrect perception of western and American weakness in the Arab world. While there were massive street demonstrations against America's war against the Taliban and al Qaeda forces in Afghanistan during the initial bombing raids, once the overwhelming military force of the United States Air Force began to devastate the terrorist military forces, the street demonstrations in Pakistan and the Palestinian-held areas of Israel almost immediately stopped.

In late December 2001 fifty U.S. Special Forces troops secretly entered Somalia and began conducting intelligence operations to identify and track down the numerous al Qaeda terrorists who use that nation as a base for their attacks on American interests.

Iran

Following the election of the moderate President Khatemi in 1997, the Iranian government has gradually begun to reduce its public support and secret finances provided to a campaign of international terrorism. Despite this reduced official support for terror attacks against Israel and the West, Iran still provides massive finance and sophisticated armaments to the following terrorist groups who cooperate in their continuing terrorist attacks on Israel: Hamas, Hizbullah, and Palestinian Islamic Jihad. Despite the changes desired by the president, Iran's feared intelligence services report directly to the extreme fundamentalist Islamic clergy of Iran, who remain totally committed to a holy war against both Israel and the United States.

A United States' grand jury completed its lengthy investigation of the 1996 terror bombing of the U.S. army troops at Khobar Towers in Saudi Arabia. Eighteen U.S. soldiers were killed. The grand jury issued an indictment on June 2001, charging that the Hizbullah terrorist organization in Saudi Arabia was responsible for this terrorist attack on American military forces. Significantly, after an in-depth examination of all of the criminal as well as intelligence data, the grand jury's indictment declared the Khobar Towers attack was "inspired, supported and directed by elements of the Iranian government."

Syria

Syria openly endorses terrorism and hatred of the Jews. Examples of Syrian officially supported government anti-Semitism are documented in a variety of Syrian textbooks, according to a study of eighty-five current Syrian textbooks completed by The Center for Monitoring the Impact of Peace. The study examined a tenth grade textbook entitled *National Pan-Arab Socialist Education* that is officially sponsored by the Assad regime. The textbook reports a speech by the late Syrian president Hafez Assad, in which he attacked the Jews, comparing them to the German Nazis, by declaring:

> Where is the difference between Nazism and Zionism? The Nazis claimed racial superiority and the Zionists

claim that they are the Chosen People. The Nazis justified occupation by the need for Lebensraum [living space], and the Zionists seize land on the pretext of a security belt for a state that was established by plunder and aggression. The Nazis expelled other peoples and the Zionists expel the Arabs.

Another tenth grade Syrian textbook teaches: "The Jews have planned the killing, pillage, and extermination of the Muslims, this is their treacherous nature." In another passage, the book declares that "the belligerence that is rooted in the Jewish personality threatens Arab and Islamic existence. Logic and justice call for one conclusion: the destruction of the Jews."[8] Syria remains the home for twenty Islamic terrorist groups.

Libya

For the past twenty years, Libya has been a leading terror-supporting nation on the United States' list of nations supporting terrorism. After seizing power in 1969, Muammar Qaddafi supported the spread of his revolutionary terrorist ideology throughout the Muslim world. Qaddafi expended enormous economic and military resources to achieve his "revolutionary goal." Qaddafi's government established ties with numerous terrorist organizations in the Middle East and Asia, providing them with financial, military, and intelligence assistance. A remarkable number of terrorist attacks were carried out during the last two decades under the direction of Libya's terrorist intelligence agencies throughout Europe, Asia, and South America.[9]

When Qaddafi addressed the Organization of Non-Aligned States in September 1986, the president of Libya declared: "I will do everything in my power to divide the world into imperialists and freedom-fighters." To Qaddafi, terrorists who attack Israel and the West are called "freedom fighters." Qaddafi declared that "national liberation can only be achieved through armed struggle." He said that any attempt by Middle Eastern nations to bargain, negotiate, or reach a compromise with the imperialists will fail and will harm the Arabs.

Libya provided state sponsorship for numerous Islamic and

left-wing revolutionary groups that opposed the policies of Israel and the nations of the West. Qaddafi set up the first professional terrorist training camps in the Libyan desert and commenced a massive flow of sophisticated arms to a multitude of terrorist organizations throughout the globe. Following the revolution in Eastern Europe against the communists, the president of Czechoslovakia admitted in March 1990 that the former communist government had sold the Libyan security agencies over a thousand tons of deadly Semtex plastic explosives. The Czech president admitted, "This quantity is sufficient to support terrorism throughout the world for 150 years."

In 1986, a terrorist bomb exploded in a West Berlin disco called "La Belle Discotheque," which was filled with off-duty U.S. soldiers. The terrorist attack killed two U.S. soldiers and one Turkish civilian and wounded two hundred civilians. The American CIA investigators declared that the perpetrators were linked to Libyan state-sponsored terrorists. When European reporters disputed the evidence, President Reagan revealed that America had intercepted radio messages from Libya to its German embassy that instructed the terrorists to attack the U.S. soldiers. In response, the American air force launched a devastating attack on numerous Libyan targets, including President Qaddafi's own coastal home. The missiles destroyed Qaddafi's home and inadvertently killed his adopted daughter.

While Libya has continued to develop secret bases in the southern deserts to produce sophisticated chemical and biological weapons of mass destruction, in the years following the 1986 retaliatory raid by American forces, the evidence suggests that Qaddafi's security forces have reduced their previous enthusiastic support for terrorist attacks against Israel and the West.

As long as these terrorist supporting nations provide funds, intelligence, and refuge to the numerous Islamic terrorists, we will never be able to free ourselves from this deadly threat to our freedom and democratic way of life. However, if this alliance against terrorism continues its relentless economic, political, and military attack against these supporters of terror, we can make it very difficult for Islamic terrorism to succeed.

In the months and years following the deadly September

11 attack on America, the U.S. led alliance should continue its determined military attacks on those states that have joined in a terrorist plot to destroy the West. If we stay the course and deal decisively with them one by one, they will be forced to stop harboring terror groups in their countries. We can, and we must win this war on terror.

Endnotes

1. "Fact Sheet: The Taliban's Betrayal of the Afghan People." 17 Oct. 2001. U.S. Department of the State Web site: http://usinfo.state.gov/topical/pol/terror/01101712.htm.

2. Shalva Weil, *The Jerusalem Report*. 22 Oct. 2001.

3. Flavius Josephus. *Antiquities of the Jews*, 13 b, xi. c v., 2.

4. Yitzhak Ben-Zvi. *The Exiled and the Redeemed*. (Philadelphia: Jewish Publication Society of America, 1957).

5. Aaron Lerner. "Arafat Told Marwan Barghouti He Wants Blood." 9 Nov. 2000. http://pages.prodigy.net/vladrjr/Them/Idhas.html.

6. "Arch-Terrorists Released by the Palestinian Authority," *The Jerusalem Post*. 19 Oct. 2000.

7. *Islamic Education for Seventh Grade*, Palestinian Authority 125.

8. *Islamic Education*, Syrian Dept. of Education, 115.

9. "Survey of Arab Affairs—A periodic supplement to Jerusalem Letter/ Viewpoints" SAA:28 29, 1 June 1992.

4

Why Do the Arabs Hate the United States and Israel?

To the surprise and shock of millions of North Americans and Europeans, the tragic destruction of the World Trade Center towers on September 11 triggered massive expressions of joy throughout the Middle East, including the supposed allies of America such as Egypt, Saudi Arabia, Jordan, and the Palestinians who have previously received billions of dollars of aid from the United States. Despite decades of continuous American diplomatic and financial support of the Palestinian aspiration for their own nation state in the West Bank and Gaza, the spontaneous expressions of glee and Palestinian public street celebrations in response to the terrible attacks against the citizens of the United States were both genuine and heartfelt expressions of the deep hatred of America that is felt by millions. These strong anti-American feelings have been powerfully promoted by the leaders of the Palestinian Authority for many decades.

A public opinion poll taken in November 2000 measured the depth of Palestinian hostility. The poll reveals: 73 percent of

Palestinians support military action against American targets in the Middle East. Regarding suicide missions against American interests in the Middle East, 73 percent supported and 22 percent opposed them. It is interesting that the support for suicide attacks against American targets among academics reached 77 percent compared to 70 percent among illiterates."[1] This public opinion poll was conducted by Beir Zet University, in Ramallah in the West Bank and was published in *Al-Hayat Al-Jadeeda*, the official daily newspaper of Arafat's Palestinian Authority.

Tens of thousands of Palestinians rushed to the streets in spontaneous celebration of the massive terrorist attacks on September 11, 2001, shooting guns in the air and exchanging sweets in their customary expression of joyful feelings. As CNN and other western media began to broadcast their ruthless expressions of hatred and contempt for the lives of thousands of innocent American terrorist victims, the leaders of the PLO realized that hundreds of millions of Americans and Europeans were horrified and disgusted by this brazen display. Yasser Arafat's Palestinian Authority took several immediate measures to counteract the broadcast of these spontaneous Palestinian celebrations.

The Palestinian Authority's Minister of Information, Yasser Abed Rabbo, demanded that western media officials immediately cease broadcasting the obscene Palestinian celebrations, and then they threatened the lives of any western journalists who would dare to televise the Palestinians rejoicing at the deaths of Americans. In addition, his security staff forcibly stole the videotapes from the cameras of western journalists who had already recorded these revealing but politically revolting displays of rejoicing at American deaths and the expression of pure hatred for the United States. Next, the Palestinian Authority officials arranged for public Palestinian displays of sympathy for America's tragedy. A conspicuous photo of PLO Chairman Yasser Arafat, the hater of Americans, donating blood for New Yorkers was provided to the western media, together with propaganda photographs of Palestinian children carrying signs (in the English language that they could not read) claiming they shared sympathy with "fellow" victims of terrorism.

The Palestinian Authority has actively supported hatred

against both the United States and Israel for several decades in its school curriculum, its daily newspapers, its public speeches, and in its endorsement of hatred taught daily within its mosques. The continuing theme of this nonstop propaganda is that the United States is an imperial power, a colonial thief of Arab historic lands, and the enemy of Arab human rights, an opposer of the Arab world, the killer of Arab men, women, and children and, worst of all, the major supporter of the State of Israel. Consider the evidence from the official newspaper of the Palestinian Authority, *Al-Hayat Al-Jadeeda*: "The suicide bombers of today are the noble successors of their noble predecessors . . . the Lebanese suicide bombers, who taught the US Marines a tough lesson in [Lebanon]. . . . These suicide bombers are the salt of the earth, the engines of history. . . . They are the most honorable [people] among us."[2] A few weeks before the attacks, the paper wrote: "[Maher Taher] a member of the political bureau of the Popular Front for the Liberation of Palestine . . . said in a press conference in Damascus: we say to the Arab nation: 'Hit American interests and threaten them. United States is a fundamental enemy which takes part and holds responsibility to the elimination of the Palestinian people and the Palestinian villages. He asked the Arab countries to take a clear and strict position towards USA, which is a fundamental enemy of the Palestinian people and Arab Nation.'"[3]

On July 11, 1997, the Palestinian Authority appointed as its authorized spiritual leader, the Mufti of Jerusalem and Palestine, Sheikh Ekrima Sabri, who preached his Friday sermon at the ancient Al-Aqsa Mosque on the Temple Mount. This is part of his sermon as broadcast on the PA controlled Voice of Palestine radio:

> Oh Allah, destroy America, for she is ruled by Zionist Jews. . . . Allah will paint the White House black! . . . The Muslims say to Britain, to France, and to all the infidel nations that Jerusalem is Arab. We shall not respect anyone else's wishes regarding her. The only relevant party is the Islamic nation, which will not allow infidel nations to interfere. . . . Allah shall take revenge on behalf of his prophet against the colonialist settlers who are sons of monkeys and pigs.[4]

In light of this evil provocation to attack America, you might wonder why the U.S.A. provides hundreds of millions in support of the Palestinian Authority.

G. J. O. Moshay, an Arab scholar who studied Islam, wrote the book *Who Is This Allah?* In it he claimed that a great deal of the Islamic incitement to implacable hatred, religious violence, and jihad is derived from a number of important passages within the Muslim's holy book, the Koran, that are directed against Jews and Christians.[5]

The Islamic text, *Holy Hadith*, declares that jihad ("holy war") is the truest method to acquire eternal spiritual benefits in heaven as well as temporal blessings during life on earth. "If there is defeat or death, there is everlasting paradise."[6]

Arab Ingratitude For America's Efforts to Save Muslims

The Arab world's fanatical hatred is fueled to an enormous degree by the virtually continuous stream of vitriolic anti-American and anti-Israel propaganda that is continuously preached in mosques, broadcast by Arab radio and television stations, and printed in articles in the Arab government-controlled newspapers and magazines. Despite the billions of dollars in foreign aid that America has donated to the various Arab nations over the last fifty years, the totalitarian governments that rule the twenty-one Arab dictatorships that surround Israel find it convenient to focus the rage and hatred of their restless and angry populations against a perceived outside western enemy to prevent this resentment from focussing on the obvious failure of their own Arab governments to meet the legitimate economic and political aspirations of their people.

Despite the perception in much of the Arab-Islamic world that America is their greatest enemy, nothing could be further from the truth. Consider the history of the last decade. The United States has gone to war several times in the 1990s—every time in defense of Muslims against a variety of enemies. Following Saddam Hussein's brutal 1990 invasion of Iraq's neighbor Kuwait and its immediate military threat to Saudi Arabia, America built up an enormous military force of more than 700,000 soldiers to expel the Iraqi army from Kuwait in the spring of 1991 and eliminate the military threat to the other Arab nations occupying the Saudi Arabian peninsula. Then, in 1995, America used its diplomatic and military power to protect the Muslims of Bosnia from their Bosnian Serb and Croatian enemies. Next, in 1999, America led powerful NATO attacks against the Serbian army to protect the Albanian Muslims in Kosovo from being wiped out by the Serb paramilitary forces.

On these three occasions in the last decade of the twentieth century America intervened at great cost to save Muslim populations from destruction by their enemies. Yet there has been virtually no gratitude expressed by Islamic clergy or governments. In fact, the propaganda attacks have continued unabated. One Arab-American commentator, Fouad Ajami, a professor at John Hopkins University's School of Advanced International Studies, wrote: "Where was Islamist gratitude for America's role in preventing Muslims from being slaughtered in Bosnia in 1995 and in Kosovo in 1999?. . . American power was used three times between 1990 and 2000 to rescue Muslims from ruin, but no Islamist has ever thanked them."[7]

What thanks has America received from its so-called Arab allies in the Middle East, whom the U.S. now attempts to placate while ignoring its only true democratic ally, Israel? Kuwait and Saudi Arabia initially refused to allow American planes to be based in their nations in defense of their sovereignty in the war against the terrorists hiding in Afghanistan. In fact, the lack of gratitude to America was so egregious that Kuwait's former oil and information minister criticized his own government for its "shameful" betrayal of the United States through Kuwait's "hesitant and timid" support for America's war against international terror.[8]

Islamic-Palestinian Hatred of Israel
The Declaration of the Supreme Fatah Movement Council

On October 8, 2000, the Supreme Council of the Fatah Movement, the major Palestinian political party of PLO Chairman Yasser Arafat, issued their response to the Israeli ultimatum of peace. The *Fatah* terrorist group is the largest faction in the PLO organization. The word *Fatah* is derived by reversing the letters of the Arabic word

Hataf that means "sudden death." The Declaration of the Supreme Fatah Movement Council was published in *Al-Hayat Al-Jadeeda*, the Palestinian Authority's newspaper and broadcast on Palestinian television. The most significant of the twelve points are:

- The Fatah movement emphasizes the continuation of the Al Quds Intifada (Uprising) in all of its activities.

- The Fatah movement calls for its brave sons who stand at the front lines in all the disturbances to continue their great struggle and even to increase it in the course of the coming days.

- The Fatah movement gives its blessings and support to our brothers in the security apparatus, security forces and police, who defend with their blood the souls of their nation. Blessings and support also to the guns of Fatah.

- The Fatah movement calls on our public to boycott Israeli products. There are substitutes in the Palestinian markets. Fatah calls on businessmen to stop the importation of goods from Israel and calls on advertising agencies not to advertise them.

- The Fatah movement calls on the masses of our nation to prevent the activity and movement of the joint patrols in areas of the Palestinian National Authority. Likewise the movement calls for an end to security cooperation.

- The Fatah movement calls for the bypass roads to be closed and that the movement of settlers to be interfered with.

- The Fatah movement blesses and strengthens all the Arab and Islamic nations in light of their historical position and their protests everywhere in the world, something that strengthens the struggle of the Palestinian people. The movement calls for them to continue and express their support in the struggle of the Palestinian people.

- The Fatah movement calls on our masses to respond to the calls of the national and Islamic forces and organize Intifada activities. The movement calls for the strengthening of Palestinian national unity and to rise above everything that divides.

- The Fatah movement calls for the negotiations to end and to dedicate attention and coverage to the goal of strengthening the Intifada. Likewise, the movement declares that it blesses the decision to hold an Arab summit.

* The Fatah movement calls on the masses of the Palestinian public and the Arab and Islamic nation to participate in processions of rage this coming Friday October 13 after Friday services. The Fatah movement blesses our nation on the liberation of Joseph's Tomb, with the assistance of the Fatah fighter, on the way towards the liberation of the rest of the strongholds and the liberation of the homeland from its chains.
* This is a revolution until victory . . . until victory . . . until victory.[9]

Arab Denial of the Holocaust

Despite overwhelming historical, photographic, documentary, and judicial evidence from the Nuremberg War Crimes Tribunal, it is common to read or hear outright denials of the reality of the Jewish Holocaust appearing in official Arab media and school textbooks. An example of officially endorsed Holocaust denial by Arab media is revealed in an article in the widely read Egyptian daily newspaper, *Al-Akhbar* that appeared on September 25, 1998. In "The Holocaust, Netanyahu and Me," writer Wahya Abu Thawkra declared:

> The Jews invented the myth of mass extermination and the fabrication that 6 million Jews were put to death in Nazi ovens. This was done with the aim of motivating the Jews to emigrate to Israel and to blackmail the Germans for money as well as to achieve world support for the Jews. Similarly, Zionism based itself on this myth to establish the State of Israel. . . . I continue to believe that the Holocaust is an Israeli myth that was invented to blackmail the world.[10]

The widespread denial of the Holocaust in the Arab nations contributes to their belief that the Jewish exiles return to the Promised Land is unjust. This popular rejection of Israel's right to exist is partially based on years of continuous Arab propaganda that denies the ancient existence of the Jewish kingdom and even denies that the Jews ever built a Temple in Jerusalem.

Arab and Islamic Extreme Hatred of Israel and America

The Islamic extremists among the Palestinians and other Arab groups have constantly used Islamic sources to defend their religious and racial hatred of the Israelis, even to the point of demanding that Arabs kill all Jews as a religious Islamic obligation and obedience to the will of Allah. The Palestinian religious leaders have publicly taught that the *Hadith* (Islamic traditions attributed to Mohammed) reveal Allah's will that Palestinian Muslims must kill Jews.

An Islamic preacher, Dr. Muhammed Ibrahim Madi, recently chastized Arab-Muslim world leaders on Palestinian TV for avoiding attacking Israel with missiles and tanks. He threatened that Allah is liable to "replace them with other men . . . that fight for Allah . . . to liberate the lands from the defilement of the Jews."[11] Sheikh Muhammed Abd al Hadi La' afi was quoted in the official Palestinian Authority newspaper *Al-Hayat Al-Jadeeda* on May 18, 2001, claiming that the Islamic writing *Hadith* declares: "The Day of Resurrection will not arrive until the Moslems make war against the Jews and kill them, and until a Jew hiding behind a rock and tree, and the rock and tree will say: 'Oh Moslem, Oh servant of Allah, there is a Jew behind me, come and kill him!'" Another PLO TV broadcast declared: "It is forbidden for anyone, Arab, Palestinian or Moslem to forgo one grain of soil of the land of Palestine, Jerusalem, and Al Aksa. . . . Whoever forgoes even one grain of soil his sin is upon him, and all the sins of the Palestinians, the Arabs and the Moslems, forever and ever."[12]

Following the brutal June 2001 suicide bombing of the Israeli dance hall in Tel Aviv that killed dozens of innocent Israeli young people, the television program that is officially sponsored by the Palestinian Authority broadcast the following message:

> Blessed is he who fights jihad in the name of Allah, blessed is he who [goes on] raids in the name of Allah, blessed is he who dons a vest of explosives on himself or on his children and goes in to the depth of the Jews and says: 'Allahu

Akbar, blessed be Allah.' Like the collapse of the building upon the heads of the Jews in their sinful dance-hall, I ask of Allah that we see the Knesset collapsing on the heads of the Jews.[13]

Israeli and Arab Conflict Over the Promised Land

The basis of the Arab-Israeli conflict includes both race, religion and the struggle for the Promised Land. We'll briefly touch on some of the areas of contention between the two peoples, each of whom feels entitled to the land the State of Israel now occupies.

Of course we are familiar with the decrees from God giving the land to Israel. God promised the land to Abraham: "Lift up now thine eyes, and look from the place where thou art northward, and southward, and eastward, and westward: For all the land thou seest, to thee I will give it, and to thy seed for ever" (Genesis 12:14–15). Later, as Joseph, Jacob's son, lay dying in Egypt, he declared to his brothers, "I die: and God will surely visit you, and bring you out of this land unto the land which he sware to Abraham, to Isaac, and to Jacob" (Genesis 50:24). Hundreds of years later God reiterated His promise through Moses, whom God chose to lead His people out of slavery in Egypt: "I will take you to me for a people, and I will be to you a God: and ye shall know that I am the Lord your God, which bringeth you out from under the burdens of the Egyptians. And I will bring you in unto the land, concerning the which I did swear to give it to Abraham, to Isaac, and to Jacob; and I will give it you for an heritage" (Exodus 6:7–8).

The Koran Declares that the Holy Land Belongs to the Jews

The Old Testament is not the only document to declare that the Jews are entitled to their Promised Land. It is fascinating to note that there are a number of passages (known as surahs) in the Koran as written by Mohammed that relate to the Children of Israel and her possession of the Holy Land. These passages in the Koran, though ignored by the Arabs, are intriguing in that they clearly acknowledge and affirm the right of the Jews to possess the land of Israel. The Koran declares:

And when Musa [Moses] said to his people [Israel]: O my people! Remember the favor of Allah upon you when He raised prophets among you and made you kings and gave you what He had not given to any other among the nations. O my people! Enter the holy land which Allah has prescribed for you and turn not on your backs for then you will turn back losers. (Surah 5:20–21)

It is worthwhile to note that this passage, Surah 5:20–21, actually declares that this territory of Israel was for the Jews and was not given by Allah to any other people. Specifically the Koran affirms to Israel that Allah "made you kings and gave you what He had not given to any other among the nations." This statement is confirmed in several other passages in the Koran, including Surah 17:104: "And We said to the Israelites after him: Dwell in the land: and when the promise of the next life shall come to pass, we will bring you both together in judgment."

The Koran clearly declares that Allah chose and blessed the Jewish people ("above the nations") and gave them the Torah ("the communications wherein was clear blessing"). The Koran states, "And certainly We chose them, having knowledge, above the nations. And We gave them of the communications wherein was clear blessing" (Surah 44:32–33). In an extraordinary statement in Surah 45:16 we find these words endorsing the Jewish Torah and even a declaration that God created Israel to "excel the nations." "And certainly We gave the Book and the wisdom and the prophecy to the children of Israel, and We gave them of the goodly things, and We made them excel the nations" (Surah 45:16).

If the Islamic peoples of the world, especially the Arabs, were to carefully read these passages, it might allow them to sit down and negotiate peace in the Middle East with the Jewish people. However, the Word of God reveals that the Middle East will not find true peace until the Prince of Peace returns to set up His kingdom on earth. Unfortunately, both history and prophecy reveal that the Middle East and the world itself will not experience true lasting peace until the conclusion of the catastrophic Battle of Armageddon that will usher in the righteous and eternal government of peace under the rule of Jesus the Messiah. He will judge the evildoers and will change the hearts of all Arabs and Jews to love peace and justice.

Islam and the Temple Mount

The Temple Mount in Jerusalem, the holiest site for the Jews, is also sacred for the Muslim peoples of the world due to its association with Mohammed, the Prophet of Islam. The Temple Mount area is called the "Haram ash-Sharif," which means "Noble Sanctuary." The area is considered to be the third most holy site for Muslims after the holy cities of Mecca and Medina in Saudi Arabia. Mecca and Medina are much more closely associated with the life and actions of Mohammed and his disciples than Jerusalem. There is no historical evidence that Mohammed ever visited Jerusalem. However, the Muslims teach that Mohammed visited the Noble Sanctuary on the Temple Mount and, according to their tradition, he departed on his mystical journey to the seventh Heaven on his white horse, Burak, from the very rock which is now located under the Dome of the Rock. The Al-Aqsa Mosque at the far southern edge of the Temple Mount is believed to be referred to in the Koran as the "far place" that is now associated with Mohammed's heavenly journey from Jerusalem. There are a number of Islamic buildings and structures on the surface of the Temple Mount today.

The Dome of the Rock

The most prominent and beautiful building on the present Temple Mount is the golden Dome of the Rock. It is one of the oldest continuously used religious shines in the world. Many people mistakenly refer to the Dome of the Rock as the Mosque of Omar. While the Dome is a shrine that is used for prayer, the only proper mosque is the Al-Aqsa Mosque, which is located several hundred yards to the south in the building on the edge of the southern wall. A mosque is used for preaching, prayers, and other religious services, while a shrine such as the Dome of the Rock is used only for contemplation and prayers.

From the date of the Muslim conquest of Jerusalem from the Persians and the building of the Dome of the Rock by Omar in

691 until 1856, the punishment for any infidel or nonbeliever for visiting the Noble Sanctuary was the death penalty. While several brave western explorers risked their lives to enter the Dome of the Rock and provide firsthand research about the Temple Mount during past centuries, serious exploration could only take place after the Turkish governor passed a decree in 1856 that allowed people of all faiths to enter under controlled conditions.

The Muslims agree with the Jews that this was the place of Abraham's offer of his son to God. The Koran often quotes passages from the Old Testament and accepts the historicity of King David and Solomon. It also contains a distinct prophecy that Jesus the Messiah will finally return to the holy site through the sealed Eastern Gate. A supreme Muslim counsel called the Waqf governs the religious affairs of the Muslims connected with the Haram ash-Sharif.

The Al-Aqsa Mosque

The Al-Aqsa mosque is known as "the furthest one," in comparison to the central mosque of Islam, which is located in Mecca, Saudi Arabia. This very large Al-Aqsa Mosque was built two years after the completion of the Dome of the Rock. The major entrance is located in its northern wall where you must remove your shoes to enter into its huge open central sanctuary, whose roof is supported by enormous and beautiful white marble pillars. Some of these pillars are over five feet in diameter, and several near the main door still bear the scars of bullets that were fired during the August 1952 assassination of King Abdullah of Jordan by a Palestinian terrorist.

The entire mosque is built on top of the ancient underground building, which dates back to the building of the Second Temple in 516 B.C. This large subterranean structure is called the ancient Aqsa-al-kadeem and leads from the southern temple wall and the lower level Hulda Gates to the ancient steps which were used by Jesus and His disciples as the major entrance up to the Temple Mount. These halls from the Double and Triple Hulda Gates, though sealed at the southern wall, still lead diagonally up under the Al-Aqsa Mosque and up ancient stone stairs to the surface of the Temple Mount just outside the doors of the mosque. My wife,

Kaye, and I personally explored and photographed with camera and video the entire underground complex in 1990, including the enormous southeastern subterranean structure known as Solomon's Stables that extends north from the southern wall of the Temple Mount. Its roof is supported by rows of huge ancient stone columns.

My Israeli archeologist sources told me that no other non-Muslim had visited and photographed in this religiously sensitive area since the 1967 visit by the late Moshe Dayan, the Israeli defense minister, following the Six-Day War. Tragically, the Muslim authorities have recently conducted an enormous and very destructive construction project on the southern part of the underground Temple Mount. This construction on the archeologically important Temple Mount violates Israeli law. Although they have illegally destroyed numerous Jewish and Muslim archeological ruins, the Muslim religious authorities are indifferent to this loss of precious historical knowledge in their determination to build an enormous underground mosque in the area that was formerly known as Solomon's Stables. Despite many protests by Jewish archeologists, the Israeli government is concerned that any attempt by the Jewish authorities to stop the Muslim building of a mosque will trigger a holy war with the surrounding Arab nations.

The Sealed Golden Gate

Then said the Lord unto me; This gate shall be shut, it shall not be opened, and no man shall enter in by it; because the Lord, the God of Israel, hath entered in by it, therefore it shall be shut. It is for the prince. (Ezekiel 44:2–3)

Another structure on the Temple Mount that is of vital importance to the Muslims, Jews, and Christians is the beautiful Eastern Gate, often called the Golden Gate. The Arab name for the sealed Golden Gate is Bab-ad-Daharia–"the occasional gate" because it was to be opened only on rare occasions. The sealed gate has two doors like most of the other ancient gates of the Temple. The northern gate is called Bab-as-Thouba, the Gate of Repentance, and the southern one is called Bab-ar-Rachma, the Gate of Mercy. The gate is 1,035 feet from the southeast corner of the mount and extends sixty-two inches out from the present eastern wall. The Eastern Gate is really a gate-building that is approximately fifty-seven feet wide and ninety feet deep.

While the subterranean foundation ashlar stones of the Golden Gate clearly date back to the reign of King Solomon, the gate was repeatedly destroyed and rebuilt like many other structures on the Temple Mount. When the Muslim caliph Omar captured Jerusalem and began to build the Dome of the Rock in 691, the gate was already sealed. When the Turkish general, Suleiman the Magnificent, rebuilt the present walls of Jerusalem in the 1600s, his Turkish workmen rebuilt the top portion of this gate-building with the much smaller stones you can see on the topmost levels of the gate and the city wall today.

As we stood on the Temple Mount several years ago and examined the inside walls of the Golden Gate, my Islamic guide told me that Muslims believed the gate was sealed centuries ago to prevent anyone other than the Prophet Jesus from entering. He claimed that they knew that it was prophesied that Jesus would enter through the Golden Gate in the last days and then judge mankind.

If you approach the sealed Eastern Gate from the outside eastern walls of the Temple Mount, you must walk through a Muslim cemetery. Centuries ago, the Arab rulers chose to build a cemetery directly in front and to both sides of the sealed gate. The graveyard now extends for a great distance along the Eastern Wall. When I last visited it, I noticed that several gravestones were placed directly in front of the gate only two inches from the base. The reason for choosing that particular place for a graveyard was due to the reluctance of the Arabs to accept the implications of the prophecy that Jesus will someday enter through the Eastern Gate and save the Jewish people. Because their priests will not spiritually defile themselves by walking through a graveyard, the Arab rulers thought that the presence of a graveyard and the sealed gate would prevent the coming of Jesus the Messiah to save His Chosen People and set up His kingdom. Interestingly, an Israeli Jew had written the words "Ba Ha Moshiach," on the huge stones sealing the gate. Translated from Hebrew, these words mean "Come Messiah."

Prophecy Declared the Eastern Gate Will Be Shut

It is for the prince; the prince, he shall sit in it to eat bread before the Lord; he shall enter by the way of the porch of that gate, and shall go out by the way of the same. (Ezekiel 44:3)

Thousands of years ago, the Lord revealed to his prophet Ezekiel that this Eastern Gate would be sealed and reserved for Jesus the Messiah, "the Prince." The gate has been sealed with stones for over twelve hundred years. Twice in the last century the Arabs attempted to open the sealed gate. First on December 9, 1917, the Muslim leaders of Jerusalem tried and failed to break the prophecy and open the gate. As the Allied Expeditionary Army led by the British general Lord Allenby approached Jerusalem, the grand Mufti, the Arab leader of Jerusalem, ordered the other gates of Jerusalem to be sealed with stones to deter the tanks of the approaching army. Since they needed one gate of the city to remain open, he ordered his workmen to open the sealed Eastern Gate. As the Eastern Gate was on a steep hill he believed that the primitive British tanks would not be able to attack that gate. As the workman picked up their sledgehammers, Lord Allenby sent a biplane flying over the city dropping leaflets warning the Turkish army to "flee Jerusalem." Miraculously, without a shot being fired, the soldiers fled the city. Jerusalem was delivered into the hands of Britain, which had already promised the Jews "a national homeland" with their famous November 1917 Balfour Declaration. The workmen fearfully put down their sledgehammers and the gate remained sealed.

Fifty years later, in June 1967, Ezekiel's ancient prophecy was tested again. Tensions were rising in the Middle East as the Arab nations mobilized a million soldiers for war and ordered the United Nations peacekeeping forces to leave the Sinai. Egypt illegally stopped Israeli shipping and moved its armed forces into attack formations to invade the Jewish state. King Hussein of Jordan had conquered the Old City of Jerusalem in 1948, including the Temple Mount. For the first time in centuries, the Jews were forbidden from 1948 until the Six-Day War in 1967 to worship at their sacred Western Wall. King Hussein planned to build a hotel for Islamic pilgrims on this section of the Western Wall, preventing Jewish worship there forever. However, the plans called for the hotel to be built over the ancient Magreb Gate, which pilgrims and tourists use to enter the Temple Mount.

The king needed to open another gate to allow Muslim worshipers entrance to the Al-Aqsa Mosque on the Temple Mount. In violation of Ezekiel's prophecy, King Hussein ordered his workmen to open the sealed Eastern Gate. On June 5, 1967, as the workmen prepared their air hammers to shatter the ancient stones, Israeli preemptively responded to the massive Arab war preparations and commenced its astonishing victory over the Arab armed forces. Israeli fighter bombers took off from their huge underground air base in the Valley of Jezreel (Armageddon) to quickly destroy their enemies' air forces and armored tank formations. As the stunningly successful Six-Day War began, King Hussein's workmen put down their tools. The Eastern Gate will remain sealed until the day when the prophesied Messiah will return to the rebuilt Temple and enter into His promised kingdom. The prophecy of Ezekiel will finally be fulfilled at the Second Coming, when Jesus Christ will descend on the Mount of Olives to save the Jewish remnants of Jerusalem from the surviving army of the Antichrist. He will then cross the Kidron Valley through the ancient Garden of Gethsemane, where he spent many hours praying. Then He will enter the Temple Mount through the sealed Eastern Gate.

The Lord declared to the prophet Habakkuk centuries ago:

And the Lord answered me, and said, Write the vision, and make it plain upon tables, that he may run that readeth it. For the vision is yet for an appointed time, but at the end it shall speak, and not lie: though it tarry, wait for it; because it will surely come, it will not tarry. (Habakkuk 2:2–3)

Endnotes

1. *Al-Hayat Al-Jadeeda.* 11 Nov. 2000.
2. *Al-Hayat Al-Jadeeda.* 11 Sept. 2001.
3. *Al-Hayat Al-Jadeeda.* 28 Aug. 2001.
4. Sheikh Ekrima Sabri, Sermon excerpts, Voice of Palestine radio, 11 July 1997.
5. G. J. O. Moshay. *Who is This Allah?* (Dorchester House Publications, 1994) 24.
6. *Mishkat Masabih*, Vol. II, 253.
7. Editorial, *Washington Times*, 4 Nov. 2001.
8. Editorial, *Washington Times*, 4 Nov. 2001.
9. Supreme Fatah Movement Council, *Al-Hayat Al-Jadeeda*, 8 Oct. 2000.
10. *Al-Akhbar*, 25 Sept. 1998.
11. Palestinian TV. 30 March, 2001.
12. Palestinian TV, 8 Sept. 2000.
13. Palestinian Authority TV broadcast. 8 June 2001.

5

Iraq's War of Revenge Against America

Iraqi president Saddam Hussein's strong hatred for the United States since his defeat by American and allied forces during the Gulf War provides powerful motivation for Iraq's policy of attacking the United States through terrorism. Iraq is the most likely nation to have the motivation, stamina, military, and intelligence organization to order the kind of terrorist attack that occurred on September 11, 2001. President Saddam Hussein's main goals are to get revenge on America, to eliminate the United Nations' economic sanctions against Iraq, to end inspection by the UN of his weapons of mass destruction, and to stop the continuing American and United Kingdom air force missile attacks on Iraqi targets. Hussein wants to be recognized as the greatest leader in the Arab world by both the leaders of his allies as well as the "Arab street." He dreams of restoring the power and glory of the ancient Babylonian empire and of becoming the strongest military power in the Gulf region.

Iraq's Threats to Exact Revenge against America

As soon as President George H. Bush declared his intention to confront Iraq's 1990 invasion of Kuwait, Saddam Hussein repeatedly threatened to destroy America for its opposition to his conquest as well as its support for his hated enemy, Israel. Iraqi's government radio service declared to the Iraqi people that they were determined to avenge this American attack. Iraq's first deputy prime minister, Taha Yasin Ramadan, announced on radio that the people of Iraq will "avenge the pure blood that has been shed no matter how long it takes."[1]

President George W. Bush recently appointed former CIA director James Woolsey to analyze the growing evidence from both secret intelligence sources as well as the criminal evidence that points to the government of Iraq as the source of the September 11 terror assault on America. Criminal evidence developed in the various trials of the numerous al Qaeda terrorists regarding their roles in the 1993 World Trade Center bombing, the simultaneous 1998 attacks on the two U.S. embassies in East Africa, and the 2000 bombing of the U.S.S. *Cole* destroyer in Yemen provides compelling evidence that Iraq may have planned and ordered these terrorist attacks. James Woolsey is now reviewing all the evidence regarding the 1993 World Trade Center bombing to determine the true role that Iraq played in the September 11, 2001 attack. Woolsey declared to Wolf Blitzer Reports—CNN that the evidence thus far "looks to me as if it's not something that a fellow sitting out in the middle of Afghanistan is going to be orchestrating—able to orchestrate by himself—even if he has several hundred million dollars."[2]

When and if the American government determines that overwhelming evidence confirms Iraq's involvement in this decade-long war of revenge against the United States, then President Bush will order his nation's powerful military and intelligence resources to destroy the Iraqi army and Saddam Hussein. The liberation of the oppressed people of Iraq, who have suffered for three decades from the incredibly repressive regime of Saddam Hussein, will be one of the greatest events in the recent history of the Middle East.

Tragically, this decade of devastating terrorist attacks against American citizens and soldiers might have been avoided if President George H. Bush had simply allowed the U.S. military to complete the military conquest of Iraq and Hussein's Republican Guard in the final days of the 1991 Gulf War. Iraq's population and thousands of Americans would have been spared from the terrorist attacks motivated by the vengeance of Saddam Hussein if the allied military forces assembled in Saudi Arabia to liberate Kuwait had only been ordered to liberate Iraq as well. Unfortunately, the president listened to the passive counsel of Russian President Gorbachev, the Arab-supporting diplomats in the U.S. State Department, and to the unenthusiastic advice of the chairman of the Joint Chiefs of Staff, Colin Powell.

Some diplomats claimed that the UN resolution that authorized the U.S.-led war in the Gulf against Iraqi forces only permitted the liberation of Kuwait but did not authorize the liberation of Iraq. However, this argument is ridiculous. If American forces had entered Baghdad, it would have allowed the United Nations to establish a peacekeeping force to oversee a temporary UN administration. This would have been followed eventually by an internationally supervised election of a true democratic regime for the first time in the history of Iraq. Hopefully, President George W. Bush will not repeat the mistake of his father. If Iraq is defeated militarily during the war against terror, there will be a genuine opportunity to liberate the long-suffering people of Iraq from a brutal and repressive dictatorship that are similar to the horrors of the Nazi regime of Adolf Hitler.

Bush Assassination Attempt in April 1993

The Iraqi government warned that they would exact personal revenge upon President George H. Bush and his associates "even if they leave office and disappear into oblivion." In April 1993, former President Bush visited Kuwait to be honored for liberating their nation from Iraqi aggression. Fortunately, Kuwaiti security forces detected a car bomb that Iraqi intelligence agents had intended to use to assassinate the former president. President Clinton addressed the U.S. Congress and declared: "This Thursday,

Attorney General Reno and Director of Central Intelligence Woolsey gave me their findings. Based on their investigation there is compelling evidence that there was, in fact, a plot to assassinate former President Bush; and that this plot, which included the use of a powerful bomb made in Iraq, was directed and pursued by the Iraqi Intelligence Service."[3]

Despite ample evidence of Iraq's involvement in a blatant terrorist attack on America's former president, President Clinton responded ineffectively by only sending cruise missiles into the Iraqi Intelligence Service's main command and control headquarters in Baghdad. Apparently, the president's attention was focused on domestic affairs at the time.

Al Qaeda's Threats to America In Defense of Iraq

In 1998, a statement was released by Osama bin Laden, the head of al Qaeda, and his second in command, Ayman al-Zawahiri, the head of the terrorist group Egyptian Islamic Jihad, using the new joint organizational name, World Islamic Front. Significantly, both bin Laden and Al-Zawahiri, al Qaeda's key terrorist planner, were indicted for the simultaneous bombings of the two U.S. embassies in East Africa. Curiously, the al Qaeda statement dealt almost exclusively with Iraq's complaints against U.S. actions against that nation during the Gulf War and in the decade that followed. The statement included three major complaints against America. The first two complaints deal with the United States' army presence in Saudi Arabia threatening Iraq as well as the continuing UN economic sanctions. It concludes with a demand that Muslims everywhere attack and kill American soldiers as well as civilian men, women, and children anywhere in the world.

> First, for over seven years the United States has been occupying the lands of Islam in the holiest of places, the Arabian peninsula, plundering its riches, dictating to its rulers, humiliating its people. . . . The best proof of this is the Americans' continuing aggression against the Iraqi people using the Peninsula as a staging post. . . .
>
> Second, despite the great devastation inflicted on the Iraqi people by the Crusader-Zionist [Christian-Jewish] alliance,

and despite the huge number of those killed, which has exceeded one million . . . despite all this, the Americans are once again trying to repeat the horrific massacres, as though they are not content with the protracted blockade imposed after the ferocious war or the fragmentation and devastation. So here they come to annihilate what is left of this people and to humiliate their Muslim neighbors. . . .

The ruling to kill the Americans and their allies—civilians and military—is an individual duty for every Muslim who can do it. . . . We—with God's help—call on every Muslim who believes in God . . . to kill the Americans and plunder their money wherever and whenever they find it. We also call on Muslim ulema, leaders, youths, and soldiers to launch the raid on Satan's U.S. troops and the devil's supporters allying with them.[4]

This signed terrorist declaration of war by al Qaeda against all American citizens throughout the world states that the U.S.'s actions against Iraq in the Gulf War and subsequent actions to control Iraq's aggressive development of weapons of mass destruction are the greatest provocations to the Islamic terrorist groups. This strongly suggests that al Qaeda is working hand in glove with Iraq's leadership and intelligence agencies to further their diabolical terrorist campaign against America, Israel, and the West. The evidence that Iraq is behind Osama bin Laden's many well-planned terrorist attacks on American targets is compelling.

Iraq Has Used bin Laden's Terrorists to Attack America

Western intelligence agencies have marshaled substantial evidence that Iraq provided the motivation, planning, support, and training for the terrorist attacks on September 11, 2001 and the numerous anthrax attacks that have followed. The prestigious defense journal *Jane's Foreign Report* states that Israel's military intelligence agency believes that Iraq is behind the massive terrorist attacks on the twin towers of the World Trade Center and the Pentagon. Israeli intelligence sources reported that senior Iraqi intelligence officers were meeting with al Qaeda terrorists as they traveled repeatedly from Baghdad to Afghanistan to set up conferences with Osama bin Laden's number-one deputy and probable successor, Ayman al-Zawahiri, the leader of the deadly terror group Egyptian Islamic Jihad. Iraq's agents also met with the chief Hizbullah terrorist, Imad Mughniyeh, in Lebanon, a man who is considered to be the most dangerous terrorist alive today. *Jane's Foreign Report* quotes the Israeli national TV news source, Arutz 7, as follows, "We've only got scraps of information, not the full picture—but it was good enough for us to send a warning six weeks ago to our allies that an unprecedented massive terror attack was expected. . . . We believe that the operational brains behind the New York attack were Mughniyeh and Zawahiri, who were probably financed and got some logistical support from the Iraqi Intelligence Service."[5]

A recent report by PBS's *Frontline* TV program on November 14, 2001, reported that the Iraqi ambassador to Turkey (the second highest official in Iraqi intelligence) offered Osama bin Laden a place of refuge in Iraq.

Iraqi Involvement in the 1993 World Trade Center Bombing

Anniversaries are very important for Arabs. In planning revenge for some perceived insult, it is common for an Arab to patiently wait for several years to exact their vengeance on the precise anniversary of the original slight. A well-known Arab proverb is, "Revenge is a dish best eaten cold." This is so well-known among counterterrorism experts that the U.S. State Department routinely issues special terrorism warnings to American bases and embassies on the anniversaries of particular historical dates. Therefore, it is very significant that the February 26, 1993, World Trade Center terrorist attack took place on the day of the second anniversary of the American army's liberation of Kuwait.

Author Laurie Mylroie has been a student of Iraq and its dictator President Saddam Hussein for many years. She claims that Iraq planned and financed al Qaeda's February 26, 1993, terrorist bombing of the World Trade Center. Mylroie suggests that the U.S. should examine the evidence that Iraqi-sponsored terrorism may be the instigator of the September 11, 2001, attack on the World Trade Center and the Pentagon. She believes that the criminal evidence revealed during the 1994 trial of the extremist Islamic defendants convicted of the 1993 attack proved that Iraq sponsored those al Qaeda terrorists. Mylroie warned that the actions of one of the prime suspects, Ahmed Ramzi Yousef, suggested that we will experience more terrorist attacks in the future. Significantly, Yousef used an Iraqi passport to enter the United States. However, he immediately fled America after the 1993 World Trade Center bombing using his new false identity, that of a Kuwaiti-born Pakistani national named Abdul Basit Karim.

Mylroie revealed that Iraqi intelligence agents altered Basit Karim's passport file in Kuwait during their 1990 military occupation of Kuwait. She points out that Iraqi intelligence agents could have doctored hundreds of Kuwaiti Interior Ministry passport files during their occupation, allowing their intelligence agents to provide numerous false identities to Saddam Hussein's terrorists. Another terrorist, Abdul Rahman Yasin, was charged with mixing the chemicals to make the huge WTC bomb. However, Abdul Rahman immediately fled to Baghdad, Iraq, to escape being arrested. He was observed in Baghdad in the spring of 1994 according to a June 1994 report by ABC News.[6] It is inconceivable that Abdul Rahman could enter and live in Iraq without the permission of Iraq's intelligence service. Mylroie suggests the September 11, 2001, attacks on the World Trade Center and the Pentagon reveal that Saddam is still engaged in his decade-long war of revenge against the United States.[7]

Many readers are unaware of the fact that while only six Americans died during the 1993 WTC explosion, the huge bomb sent over 1,000 injured citizens to hospital, more victims than any other peacetime terrorist incident in the U.S. to that point in time. The Islamic terrorist who led the plot, Ramzi Yousef, admitted to FBI agents that he fully intended his bomb would topple the North Tower into the South Tower with the goal of killing up to 250,000 American citizens. The terrorists laced 1,200 pounds of explosive urea nitrate with sodium cyanide in the hopes of poisoning up to 50,000 additional office workers. Providentially, the enormous heat generated by the main explosive burned the cyanide before it could vaporize and poison thousands of additional innocent office workers.[8] Most U.S. citizens did not appreciate the enormous power of the 1993 terrorist bomb because the towers did not fall as the huge explosion occurred below the ground level. The bomb pulverized 15,000 square feet of concrete and steel creating a massive crater that extended six stories deep leaving a pile of burning rubble over thirty feet deep.

Jim Fox, the former head of the New York City FBI office who was in charge of the investigation of the 1993 World Trade Center bombing, declared in a March 5, 1993, interview with the *Chicago Sun Times* newspaper that overwhelming evidence points to the intelligence service of Iraq as the supporter, instigator, and planner of this terrible terrorist attack using a group of Islamic terrorists from bin Laden's al Qaeda group. This FBI conclusion regarding Iraqi responsibility was confirmed in a May 12, 1998, speech by FBI Director Louis Freeh, who declared that the Iraqi terrorist Abdul Rahman was now living in Iraq.[9] Despite the overwhelming evidence from the FBI investigation, President Clinton refused to pursue the matter further.

The 1998 Bombings of Two U.S. Embassies in East Africa

On August 7, 1998, Osama bin Laden's terrorists launched a devastating simultaneous terrorist bombing attack on two American embassies in East Africa. The first truck bomb was detonated at 10:30 a.m. at the U.S. embassy in Nairobi, Kenya, which killed 213 people and injured approximately 4,500 civilians. Only ten minutes later, another terrorist truck bomb was detonated at the American embassy in Dar Es Salaam, Tanzania, which left 11 citizens dead and another 85 injured.

Only two days before the August 7, 1998, embassy bombings, Iraq's National Assembly issued a decree that totally rejected the continuing weapons inspection by the United Nations. Weapons inspectors had already destroyed massive amounts of chemical, biological, and nuclear weapons facilities despite constant Iraqi cat-and-mouse techniques of hiding whatever weapons labs and armories they could from the UN teams. On August 5, the Iraqi government announced that they were renouncing their previous signed agreement with the United Nations following their defeat in the Gulf War that allowed the UN commission to completely inspect and destroy their weapons of mass destruction (UNSCR 687).

It is significant that this massive simultaneous terror attack on two American embassies came just two days after the Iraqi government's dismissal of the UN inspections. A few hours before the bombs exploded "claims of responsibility were sent by facsimile to London, England, in the name of the 'Islamic Army for the Liberation of the Holy Places' for further distribution by co-conspirators."[10] The subsequent investigation and trial of the terrorists who committed this outrageous 1998 attack on American embassies provided compelling evidence that they belonged to bin Laden's notorious al Qaeda terrorist group. However, President Clinton carefully avoided announcing the accumulated evidence that Iraq's intelligence agency was working hand-in-glove with bin Laden's Islamic terrorists.

On August 20, 1998, President Clinton authorized a militarily useless attack against several of bin Laden's al Qaeda deserted terrorist training camps in the mountains of Afghanistan by launching sixty-six Tomahawk cruise missiles (costing $1 million each) that accomplished virtually nothing. Unfortunately, intelligence sources have revealed that it is possible that, when the United States attacked bin Laden's Afghanistan bases in August 1998, al Qaeda acquired the unexploded missile warheads. In the raid, 70 missiles were fired, but reports from Debka, an Israeli intelligence source (http://www.debka.com/) on December 19, 2001 suggest that only 30 of the cruise missiles exploded on impact. If this report is correct, then bin Laden's al Qaeda may have acquired some very deadly additional weapons to use against the West.

Then, in an even more dubious military intelligence command decision, Clinton ordered another thirteen cruise missiles to be fired at the El Shifa pharmaceutical plant in Khartoum, Sudan. Clinton claimed it was partly owned by Osama bin Laden and was a manufacturer of deadly VX nerve gas. However, the only evidence that U.S. intelligence could offer in support of Clinton's theory was their claim that a CIA investigator had discovered a chemical, EMPTA, in the soil outside the plant. EMPTA is a precursor chemical that was previously used by Iraq to manufacture VX nerve gas (according to UN weapons inspectors). Subsequent independent investigations revealed that there were no chemical traces of EMPTA in the soil around the plant or in the debris. In addition, a respected American investigation firm, Kroll Associates, completed their investigation that concluded that bin Laden was not an owner of the plant. Finally, the U.S. government relented quietly in 1999 and compensated the owners of the destroyed factory.[11]

Unfortunately, the Clinton administration refused to consider the implications of the evidence that Iraq was orchestrating and funding the continuing series of terrorist attacks on America by bin Laden's al Qaeda group throughout the 1990s. Apparently, the Clinton administration felt that if they publicly acknowledged the evidence of Iraq's involvement in this series of terrorist attacks against America, they would be forced by the U.S. Congress and an aroused American public to launch a decisive war against Iraq. It appears that the president decided to ignore the mounting evidence that Iraq had launched a war of revenge against America to avoid being distracted from his domestic political agenda.

The October 12, 2000 Terrorist Attack on the U.S.S. *Cole*

The extensive intelligence and the sophisticated terrorist resources required to successfully infiltrate the military security of the port of Aden strongly suggests that a state such as Iraq is behind this attack on the U.S.S. *Cole*. Saddam Hussein had both the motive and the intelligence resources as well as the technical means to achieve this devastating terrorist attack on the U.S. military presence in the Middle East. It would have required the advanced technical capabilities of a state such as Iraq to gather intelligence on the U.S.S. *Cole*'s position and precise scheduled naval movements. Iraq has friendly relations with the government of Yemen, and both governments contain elements that are extremely hostile to U.S. interests. It is significant that Saddam Hussein has strong political and financial ties with President Ali Abdallah Salih, the leader of Yemen. It is also noteworthy that President Abdallah Salih insisted that the October 12, 2000, attack on the U.S.S. *Cole* was simply an accident for several weeks until the evidence was simply overwhelming that Islamic terrorists had attacked this U.S. naval vessel.

In 1996, Osama bin Laden, whose family comes from Yemen, released his now famous "Declaration of War," (see appendix A) that emphasized the importance of south Yemen in the radical Islamic struggle of al Qaeda against both the West and Israel. Bin Laden declared, "The presence of a population of fighters in the south of Yemen, fighting in the cause of Allah, is a strategic threat to the Zionist-Crusaders alliance in the area." A report in the *New York Times* in October 20, 2000, revealed that an intelligence warning was received in mid-September 2000 that referred to a possible terrorist attack against an American warship without any details about timing or location. The October 23, 2000, issue of *Newsweek* claimed that since 1998 U.S. intelligence has thwarted at least two additional terrorist plots aimed at U.S. ships that were visiting seaports in the Arabian Peninsula.

The former head of the U.S. Central Intelligence Agency's counterterrorism operations, Vincent Cannistraro, is an expert on the Middle East and Islamic terrorism. Mr. Cannistraro declared that the location, the precise timing, and the chosen method of attack on the U.S.S. *Cole* strongly suggested that al Qaeda is the group responsible for this atrocity. Cannistraro pointed to the sophistication of the huge terrorist bomb, which consisted of six hundred pounds of high explosives and thereby caused enormous damage, including a thirty-eight-foot-wide hole in the side of the ship and the death of seventeen U.S. naval personnel. The terrorist bomb was specially shaped in a concave mold inside a strong metal container to direct the resulting blast to penetrate the heavily armored hull of the American destroyer. He suggested that the design certainly pointed toward a professional intelligence and military involvement by a state such as Iraq. Mr. Cannistraro declared, "The Iraqis have wanted to be able to carry out terrorism for some time now. . . . Their military people have had liaison with al Qaeda in Afghanistan, and could well have supplied the training."[12]

Yemen is a vital refueling Persian Gulf port for both military and civilian ships. However, the well-known Islamic terrorist support for bin Laden in Yemen and the several intelligence warnings received by American intelligence agencies made this port an exceedingly dangerous place for the U.S. navy to refuel their ships. However, the navy had no choice but to refuel their ships in this dangerous port because of a disastrous decision by President Bill Clinton in the early 1990s. Until the end of the 1991 Gulf War, the U.S. navy had a fleet of thirty-two huge refueling tanker ships to safely refuel their naval vessels in the deep oceans, far from any threat. Tragically, in his contempt for the military needs of the nation, the president ordered a massive 75 percent cutback in this vital refueling fleet. Today there are only eight remaining tankers. A report by FreeRepublic.com by Col. David Hackworth, an expert on the U.S. military, reported that this reduction in refueling capability forced the U.S.S. *Cole* to enter the dangerous waters of the Yemeni port where al Qaeda's terrorists were waiting to attack her with a small fishing vessel containing a huge suicide bomb.[13]

The Terror Planning Conference in Baghdad in August 2001

President Saddam Hussein hosted a three-day terrorism planning conference in Baghdad, only three weeks before the September 11 bombing. Sponsored by the Iraqi intelligence service, bin Laden's al Qaeda, Egypt's Gamaa al Islamiya, Iraq's Jund al Islam, and numerous other Islamic terrorist groups including Hamas and Islamic Jihad from Israel's West Bank, joined in a terrorism conference to plan attacks against western targets as reported in the October 28, 2001 issue of the British newspaper *The Sunday Telegraph*. In addition to President Hussein, two of Iraq's vice presidents, Taha Ramadan and Izzet Douri, together with senior Iraqi intelligence officers sat at the head table. More than six thousand terrorist volunteers were recently recruited around the world to join Iraq's war against America. In the weeks following this terrorism conference, more than 100 participants engaged in intense training courses with Iraqi intelligence officers. Following the conference, senior Iraqi intelligence officers were dispatched by Saddam Hussein to meet with Osama bin Laden's network.[14]

Mohammed Atta, the leader of the nineteen Islamic terrorist hijackers who destroyed the World Trade Center and the Pentagon, met secretly in Prague, the Czech Republic, with Ahmed Khalil Ibrahim al Ani, a senior Iraqi intelligence officer who posed as an Iraqi diplomat until he was expelled from the republic for "engaging in activities beyond his diplomatic duties." Since the September 11 attack, there have been numerous meetings between Iraqi intelligence agents and al Qaeda terrorists. On September 20, Mohammed Nouri, a colonel in Iraqi intelligence, traveled to Bangkok, Thailand, to meet with a terrorist associated with bin Laden's network. Four days later, Iraqi brigadier Abdul Khader Majid traveled to Bangladesh with several other senior Iraqi intelligence agents to meet al Qaeda representatives.[15]

Iraqi Terrorist Training Camps for Hijackers in Baghdad

In mid-October 2001, a former Iraqi intelligence officer reported that there is a training facility in the suburbs of Baghdad that trains Islamic terrorists in the arts of hijacking and assassination.[16] On November 14, 2001, the PBS show *Frontline* declared that its research confirmed that Iraqi intelligence trained forty Islamic terrorists between 1995 and 2000 in sophisticated hijacking techniques using a Boeing 747 passenger plane in a terrorist training institute in Baghdad.

During the UN weapons inspections of Iraq in the summer of 1996, a team led by Scott Ritter found evidence of a vast terrorist training program under the direction of Directorate M-21 of Iraqi intelligence. "Document after document outlined an international program of terror."[17]

The Anthrax Attacks Since September 11, 2001

In the months following the World Trade Center bombing a series of anthrax terrorist attacks have produced infection, death, and deep fear in many people, especially because the secret source of the mailed anthrax has been difficult to locate. Anthrax is an extremely deadly weapon. Just one gram of anthrax, a tiny amount that could fit in the bottom of a tiny spoon, theoretically contains enough anthrax spores to kill 100 million people if the weapon was efficiently distributed. The U.S. Defense Department stated in their Defense Department Fact Sheet that anthrax is "100,000 times deadlier than the deadliest chemical warfare agent."[18]

It is important to recognize that anthrax is a very difficult biological agent to utilize as an effective weapon by a terrorist group. The Japanese terrorist group Aum Shinrikyo tried and failed almost a dozen times to utilize anthrax as a terrorist weapon and could not make anyone sick.[19]

Only a nation state like Iraq with sophisticated biological labs with expensive milling equipment, professional chemical experts, experience with anti-clumping chemicals, and an efficient distribution device could actually produce an effective anthrax weapon that would kill significant numbers of people. Most anthrax infections are cutaneous (through skin cuts or abrasions) and are treatable through penicillin or Cipro with a great expectation of recovery. However, airborne anthrax attacks are extremely deadly. By the time a victim of airborne anthrax begins to manifest symptoms, in most cases it is too late to begin effective antibiotic treatment because the anthrax spores have already produced their deadly toxins within the lungs of the victim. Less than 10 percent of the infected patients are expected to survive if they do not receive antibiotics prior to the appearance of flu-like symptoms that follow exposure to airborne anthrax.

Biological weapons experts such as Richard Spertzel, a former UN weapons inspector in Iraq, report that the anthrax used in these attacks since September 11, 2001 is not homegrown or produced in a basement lab by a domestic terrorist. Spertzel told the *Sunday Telegraph* on October 27, 2001, "It has to be someone with an existing biological program. These are Russia, Syria, Iran, and Libya. Top of my list, though, is Iraq. There are known associations with intelligence personnel and al Qaeda. Also they have the capability, and the know-how." Normally, anthrax spores clump together, making them heavier than air and preventing them from becoming airborne. In order to make airborne anthrax, it is necessary to mill it with sophisticated milling equipment to separate the spores as well as the addition of an anti-clumping chemical to prevent spores from sticking together. Iraq has developed anthrax that is airborne or "weapons grade" according to the weapons inspectors of the United Nations. In 1973, President Hussein developed the Al Hassan Ibn Al Haithem Institute in Iraq that was responsible for the manufacturing of nuclear weapons, poison gases, and toxins such as anthrax. Since then, the Military Industrialization organization has taken over the development of weapons of mass destruction.

Compelling evidence of Iraq's part in supplying this airborne anthrax was discovered by American laboratories that tested the anthrax that was recently sent by letter to Senator Tom Daschle, the U.S. Senate Majority leader. The crime lab discovered the presence of microscopic amounts of the chemical betonite. Iraq is the only nation that has ever used betonite in the manufacture of its weapons-grade airborne anthrax. Timothy Trevan, a UN weapons inspector, said, "It means to me that Iraq becomes the prime suspect as the source of the anthrax used in these letters." (ABC News.com, October 29, 2001)

New Evidence that Iraq Sponsors Bin Laden's Attacks

An article in the *New York Times* entitled "Iraqi defectors tell of saboteurs, sites" on December 21, 2001, reported that a defector, Adnan Ihsan Saeed al-Haideri, claimed Iraq recently renovated secret underground sites to store nuclear, chemical, and biological weapons after exiling the UN weapons inspectors from the country in 1998 to prevent their continued monitoring of their weapons of mass destruction.

An article in the January 9, 2002, issue of the magazine *Vanity Fair* included an interview with Abu Zeinab al-Qurairy, an Iraqi defector who was formerly a brigadier general in Hussein's dreaded Mukhabarat intelligence service. Abu Zeinab al-Qurairy was a close aide to Uday Hussein, President Saddam's son. He claimed that Uday was the head of a top secret 1200-strong terrorist force called *The Strikers*. Uday ordered him to hand-pick a team of 30 of these Iraqi terrorists and give them false identities provided by a corrupt official in the United Arab Emirates. Al-Qurairy warned that this elite terrorist group was trained in "sabotage, urban warfare, hijacking, and murder." However, they have now vanished and could be underground anywhere in the West. Al-Qurairy said that Iraq was definitely involved in the September 11 terrorist attacks using their undercover Iraqi teams in the West.

Iraq's Development of Weapons of Mass Destruction

Significantly, the Scriptures contain thirty specific prophetic warnings regarding plague and pestilence occurring during the terrible events of the last days Tribulation period that will usher in the return of Christ. The prophet John warned in Revelation that the fourth horseman of the apocalypse will ride forth during the seven years of tribulation and take the lives of a quarter of the world's population with plague. Jesus Christ also warned, "For nation shall rise against nation, and kingdom against kingdom: and there shall be famines, and pestilences, and earthquakes, in divers [strange] places. All these are the beginning of sorrows" (Matthew 24:7–8).

A web site produced by the British Foreign and Commonwealth Office and the Ministry of Defense (http://special.fco.gov.uk/) reveals the latest news updates on Iraq and the United Nations (UNSCOM) weapons inspections. According to UNSCOM reports, *prior to the Gulf War, Iraq produced enough chemical and biological weapons material to kill the world's population several times over.* It is still trying to acquire deadly nuclear, chemical, and biological weapons technology. UNSCOM has destroyed more Iraqi weapons than were destroyed by American bombs during the whole of the Gulf War. Its work is vital to the security of the entire Middle East.

Time magazine reported in April 1977 about the incredible dangers from the unlimited development of DNA genetic manipulation of biological weapons:

> Appearing before a Senate subcommittee. . . . HEW Secretary Joseph Califano asked Congress to impose federal restrictions on recombinant DNA research, a new form of genetic inquiry involving *E. coli* . . . DNA with the DNA of plants, animals, and other bacteria. By this process, they may well be creating forms of life different from any that exist on earth. . . . What would happen, they ask, if by accident or design, one variety of re-engineered

E. coli proved dangerous? By escaping from the lab and multiplying . . . it could find its way into human intestines and cause baffling diseases . . . Caltech's biology chairman, Robert Sinsheimer, concludes: 'Biologists have become, without wanting it, the custodians of great and terrible power. It is idle to pretend otherwise.'[20]

Overwhelming evidence in the hands of UNSCOM and western intelligence agencies suggests that Iraq is still engaged in the production of illegal and forbidden weapons of mass destruction, including nuclear bombs as well as biological and chemical programs to produce deadly anthrax and small pox infections. Jeff Stein, a special correspondent on terrorism for the *San Francisco Chronicle*, coauthored the book *Saddam's Bombmaker* with Khidhir Hamza, the father of Iraq's nuclear program who defected from Iraq. Stein reported that Iraq is the only Arab regime that has already repeatedly used chemical and biological weapons against its enemies, both civilian and military, on the battlefield during the eight-year war with Iran.

In 1984, Iraqi intelligence sent one hundred Muslim Shiite prisoners to a pesticide factory in the city of Samara. The prisoners were subjected to various chemical weapons, which killed all subjects. A year later, another fifty prisoners were subjected to lethal biological experiments at a weapons facility at Salmon Pak. Other prisoners were injected with biological weapons in a vaccine. In the months that followed, they became sick with flu-like symptoms and later died. Iraq aircraft tested the lethality of chemical weapons by dropping chemical canisters on Shiite prisoners in trenches. Saddam Hussein ordered the massive use of chemical weapons against the huge Iranian human-wave assaults in the final months of the Iran-Iraq war. Iraq used nerve gas to kill five thousand Kurdish civilians living in the village of Halabjah in northern Iraq in March 1988. Therefore, Iraq is the only nation on earth that has not only produced enormous quantities of biological and chemical weapons, but has proven willing and able to use these diabolical weapons of mass destruction against their enemies.[21]

A February 1998 article by the *Near East Report* revealed

that the *Washington Post* and the *New York Times* confirmed that UNSCOM weapons inspectors had discovered a 1995 bilateral agreement between Russia and Iraq in which Russia promised to provide Saddam Hussein with sophisticated biological and chemical manufacturing facilities to allow Iraq to produce enormous quantities of biological and chemical weapons including anthrax and nerve gas. In addition, UN inspectors found documentary evidence that the required Russian machinery was delivered.[22]

The CIA recently reported that Iraq has developed an unmanned air vehicle that is capable of launching chemical or biological weapons of mass destruction. The U.S. intelligence agency said that Hussein had acquired and modified the unmanned air vehicle, the L-29, originally built as a jet trainer aircraft. "It is believed that Iraq has conducted flights of the L-29, possibly to test system improvements or to train new pilots. These refurbished trainer aircraft are believed to have been modified for delivery of chemical or, more likely, biological warfare agents."[23]

Since the UN was forced by Iraq to suspend weapons inspections in 1998, Saddam Hussein has acquired dual-use [civilian-military] equipment from western companies. This has allowed him to restore his missile factories and secret underground installations manufacturing weapons of mass destruction, including work on developing an Iraqi nuclear bomb. The CIA report warned that Iraq is close to completing the manufacture of a liquid propellant–driven, short-range ballistic missile named Al Samoud to deliver its chemical or biological warheads.[24] The UN weapons inspection teams discovered that Iraq had developed sophisticated aerial spray tanks that could be attached to either manned or pilotless planes that would disseminate deadly biological or chemical weapons over the territory of its enemies. The UN teams issued a report that declared this weapons system to be "the most efficient means for the delivery of biological warfare agents produced by Iraq."[25]

Iraq's Quest for the Islamic Nuclear Bomb

Iraq conspired for the last twenty-five years with a large number of western and Russian high-tech companies to thwart western customs restrictions designed to prevent nuclear technology getting into the hands of Third World countries. Billions of dollars were spent in setting up advanced nuclear labs and research reactors. With an abundance of cheap oil, Iraq's only logical purpose in building a nuclear program was the creation of nuclear weapons. These weapons of mass destruction would transform it in one short moment into a superpower potentially capable of devastating Israel or any other enemy.

In August 1989, an enormous explosion occurred at a secret underground weapons lab at Al-Quaqua, Iraq. The Iraqis were developing high-melting-point explosives and rapid-detonation explosives. These particular explosives are used solely for the production of nuclear implosion devices. In the early 1980s, Iraq purchased three hundred tons of yellow cake, a basic raw material used only in the production of nuclear weapons. This yellow cake produces gaseous uranium hexafluoride, which can be utilized in a series of cascading gas centrifuges to separate out the essential three percent uranium 235 from the militarily useless 97 percent of uranium 238 to produce weapons-grade uranium. American satellite photos detected a new uranium mine in northern Iraq that will allow them to produce as much yellow cake as they need for the future. Iraq's attempt to import forty nuclear high-capacity bomb triggers in the spring of 1990, combined with the importation of gas centrifuges from Switzerland for refining the uranium 235, provides overwhelming evidence that Iraq is working constantly on their own "Manhattan Project." We are moving closer to the moment when Iraq will have weapons of mass destruction in their arsenal to use against Israel and the West. Whether the world wants to admit it or not, we are now two minutes until midnight on the doomsday clock for Armageddon in the Middle East.

Israel's June 7, 1981, attack on Iraq's nuclear reactor facility at Osirak set back Saddam Hussein's nuclear warhead project for several years. Many nations publicly condemned Israel at the time for its preemptive action. However, many of the West's leaders were secretly grateful for Israel's action in significantly delaying Hussein's development of nuclear weapons. Unfortunately, his French-built reactor had already produced enough plutonium to create one or two very primitive weapons. If Israel had not bombed the Osirak reactor, the U.S. forces in Saudi Arabia would have been vulnerable to an Iraqi nuclear attack during the War in the Gulf.

In March 1990, British and American authorities announced that they had seized forty nuclear triggers known as high-speed capacitors that were on the way to Iraq. Two months later, a smiling Saddam Hussein held one of these sophisticated nuclear trigger devices and displayed it to TV cameras. He revealed that Iraq had already imported a number of these highly secret devices that are needed to control the sophisticated electronic triggering sequence to detonate a nuclear bomb. Iraqi scientists have developed the Tammuz I and II missiles, which have a current range of 1,200 miles. If such a missile were fired from Iraq's missile test range in Mauritania in North Africa it could deliver a warhead on Paris or London. Iraq will soon have intercontinental-range missiles. Unfortunately, western intelligence agencies have consistently underestimated by many years the length of time it would take nations such as Iraq to develop advanced weapons technology.

Another very unpleasant scenario involves the Iraqi creation of a primitive radiological weapon, a conventional warhead that can be filled with radioactive waste products (such as strontium 90 and thorium) from their nuclear reactor program. Such a "dirty atomic weapon" could be fired at an enemy target with a modified Scud-B missile. When such a warhead explodes in the air, a huge amount of deadly radiation will float down on the target city or oil field, making the area uninhabitable for up to a hundred years until the radioactivity finally decays. During World War II, U.S. and British nuclear scientists in the Manhattan Project suggested that bombs composed of radioactive material might be dropped on Germany and Japan, poisoning their cities for decades. The idea was rejected in favor of the more selective targeting of cities and bases with the powerful nuclear fission bombs.

When we consider the devastating destructive power that our western technology has placed in the hands of Third World nations, we should realize that we are approaching the last days described in the Bible as the time leading to the battle of Armageddon. The Lord declared in the book of Revelation He would, "destroy them which destroy the earth" (Revelation 11:18). The world is quickly approaching the time when only the coming of the Messiah, the Prince of Peace, will save mankind from destruction.

America's War against Terror Must Deal with Iraq

Although the publicly available evidence is overwhelming, the secret intelligence available to the American government provides additional powerful confirmation that Iraq is using Osama bin Laden's al Qaeda group to launch a series of deadly terrorist attacks on American targets. President George W. Bush appointed James Woolsey, the former director of the CIA, to review all of the available intelligence to determine if Iraq or some other terrorist-supporting state is behind al Qaeda's September 11 attack on the United States of America. The evidence is compelling that Iraq has supported and been intimately involved with a whole series of terrorist attacks on American interests throughout the last decade. James Woolsey warned in late October 2001: "This war began with the direct and immediate murder of thousands of Americans, and, if we find that we have a reasonable target along with Osama bin Laden in the government of Iraq, we must wage this war quickly. We must wage it powerfully. . . . We must wage it cleverly. And we must wage it ruthlessly."[26]

Iraq is a very real threat to the West because of President Saddam Hussein's implacable hatred of America, the United Kingdom, and Israel. Saddam Hussein has devoted an enormous amount of effort and money toward the development of weapons of mass destruction. His previous thirty-nine SCUD missile attacks on Israel and Saudi Arabia in 1991, his numerous chemical and biological attacks on civilians as well as Iranian soldiers, and his support of terrorist attacks on America provide powerful evidence that he is willing to use any of his weapons of mass destruction—nuclear, biological, or chemical. While the coalition against terror has wisely chosen to first deal with the Taliban government of Afghanistan that hid and supported bin Laden's al Qaeda terrorists, it will soon arrive at the point where the West must deal with Saddam Hussein and his army.

A war to destroy President Hussein and his elite Republican Guard to the point where American and allied military units can travel throughout Iraq and destroy his weapons programs will not be easy. Such a war against Iraq will potentially cost the lives of many American and allied soldiers. But we have no choice. If we wait, Iraq will eventually develop weapons of mass destruction, and Hussein will use them against Israel and the West. We can deal with Iraq either now or later. But if we delay our military response until Iraq first launches devastating weapons of mass destruction, the massive casualties that occurred on September 11, 2001, will be only a footnote to the coming Third World War, a devastating war of global proportions.

Endnotes

1. Taha Yasin Ramadan, *Baghdad Domestic Service*, 15 February 15. 1991.
2. CNN, Wolf Blitzer Reports, 21 Sept. 2001. http://www.dgss.com/aoa/cnn/met_with_Iraq.html.
3. Presidential Address to Congress, 26 June 1993, web site: http://www.fas.org/irp/news/1993/930626i.htm.
4. Declaration of War: See Appendix.
5. *Arutz 7*, 20 Sept. 2001.
6. Laurie Mylroie, *Study of Revenge*, Washington: The AEI Press, 2000.
7. http://www.rferl.org/welcome/english/releases/2001/09/55-280901.html.
8. *The New York Times*, 23 Oct. 1997.
9. Laurie Mylroie, *Study of Revenge*, Washington: The AEI Press, 2000, p. 112.
10. Indictment of Usama bin Ladin et al., S 6 98 CR. 1023 LBS, p. 37.
11. *Washington Post*, 7 May 1999.
12. Julian Borger, *The Guardian*, 19 Oct. 2000.
13. http://www.freerepublic.com/forum/a39e8d3cd31bb.htm.
14. *Sunday Telegraph*, 28 Oct. 2001.
15. *Sunday Telegraph*, 28 Oct. 2001.
16. *Sunday Telegraph*, 28 Oct. 2001.
17. Scott Ritter. *Endgame: Solving the Iraq Problem—Once and for All*. New York: Simon & Schuster, 1999, p. 121.
18. "Anthrax Is Preferred Biological Warfare Agent," United States Information Service, 20 Feb. 1998.
19. W. Seth Carus. "Biohazard: Assessing the Bioterrorism Threat." *New Republic*, 2 Aug. 1999.
20. Time, 1 April 1977.
21. Jeff Stein. 'The Iraq Factor." http://www.nyu.edu/globalbeat/syndicate/. 26 Sept. 2001.
22. *Near East Report*, 4 Feb. 1998.
23. *Middle East News Line*. www.bridgesforpeace.com. 11 Sept. 2001.
24. *Middle East News Line*, www.bridgesforpeace.com. 11 Sept. 2001.
25. UNSCOM Report to the UN Security Council, 3 June 1998.
26. *Sunday Telegraph*, 28 Oct. 2001.

6

The War Against Babylon
The First Prophetic War

> For, lo, I will raise and cause to come up against Babylon an assembly of great nations from the north country: and they shall set themselves in array against her; from thence she shall be taken: their arrows shall be as of a mighty expert man; none shall return in vain. (Jeremiah 50:9)

The prophets predicted that as we approach the time of the Great Tribulation and the return of Christ, the ancient city and kingdom of Babylon would rise again to take its place on the stage of world history. Many of the biblical prophecies foretell that this great ancient city of Babylon will rise again to be destroyed in the last days in one hour and that smoke will forever ascend from its ruins. "And Babylon, the glory of kingdoms, the beauty of the Chaldees' excellency, shall be as when God overthrew Sodom and Gomorrah" (Isaiah 13:19). This prophesied destruction did not occur during the last four thousand years, nor did it happen during the 1991 Gulf War. While the city of Babylon was conquered many times, it was never destroyed by fire from heaven as "Sodom and

Gomorrah." The cities of Sodom and Gomorrah were destroyed in a supernatural firestorm from heaven, which obliterated these cities without a trace. Therefore, many prophecy scholars have concluded that Isaiah's prophecy of the spectacular future destruction of Babylon demands that the ancient city will be rebuilt in order for this prediction to be fulfilled. Since hundreds of biblical prophecies were fulfilled precisely, this particular prophecy about Babylon's destruction must also be fulfilled at some point in the future.

There are three phases in the rise and fall of Babylon as described in the prophecies of the Bible. The first phase was

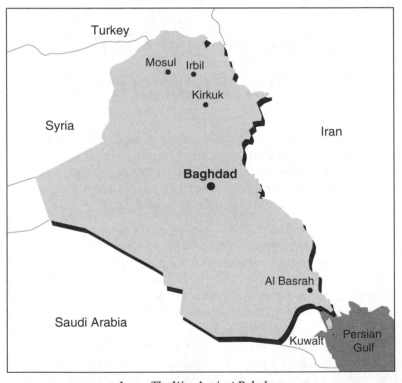

Iraq—The War Against Babylon.
"For, lo, I will raise and cause to come up against Babylon an assembly of great nations from the north country." Jeremiah 50:9

fulfilled during the lifetime of the prophets themselves, when the Medes and Persians led by King Cyrus destroyed Babylon in 538 B.C. The second phase will witness the future military destruction of Iraq as described in Jeremiah 50. The third and final phase will occur during the last days of the Great Tribulation leading up to the Battle of Armageddon; God will then supernaturally destroy Babylon forever with fire from heaven as "Sodom and Gomorrah."

The Bible prophesied that ancient Babylon would arise in the last generation leading to the return of Jesus Christ. The prophets Ezekiel, Jeremiah, Daniel, Isaiah, and John each wrote extensively about the prophetic future of the great Babylonian empire, which has always battled against Israel. The prophets predict both an immediate and a future final destruction of Babylon.

The Babylonian empire dominated the Middle East for only seventy years, from 608 B.C. until its defeat by the Media-Persian empire in 538 B.C. Why then does the Bible contain so many extensive prophecies about this historically brief kingdom? Is the answer found in the rebuilding of the fabled city of Babylon in these last days by Iraqi President Saddam Hussein? Many prophecies describe a great alliance of northern nations that will arise to attack Babylon in the last days. Several of these prophets describe a final destruction of the city of Babylon by a supernatural fire that will burn forever. Several prophecies describe the city being destroyed "in one hour" and mention that the merchants of the world will weep for the loss of their profits.

When the Media-Persians overthrew Babylon in October 538 B.C. part of the city was burnt, but the city continued to exist as the capital of the new Persian kingdom. The apostle Peter wrote his letter to the churches from Babylon, where many of the Jews lived in exile during the centuries following Christ. The Babylonian Talmud, the great Jewish commentary on the Torah, was written over a period of five hundred years by the Jewish scholars of Babylon from 100 B.C. to A.D. 400. Since Babylon's total destruction has not yet occurred, the military destruction must happen at some point in the future.

In Revelation 18, the prophet John declared that the great city of Babylon will be destroyed in a spectacular manner that will cause the merchants and kings to weep and mourn for her loss. Isaiah 13:1, 6 also refers to this supernatural destruction specifically at the "day of the Lord." The prophet says, "The burden of Babylon, which Isaiah the son of Amoz did see. . . . Howl ye; for the day of the Lord is at hand; it shall come as a destruction from the Almighty." Isaiah's prophecy confirms that Babylon's final supernatural destruction will occur at the end of the Great Tribulation at the Battle of Armageddon known as the "day of the Lord."

Ancient Babylon

Ancient Babylon was the most powerful empire to arise in the Middle East. It swept before it all previous kingdoms and established an incredibly wealthy and ruthless empire that became a symbol of imperial power for thousands of years. King Nebuchadnezzar and his successors created an enormous military power that defeated nation after nation in its rapid rise to world supremacy. The writings of the Greek historian Herodotus and the discoveries of Robert Koldewey, the German archeologist who excavated a significant portion of Babylon from 1899 to 1912, confirm the Bible's description of "Babylon, the glory of kingdoms, the beauty of the Chaldees' excellency" (Isaiah 13:19).

A twenty-mile drive south of Baghdad leads to one of the most amazing historical and archeological sites in the world. Here, in the land that was once the cradle of all civilization, lie the ruins of the greatest city of the ancient world, Babylon. In the ruins of the ancient past, Iraq has rapidly constructed new buildings, gates, temples, and massive city walls in the largest ancient city reconstruction project ever attempted. For the first time, an entire city is being rebuilt from the dust and ashes left by their ancestors thousands of years ago. Many foreign construction workers from South Korea, China, Egypt, and Sudan are now working on the project. I have an unusual booklet produced by the Iraqi government in 1982 that is entitled *Babylon*. The book contains numerous illustrations and photographs of the ruins as well as plans for the reconstruction of the city. The back cover contains this declaration: "Archaeological Survival of Babylon is a Patriotic, National, and International Duty."

Nimrod, "the great hunter," founded Babylon. The book of Genesis describes Babylon as the site of the first great organized religious rebellion against God. Many mystery pagan religions have grown out of the satanic spiritual seeds first planted in Babylon. When men first rebelled against God after the Flood, they tried to build a tower to heaven to assert their rejection of God. The Lord confounded their unified language to prevent them from working together. This differentiation of language forced humanity to split into the different language groups, and they consequently moved out from the fertile Mesopotamia area to explore further into Asia, Africa, and Europe.

The city of Babylon was built around the ancient ruins of the Tower of Babel. Babylon's fifty-six miles of walls were three hundred feet in height and over eighty feet wide, large enough to allow six chariots to run abreast along the walls. These massive fortified walls made of clay bricks were built on enormous foundations that extended thirty-five feet below ground. The walls were surrounded by deep moats filled with water diverted from the Euphrates River to prevent access or tunneling. One hundred huge ornate gates of polished brass, emblazoned with figures of bulls and dragons composed of glazed tiles, opened into the city. The great Euphrates River divided the city into two equal halves, flanked by huge brick walls with twenty-five enormous brass gates opening into vast boulevards crisscrossing the metropolis.

King Nebuchadnezzar created the famous Hanging Gardens of Babylon, a huge seventy-five-foot-high artificial mountain that could be seen fifty miles away, for his beloved queen, who came from a mountainous area and hated the flat plains of Mesopotamia. A series of magnificent terraces held trees, vines, and flowers watered by an ingenious system of wells and fountains. Babylon's Hanging Garden was one of the seven wonders of the ancient world. The great temple of Marduk (Bel) contained a huge golden statute of the pagan god Bel and a golden table, made with fifty thousand pounds of gold, costing over $320 million in today's dollars. The prophet Daniel described Babylon as the "head of gold" in his prophecy of a metallic statue representing world empires. But Babylon was dedicated to Satan,

The Rebuilt City of Babylon. Over $2 Billion Spent To Date By Iraq.
(Photo: courtesy of Dr. Charles Pack)

The Rebuilt Ishtar Gate in Babylon. Daniel and the Jewish Captives
Were Led Through This Gate Twenty-five Centuries Ago.

as indicated by its fifty-three temples and one hundred and eighty golden altars dedicated to Ishtar.

Rebuilding the City of Babylon

It is ironic that the modern nation of Iraq, under the brutal rule of President Saddam Hussein, has chosen the image of ancient Babylon and King Nebuchadnezzar to symbolize its determination to rule the Middle East. Every village and city throughout Iraq contains massive billboards showing an image of President Hussein shaking the hand of the ancient King Nebuchadnezzar, the conqueror of Israel. In this display of imperial conceit, Saddam Hussein reveals his lust to re-establish the former Babylonian empire to dominate his Arab neighbors. In 1971, UNESCO publicly announced that the United Nations would provide assistance to Iraq to rebuild the ancient city of Babylon. In a fascinating article about the rebuilding of Babylon in the *Philadelphia Inquirer*, on October 10, 1986, Subhy Haddad reported that the governor of Babylon, Gita Suheil, declared, "[Saddam Hussein] has signed an open check to reconstruct the ancient city and revive the marvelous shape it had before the Persian aggression which destroyed it more than twenty centuries ago."

Many Bible scholars have dismissed the reports that Iraq is rebuilding Babylon as nothing more than the creation of an Iraqi "Disneyland" project to satisfy the curious ego of Saddam Hussein. However, evidence from eyewitnesses as well as numerous media reports confirms that this is an enormous construction project first begun in 1978 that remains a huge priority of both Hussein's government as well as the Iraqi people. For example, Paul Lewis wrote an article in the *San Francisco Chronicle* in 1989 that confirms the importance of this major construction project. "When King Nebuchadnezzar ran things around here some 2,500 years ago, he left clear instructions for the future kings of Babylon that are finally being carried out. Writing in cuneiform script on tablets of clay, the royal scribes urged their master's successors to repair and rebuild his temples and palaces. Today, in a gesture rich in political significance, President

Saddam Hussein, Iraq's strong-armed ruler, is sparing no effort to obey that now-distant command."[1] Immediately following the cease-fire between Iran and Iraq on August 20, 1988, Hussein declared publicly that Iraq would resume the rebuilding of Babylon as a top-priority national project.

Despite the earnest objections of international archaeologists who protested Iraq's decisions to rebuild on top of the ancient ruins, Hussein ordered his officials to rebuild on the exact site of ancient Babylon. They have rebuilt the huge Southern Palace of Nebuchadnezzar, a Greek theater, numerous temples, the main Procession Street, Nebuchadnezzar's throne room, and the Ishtar Gate. There are reports that Hussein plans to rebuild the ancient Hanging Gardens. The fifty-six miles of ancient city walls, constructed of mud bricks and asphalt have now been reconstructed with over sixty million new bricks, with many of them inscribed with a seal that reads "The Babylon of Nebuchadnezzar was reconstructed in the era of Saddam Hussein."

Charles Dryer, the author of *The Rise of Babylon*, wrote about a surreal experience he had in 1988 when he was present with the Iraqi president in the ancient city of Babylon to witness an evening ceremony celebrating the International Babylon Festival. Dryer wrote:

It is a cloudless September night, and the moon casts its shining image on the banks of the gentle Euphrates River. Thousands of guests and dignitaries walk by torch light to Babylon's Procession Street and enter the city from the north. Instructed to line the streets along the massive walls, the guests obediently follow orders. When the audience is in place, the dark-eyed man in charge nods, and the procession begins. Rows and rows of soldiers parade in, dressed in Babylonian tunics and carrying swords, spears, and shields. Interspersed among the ranks of soldiers are groups of musicians playing harps, horns, and drums. Clusters of children carry palm branches, and runners bear bowls of incense. Then come soldiers and still more soldiers in a seemingly endless line of men and weapons.

After the procession, the guests attend a ceremony paying tribute to Ishtar, the mother goddess of Babylon.

The director of that event, the International Babylon Festival, was none other than Saddam Hussein. He was celebrating the revival of the city from ancient times. By 1990, over sixty million bricks inscribed with Hussein's name were on top of the very bricks that Nebuchadnezzar had laid.[2]

The official seal of the International Babylon Festival shows a double portrait with a mirror image of King Nebuchadnezzar and Saddam Hussein. The festival theme is: "From Nebuchadnezzar to Saddam Hussein—Babylon undergoes a renaissance." In 1987, the festival opened with a statement from President Hussein in which he glorified the achievements of "Nebuchadnezzar, the national hero who was able to defeat the enemies of the nation on the land of 'Kennan' [Canaan] and to take them [Jews] as prisoner of war to Babylon. What we need now is to increase awareness in this regard."

The ruins of the six-hundred-room palace of King Nebuchadnezzar are now being replaced by the construction of a vast new edifice that is rumored to be the future main palace of President Hussein. Many western intelligence agents are concerned that Saddam might have built a massive chemical and biological weapons laboratory deep in the earth beneath the new palace. Hussein has a history of hiding his valuable military assets near ancient archeological ruins in his belief that our western cultural sensitivities would prevent us from bombing such a target.

President Hussein has repeatedly compared himself to King Nebuchadnezzar and has declared that his great goal is to recreate the ancient Babylonian empire in all its glory, wealth, and military power. His vision has influenced Iraqi society so profoundly that it is probable that this plan to rebuild Babylon and its empire would continue even when Saddam dies. In considering Hussein's inner motivation regarding the dead King Nebuchadnezzar, we should consider his 1979 speech, quoted by David Lamb in the *L.A. Times*, October 12, 1990. Saddam declared,

What is most important to me about Nebuchadnezzar is the link between the Arab's abilities and the liberation of

Palestine. Nebuchadnezzar was, after all, an Arab from Iraq, albeit ancient Iraq. Nebuchadnezzar was the one who brought the bound Jewish slaves from Palestine. That is why, whenever I remember Nebuchadnezzar, I like to remind the Arabs, Iraqis in particular, of their historical responsibilities. It is a burden that should not stop them from action, but rather spur them into action because of their history.

This remarkable speech reveals that Saddam Hussein wishes to emulate King Nebuchadnezzar's "liberation of Palestine," a code phrase for the Arabs meaning "the killing of the Jews." The goal that Saddam has set for himself and Iraq is the repetition of history in taking "bound Jewish slaves from Palestine." This satanically inspired vision motivates many of the Arab leaders throughout the Middle East. Despite the enormous economic and social problems facing these twenty-one Arab nations, their greatest goal remains the elimination of Israel.

Saddam Hussein: The Butcher of Baghdad

Saddam Hussein was born to a poor, landless peasant family near the village of Takrit on April 28, 1937. He was hated by his stepfather and ultimately forced to live with his uncle at the age of ten. His uncle, Khayrallah Tulfah, was dismissed from the Iraqi army for attempting a pro-Nazi coup against the British during World War II. This led to his abiding hatred for the British and Zionists, which he passed on to his nephew. Saddam went to Egypt, where he studied politics and law. When he returned, his uncle had become the mayor of Baghdad and assisted in Saddam's rise to power in the socialist Baath Party. Hussein spent eighteen months working in the torture and interrogation center of the Iraq Intelligence Division.

In the mid-1970s, Saddam rose to second-in-command. He remedied his total lack of military experience by appointing himself as lieutenant general of the Iraq army.

Within days of becoming President, Saddam personally executed twenty-one of his close friends and cabinet members. His personal brutality is legendary in Iraq. Whenever a general achieved some measure of success during the Iraq-Iran War, Saddam ordered him executed as a possible threat to his regime. Hussein ordered chemical attacks on thousands of Kurdish villagers in northern Iraq and launched repeated chemical weapons against the armies of Iran. Death squads were sent out to kill Iraqi dissidents throughout the Middle East and Europe. Amnesty International interviewed hundreds of refugees who were able to escape the savage Iraqi killers sent into Kuwait to subdue the population. These refugees detailed forty-eight specific methods of torture and execution that the Iraqis used to kill the people who fell into their hands.

Many in the Middle East refer to Hussein as "the butcher of Baghdad" because of his personal involvement in torture and murder. When Janet Cawley interviewed Saddam in August 1990, only a day before his invasion of Kuwait, she asked him to comment on his nickname. Hussein replied, "Weakness doesn't assure achieving the objectives required by a leader."[3]

On August 2, 1990, Saddam Hussein invaded his former ally Kuwait. Significantly, this was the very day that ended the Jewish fast of Tisha be'Av, the most solemn fast in the Jewish calendar that marks the day of the Babylonian army's destruction of Solomon's temple in 587 B.C. and the burning of the second temple by the Roman legions on the exact same day in A.D. 70. When 120 of Iraq's senior military officers protested his invasion of a friendly Arab neighbor, Saddam ordered their immediate torture and execution.

Although he publicly claims overwhelming popular support from his oppressed people, according to a special report by Dennis Eisenberg to the *Toronto Sun,* from Jerusalem in September 1990, Saddam admitted to PLO chairman Yasser Arafat that "he doesn't trust a single man, woman, or child in Iraq." Saddam's regime of terror is so despised by his own Iraqi people that he was forced to turn to Yasser Arafat to obtain a special group of one thousand PLO terrorist bodyguards to protect him against assassination attempts. Over ten thousand PLO terrorists were flown in from their headquarters in Tunis and Lebanon and set up quarters in a secret army base in Baghdad where Hussein often sleeps. Hussein follows the same secretive and elusive practice of Osama bin Laden, in that he changes his location several times each night to minimize the opportunities for his many enemies to assassinate him.

President Hosni Mubarak of Egypt reported that Saddam told him that "when I am killed, the largest part of me which will remain will be the size of my little finger." Saddam's passion for his personal security rose to such a level that he hired three Saddam Hussein "doubles" to appear at various locations in the country, complete with a retinue of security men. These look-alikes were intended to fool potential hit teams who might try to get revenge for the many thousands of Iraqis and Kurds that Saddam has killed.

In 1977, Saddam wrote and published a book entitled *Unser Kampf,* or *Our Struggle.* The West totally ignored this book, just as western politicians in the 1930s tragically ignored the threats found in Adolf Hitler's book, *Mein Kampf (My Struggle)* Saddam's hero. The Reuters News Service and the German magazine *Hamburger Rundschau* reported on February 23, 1991, that Saddam's book outlined three main goals for "the Arab nation."

1. "We believe in a policy of international tension and preparation for war." He argued that this situation would help produce a stronger sense of belonging among the Arabs. "We believe that in times of tension, the Arabs find their unity again."

2. To "divide Europe, the United States, and Japan over their oil policies." He believed that Iraq could play each of these nations against each other to achieve his goal to "divide and conquer."

3. To achieve "the expulsion of the Jews" and to create "the establishment of a Palestinian state in place of Israel." This third goal became the most important in Saddam's plan for the recreation of the Babylonian Empire—with himself occupying the place of "King Nebuchadnezzar," the conqueror of the Jews.

Iraq's Plans to Re-establish the Babylonian Empire

In the book of Jeremiah we find a prophetic description of the future war against Babylon (ancient Iraq) that will occur in the last days: "For, lo, I will raise and cause to come up against Babylon an assembly of great nations from the north country: and they shall set themselves in array against her; from thence she shall be taken: their arrows shall be as of a mighty expert man; none shall return in vain" (Jeremiah 50:9).

Jeremiah's prophecy describes "an assembly of great nations from the north" coming against Babylon. The nations of the coalition against terror are led by North America and include a large number of supporting northern European nations. When the city of Babylon was first destroyed in October 538 B.C. the attack came from two eastern provinces, the Medes and the Persians. Therefore, Jeremiah's prophecy of an alliance of northern nations against Babylon was not fulfilled at that time. Note that the prophet Jeremiah commented on the astonishing accuracy of the missiles or "arrows" which are sent against the future Babylon by "mighty expert men." Could Jeremiah have seen in his vision weapons such as Tomahawk cruise missiles and smart laser-guided weapons hitting targets with great technical precision as "none of them shall return in vain"?

Babylon has been a religious symbol of Satan's hatred of God and His Chosen People, the Jews, throughout history. After thousands of years of spiritual warfare, the verdict of God against Babylon remains unchanged. Jeremiah 50:31 describes God's final sentence at the time of Armageddon on that wicked city and the evil rebellion of its inhabitants: "Behold, I am against thee, O thou most proud, saith the Lord God of hosts: for thy day is come, the time that I will visit thee."

We witnessed the beginning of the fulfillment of Jeremiah's prophecies about the war against Babylon during the 1991 Gulf War. However, the failure of the 1991 alliance to militarily defeat Iraq's army indicates that the prophecy of Jeremiah 50 concerning Babylon's military destruction must still be fulfilled at some point in the future. Jeremiah foretold the identify of several nations that will participate in this alliance of northern nations against Iraq. "Set ye up a standard in the land, blow the trumpet among the nations, prepare the nations against her, call together against her the kingdoms of Ararat, Minni, and Ashchenaz; appoint a captain against her; cause the horses to come up as the rough caterpillars" (Jeremiah 51:27). Ararat is an ancient tribal name associated with the modern nation of Turkey, an ally of America in the war against terror. Minni is associated with southern Russia. Ashchenaz is a tribe descended from Noah that settled in Europe. Significantly, while the northern alliance is led by America, it is interesting that Jeremiah mentions these three additional key allies in this coalition.

The remaining prophecies concerning Babylon's future role as a major economic and religious power will finally be fulfilled during the seven-year tribulation period that will conclude with the return of Christ to set up the kingdom of God. The book of Isaiah and Revelation 18 clearly describe the ultimate supernatural destruction of a future Babylon by fire and brimstone for its part in the terrible persecution of Israel and the martyrdom of the Tribulation saints.

Following the Gulf War, Iraq returned to the project of rebuilding the ancient city. When the UN economic sanctions are finally lifted, Iraq will be able to use its awesome oil revenues of over $100 million a day to become the major Middle Eastern economic power as prophesied in the Bible.

Although the prophecy in Ezekiel 38–39 indicates that Iraq will participate in the future Russian-Arab invasion of Israel, Babylon will still survive to become one of the leading centers of satanic pagan worship in the last days. In that regard, it is fascinating to observe that Saddam Hussein changed the law of Iraq several years ago to grant citizenship to Satan worshipers, allowing them to build communities to worship the devil near ancient Babylon. He has surrounded himself with witch doctors from Africa to cast spells to protect him during times of crisis. Iraq is currently rebuilding many of the ancient pagan temples in Babylon and is allowing priests to be trained in pagan festival worship. Babylon is once more becoming an abode of devils, just as the ancient prophets warned.

"Babylon The Great Is Fallen"

The prophet Isaiah warned that God's final destruction of the city of Babylon will be supernatural, "as Sodom and Gomorrah" (Isaiah 13:1). Revelation 19:3 prophetically describes that the fire and "smoke rose up forever" following the destruction of the great city, which was filled with "the blood of the prophets and of saints and of all that were slain upon the earth" (Revelation 18:24). "Babylon the great is fallen, is fallen, and is become the habitation of devils, and the hold of every foul spirit, and a cage of every unclean and hateful bird" (Revelation 18:2).

Babylon will play a terrible role as a spiritual center for satanic worship during the last days. A spiritual war has been waged for thousands of years between the spirit of Babylon, the city of Satan, and the spirit of Jerusalem, the city of God. All false religions trace their rituals, beliefs, and origin back to Babylon and its initial rebellion against the law of God. The essence of the Babylonian mystery religion is the attempt to transcend oneself and "become as God," as we see in the manifestations of New Age spirituality today. As the world approaches the final conflict of the ages, it will take on a physical as well as spiritual form as indicated by the specific prophecies about the rebuilding of Babylon and its religious system.

If you were to visit Babylon in the summer, you would see large amounts of warm, sticky asphalt oozing up out of the ground on hot days. The ancient builders used this pitch as a mortar in constructing the walls. The scientists tell us that the entire city has been built upon an underground lake of thick oil-based pitch or asphalt lying eight feet beneath the surface. This material is molten and expands through cracks in the clay when it is heated. This flammable material may provide the fuel for the eternal burning of the city of Babylon. This is additional evidence of the absolute reliability of the Word of God and its divine prophecies about the last days leading to the glorious return of the Messiah.

Endnotes

1. Paul Lewis, "Nebuchadnezzar's Revenge: Iraq Flexes Its Muscles by Rebuilding Babylon," *San Francisco Chronicle*. 30 April 1989.
2. Charles Dryer, *The Rise of Babylon*. Wheaton, Ill.: Tyndale.
3. Janet Cawley, "Hussein Doesn't Deny 'Butcher of Baghdad' Nickname." *Chicago Tribune*. 3 Aug. 1990.

7

The Coming Russian and Arab Invasion of Israel The Second Prophetic War

Despite constant liberal western media propaganda to the contrary, Russia's huge military machine still represents a serious threat to the nations of the West and to Israel. While western nations have reduced their armed forces and their levels of military preparedness, Russia has continued to build up their powerful military forces. The ongoing economic and political problems within Russia should provide little comfort to the NATO chief officers charged with the defense of the West. History reveals that Russia has often attacked her neighbors during times of internal Russian economic and political crisis as a means of uniting the nation against perceived external enemies. There are growing indications of renewed imperialism in the Russian military, its intelligence agencies, and former KGB agents forming the "Russian mafia" who are ruling the nation from behind the scenes. The brutal invasion and wholesale bombing of thousands of Russian civilians in Chechnya, a southern Islamic republic of Russia that wants independence, is one more indication that the real leaders in Moscow are reverting to their historic totalitarian and imperialistic methods.

Russia Is Preparing for an Invasion of the Middle East

The Russian military buildup is not confined to Russia. Some of Russia's largest military bases are now located in the Middle East. Russia maintains major air bases in Libya with hundreds of Russian combat aircraft. In addition, Russia has pre-positioned thousands of Russian tanks and armored personnel carriers in Libya. The North African nation of Libya has only three million citizens and no significant enemies. Libya has no objective need for such enormous quantities of Russian armaments.

Why would Libya's Colonel Qaddafi require such a large air force and armored units? Obviously, Libya does not have the capability to utilize such a huge military force. This enormous military buildup in Libya and other Middle Eastern countries may be used by Russia and her allies in a future war against Israel and in the conquest of the strategic oil interests in the Middle East.

Despite decades of Middle East diplomacy and peace talks, the area remains the most likely place in the world for the next great war to occur. During the last ten years, Russia supplied over $25 billion in new advanced weapons to Syria without any hope of repayment of billions of dollars for past arms sales. During the 1990s, both Iran and Iraq received a staggering $20 billion each in sophisticated weapons, while billions of dollars in arms were also sent to Yemen to threaten Saudi Arabia.

Russia's Secret Agenda in the Middle East

While attempting to present itself as a good world citizen and peace-loving democratic member of the United Nations, the truth is that Russia continues to maneuver behind the scenes to achieve her long-term aim of political-military control of the Middle East. During the Gulf War, Russia publicly stood on the side of the United States and its UN allies against Iraq's naked aggression. Behind the scenes, however, Russia did everything in its power to assist Iraq in its plans to conquer Kuwait and Saudi Arabia.

Russia was Iraq's main arms supplier during the last three decades. They sold Hussein every weapon in the Soviet arsenal except for nuclear warheads. In turn, the Iraqis provided the Russians with oil and desperately needed western hard currency. Iraq's well-paid German engineers retrofitted Russian Scud missiles to dramatically increase their range from 450 miles to 1,000-plus miles to enable them to hit Israel. The tradeoff to achieve the longer range involved a smaller warhead, either conventional, chemical-biological or, in the future, a very small tactical nuclear warhead (.2 megaton).

UN Resolutions: A Russian-Arab Opportunity

One of the most significant developments in the war against terrorism is the American utilization of UN Security Council resolutions to provide legal justification to attack the Taliban and al Qaeda terrorist forces. The Russians and Arabs have repeatedly demanded that the United Nations pass resolutions ordering Israel to surrender the West Bank, East Jerusalem, and Gaza to the Palestinian Authority.

When Israel resists this political pressure in an attempt to avoid committing national suicide, the UN will probably vote for economic sanctions, an arms embargo, et cetera, to attempt to force Israel to allow the creation of a Palestinian state in the West Bank and Gaza. We may ultimately see resolutions calling on the UN to send in peacekeeping troops "to protect Palestinians." Eventually, if Israel continues to say no, it is possible that the Russians and the Arabs may use UN Security Council resolutions as the legal pretext for the coming Russian-Arab invasion of Israel. This invasion will be a key event in Bible prophecy. The new coalition against international terrorism may set the stage for the coming Russian-Arab invasion of Israel—the prophesied War of Gog and Magog described by Ezekiel 38–39.

Many of the Islamic and Arab nations in the current coalition against terror have already demanded that this alliance put political pressure on Israel as "a terrorist nation." Muslim nations have falsely claimed that Israel's legitimate acts of military defense against terrorists and suicide bombers are also terrorist acts. Naturally, America, Canada, and the United Kingdom would refuse to use the alliance against terror to attack Israel, the only democracy in the Middle East. However, it is possible that the Arab and Islamic nations will join with Russia to direct the remaining alliance members against Israel at some point in the future. As these events begin to unfold, we can have confidence that the time is rapidly approaching for the Second Coming of Christ.

Identification of Ancient "Gog and Magog" as Russia

"Gog and Magog" are famous in biblical prophetic literature and rabbinical writings because of their future role in the great War of Gog and Magog, as predicted by the prophet Ezekiel (chapters 38–39).

The prophecies indicate that three great wars will convulse the planet during the apocalyptic period known as "the last days." The first war as described by Jeremiah is the war against Babylon (Iraq) that will involve a northern alliance of nations militarily defeating Iraq (Jeremiah 50) as described in Chapter Six. The second war is the War of Gog and Magog, the coming Russian-Arab invasion against Israel described in this chapter. The third battle, seven or so years later, is described in Joel, Zechariah, and the book of Revelation (16:16). The third and final war is known as the Battle of Armageddon. This cataclysmic conflict will involve the armies of the West under the Antichrist world dictator pitted against the enormous armies of the Kings of the East and then, against the victorious heavenly armies of Jesus Christ.

Revelation tells us about a fourth war, a battle at the end of history that will occur one thousand years after Armageddon at the end of the Millennium. "And when the thousand years are expired, Satan shall be loosed out of his prison, And shall go out to deceive the nations which are in the four quarters of the earth, Gog and Magog, to gather them together to battle: the number of whom is as the sand of the sea" (Revelation 20:7–8). The book of Revelation records that millions will join with the nations represented by "Gog and Magog," led by Satan, in a final attack against the beloved city and camp of the saints a thousand years later at the end of the Millennium. This final war will be the last battle in human history. A great number of people born during the Millennium to those who survive the tribulation period will choose to join Satan in his final attack against the City of God, once more led by Gog and Magog—Russia and other nations to the extreme north of the Holy Land. After God supernaturally destroys His enemies, there will never be war or rebellion again.

The question of the proper identification of the nation of Magog is of abiding interest to Bible students who wish to clearly understand the meaning of these great biblical prophecies. "Magog" is a real nation occupying a territory that was known to Ezekiel and his Jewish readers in the fifth century before Christ. I believe the historical evidence supports the conclusion that Magog refers to the territory that is currently occupied by the nation called Russia and several of the southern republics of the former USSR including Kazakhstan, Tajikistan, and Georgia.

Many prophecy teachers have concluded that Magog refers to the ancient tribal groups that once occupied the geographic area known today as Russia. However, in recent years, a number of liberal Christian scholars have challenged this identification of Magog with the Russian nation. Some scholars suggest that Magog was connected with some small tribal groups in ancient Mesopotamia in the area of Iran. Others suggest Magog was connected with the tribes led by Gyges in the area of Turkey, known to the ancients as Lydia, to the south of Russia. Many liberal scholars reject any "literal" interpretation of this prophecy. They tend to interpret Ezekiel's prophecy about the future war of Gog and Magog as merely a symbolic, apocalyptic war between good and evil.

If we want to understand the prophetic message of God regarding the events in the last days we need to determine the correct identification of Gog and Magog. The following is a summary of the research material I have collected during the last few years relating to this question.

Jewish Scholarship Identifying Magog with Russia

The first area we will examine includes a review of the Jewish scholarship concerning this identification. Since the passages in Ezekiel were studied in great detail for thousands of years by Jewish sages, their conclusions should throw some light on the true meaning of the Hebrew words "Gog and Magog." Genesis 10 lists Magog as a literal grandson of Noah who ultimately gave birth to a nation. This name Magog was well-known to every Jew who studied this Genesis passage. The prophet Ezekiel included the name Magog together with the names of other specific countries such as Libya, Persia, and Ethiopia in his prophecy about this future war. Ezekiel naturally expected the name Magog would be understood by his Jewish readers as a real nation, not as an abstract symbol of evil.

A recent commentary on the book of Genesis, *Bereishis–Genesis: A New Translation with a Commentary Anthologised from Talmudic, Midrashic and Rabbinic Sources*, includes this commentary on Genesis 10:2. "Magog is mentioned several times in Scripture, e.g. Ezekiel 38:2; 39:6 as the name of the land of Gog. . . . He also cites Arab writers who refer to the Great Wall of China as the wall of Al Magog." Dr. J. H. Hertz, the late chief rabbi of the British Empire edited *The Pentateuch and Haftorahs* comments on Genesis 10: "Magog—The Scythians, whose territory lay on the borders of the Caucasus." Dr. Alfred Edersheim, a Jewish-Christian scholar, in his book *Bible History—Old Testament*, also identified Magog as the Scythians of Russia.

A 1980 Jewish commentary on *Daniel*, published by The Art Scroll Tanach Series, comments on the identity of Magog: "The various traditions concerning the identity of Magog, who in Genesis 10:2 is listed among the sons of Noah's son Japheth, tend to place the land of Magog in what today is southwest Russia—the Caucasian region, which lies between the Black and Caspian Seas. . . ."[1]

This highly acclaimed Art Scroll commentary concludes with this fascinating comment. "In this light one may understand an oral tradition passed down from the Vilna Gaon (see *Chevlei Mashaiach BiZemaneinu* p. 134), that when the Russian navy passes through the Bosporus (that is, on the way to the Mediterranean through the Dardanelles) it will be time to put on Sabbath clothes [in anticipation of the coming of the Messiah]." The Jewish sages warned that the generation that witnessed the Russian preparation to invade Israel should prepare their hearts because the coming of the Messiah was at hand. The famous Jewish historian Flavius Josephus, who lived at the time of Saint Paul, wrote a definitive history of the Jewish people called the *Antiquities of the Jews*. In his history, Josephus identified Magog as follows. "Magog founded those that from him were named Magogites, but who are by the Greeks called Scythians."[2]

Christian Scholarship Identifying Magog with Russia

The section of Dr. R. Young's book, *Analytical Concordance of the Holy Bible*, dealing with Magog speaks of ancient Scythia or Tartary, describing southern Russia. Professor Young said that Ezekiel 38 referred to "a prince of Rosh, Mesheck, Tubal, and Tiras, in ancient Scythia or Tartary."[3] Young also described "the descendents of Magog and their land, called Scythia, in the N. of Asia and Europe." The authoritative 1973 reference work *Eerdman's Handbook to the Bible*, came to the same conclusion, "Magog, Meshech, Tubal and Gomer were all sons of Japheth (Noah's son). They gave their names to Indo-European peoples living in the Black Sea/Caucasus region, on the northern fringe of the then-known world." *The Comprehensive Commentary of the Holy Bible*, edited by Dr. William Jenks declared: "Magog was the son of Japheth (Genesis 10:2), from whence the Scythians are generally supposed to be derived."

Dr. Dwight Pentecost is the author of an excellent study of Bible prophecy entitled *Things to Come*. Dr. Pentecost quoted: "Magog's land was located in, what is called today, the Caucasus and the adjoining steppes. And the three, Rosh, Meshech and Tubal were called by the ancients, Scythians. They roamed as nomads in the country around and north of the Black and the Caspian Seas, and were known as the wildest barbarians."[4]

One of the most important scholarly tools employed in the exegesis of Scripture is *Gesenius' Hebrew and Chaldee Lexicon*. For many years numerous scholars referred to this book as a major authority on the precise meaning of Hebrew and Chaldean words in the original manuscripts of the Old Testament. He wrote, "Magog - PR. N. of a son of Japheth, Genesis 10:2; also of a region, and a great and powerful people of the same name, inhabiting the recesses of the north, who are at some time to invade the Holy Land Ezekiel 38, 39." We are to understand just the same nations as the Greeks comprised, under the name of Scythian (Josephus *Antiquities of the Jews* 1.6.1.)" Professor Gesenius referred to "Gog" as a "prince of the land of Magog . . . also of Rossi, Moschi, and Tibareni, who are to come with great forces from the extreme north (38:15; 39:2), after the Exile (38:8,12) to invade the holy land, and to perish there, as prophesied by Ezekiel."

The Coming Russian-Arab Assault

The prophecies of Ezekiel 38–39 tell us that Russia (Magog) will lead a confederacy of Arab and North African nations in an overwhelming military invasion of Israel in the last days. The miraculous defeat of Russia by the hand of God will set the stage for the final rise of the one-world government of the Antichrist. This will prepare for the rise of Antichrist over the ten nations that will arise within the confines of the ancient Roman Empire.

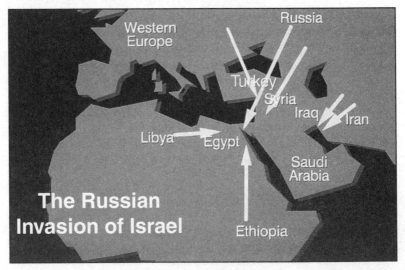

The Russian Invasion of Israel. The War of Gog and Magog.

Ezekiel's prophecies describe an enormous military power to the extreme far north of Israel that will lead a huge alliance of Russian, Arab, North African, and Middle Eastern nations in an overwhelming assault on Israel in their attempt to destroy the Chosen People. Ezekiel prophesied to "Gog," the leader of Russia as follows:

In that day when my people Israel dwelleth safely, shalt thou not know it? And thou shalt come from thy place out of the north parts, thou, and many people with thee, all of them riding upon horses, a great company, and a mighty army: And thou shalt come up against my people of Israel, and a cloud to cover the land; it shall be in the latter days, and I will bring thee against my land, that the heathen may know me, when I shall be sanctified in thee, O God, before their eyes. (Ezekiel 38:14–16)

Despite the overwhelming military strength of the coming Russian-Arab assault, Israel will be victorious because the Lord will intervene supernaturally to save the Jewish people at their greatest moment of danger. After moving their troops into the nations surrounding Israel, the Russian and Arab armies will prepare to launch their invasion of the Holy Land to defeat the Jewish nation. However, Ezekiel warns that the Lord will then unleash the greatest earthquake in history to destroy the armies of the Russian-Arab invaders. "Surely in that day there shall be a great shaking in the land of Israel. . . . And I will plead against him with pestilence and with blood; and I will rain upon him, an upon his bands, and upon the many people that are with him, an overflowing, and great hailstones, fire, and brimstone" (Ezekiel 38:19, 22).

The Russian-Arab armies will be utterly destroyed by earthquake, plague, hailstones, fire, and brimstone sent from God. The Lord will also afflict the Russian-Arab armies with a madness that will cause soldiers to attack their brother soldiers until 85 percent of the invading army will be left dead on the mountains surrounding the borders of Israel (Ezekiel 39:2). The number of dead soldiers will be so overwhelming that the prophet tells us that it will take seven months to bury the dead following God's devastating destruction of the enemies of Israel (Ezekiel 39:12). The coming War of Gog and Magog will eliminate the great military power of Russia and its plans to defeat the western democracies. It will take seven years to burn the weapons for fuel (Ezekiel 39:9). When Russia joins with the Arab nations to attack Israel, their conscious motive will be to conquer the strategic territory of the Middle East and seize its enormously valuable oil reserves. God's supernatural defeat of Russia and her Arab allies will drastically alter the geopolitical balance of power.

God explains why He will supernaturally destroy the Russian-Arab armies when they are about to destroy His Chosen People. First, God promised that He would never allow the Jews to be exiled from their Promised Land after they returned to Israel in 1948. Second, the Lord will demonstrate His supernatural power and glory to the gentile nations. "Thus will I magnify myself, and sanctify myself; and I will be known in the eyes of many nations, and they shall know that I am the Lord" (Ezekiel 38:23). Third, God will demonstrate His power and glory to the Children of Israel. "So will I make my holy name known in the midst of my people Israel; and I will not let them pollute my holy name any more: and the heathen shall know that I am the Lord, the Holy One in Israel" (Ezekiel 39:7).

When Russia is defeated by God's miraculous power, the newly united European Union will emerge as the greatest economic, political, and military power on earth (Daniel 2:40–43). These pivotal events will set the stage for the rise of the new European superstate and the emergence of the new leader who will ultimately become the Antichrist, the final world dictator who will rule the planet during the last seven years leading to the climactic Battle of Armageddon and the return of Jesus Christ to set up His eternal kingdom.

Endnotes

1. *Daniel* (New York: Mesorah Publications, Inc., 1980).
2. Flavius Josephus , *Antiquities of the Jews,* Book 1, vi, 1.
3. R. Young, *Analytical Concordance of the Holy Bible* (London: United Society For Christian Literature, 1971).
4. Dwight Pentecost, *Things to Come* (Grand Rapids: Zondervan Publishing House, 1958).

8

America's Counterterror War

The United States and its allies began their response to September 11 by attacking the soldiers and terrorist training camps of bin Laden's al Qaeda group in Afghanistan, Yemen, and other Islamic nations. However, it is vital that this war on terrorism include powerful and sustained attacks against those nations and terrorist groups throughout the Middle East that have supported terrorist attacks against the West and Israel during the last several decades. The first phase of this war necessarily targeted the individual terrorists and the thousands of Taliban supporters in Afghanistan that provided housing, vehicles, intelligence, financial resources, and disguises through stolen passports, etc. However, we will never destroy the global threat of Islamic extremist terrorism until we marshal our powerful military, political, intelligence, and financial resources against the many nations, groups, and individuals that have provided support to these despicable terrorists who kill thousands of innocent victims throughout the world.

Western intelligence and security forces have known for

years that there are several nations who have provided financial, intelligence, and military resources that protected and enabled these terror groups to attack western interests throughout the globe with virtual impunity. The list of terrorist-supporting nations is well known to the intelligence agencies of America, Britain, and Canada, as well as to the United Nations. The major terrorist-supporting states include Afghanistan, Iraq, Iran, Syria, Lebanon, Yemen, Sudan, Somalia, Libya, and the Palestinian Authority of Yasser Arafat.

First, the U.S.-led western coalition against terror wisely chose to attack the military forces of Afghanistan and its extremist Islamic Taliban regime, which wholeheartedly supported al Qaeda and its September 11 attacks against the West. President Bush correctly decided that it was essential to destroy the Taliban in order to eliminate the physical protection and support of bin Laden's terrorist group. As long as the Taliban remained in power in Afghanistan, it would have been virtually impossible to effectively send in our western military's special forces such as Britain's SAS (Special Air Service) and America's highly effective Rangers and Delta Force to locate and destroy bin Laden's terror network. Without American air cover and the suppression of al Qaeda's deadly anti-aircraft guns and its surface-to-air Stinger missiles, it would have been virtually impossible to safely send in our troops with silenced helicopters for insertion as well as the rescue teams to safely pull our elite troops out at the conclusion of their dangerous search-and-destroy missions.

It is significant that immediately following the American victory over the Taliban forces in Afghanistan US and UK special forces teams were sent to Somalia and Yemen where they are now working secretly to identify al Qaeda terrorists and their terror training camps.

Following the successful completion of Phase One of the war on terror against the al Qaeda terrorists and their Taliban supporters in Afghanistan, the alliance will turn its attention in Phase Two toward the next major supporter of Islamic terrorism—Saddam Hussein's regime in Iraq. The first step America will probably take is to marshal the overwhelming evidence from the criminal trials of the 1993 World Trade Center bombing and the 1998 U.S.

embassy bombings in Africa together with the secret intelligence sources acquired since September 11 that proves Iraq was behind the wave of al Qaeda terrorist attacks for the last ten years. This compelling evidence will be presented to America's allies in the war against terror and the United Nations together with recently acquired evidence of Iraq's continued illegal development of weapons of mass destruction. Then the president will be able to publicly present the appropriate evidence of Iraq's complicity to the U.S. Congress and the American public.

The massive media presentation will include enormous documentation of Iraq's guilt in supporting al Qaeda's terrorism together with evidence of Saddam Hussein's continued illegal development of weapons of mass destruction that threaten all western nations and Israel. The western nations together with our allies will undoubtedly begin Phase Two with massive air strikes against Iraq's army and air force targets, Hussein's intelligence and national security infrastructure including his elite Revolutionary Guard. While Iraq is only 65 percent the size of Afghanistan, it has a million-man professional army (regular and reserves) that is 15 times larger than the combined Taliban and al Qaeda forces. In addition, Iraq has extremely sophisticated air defences. However, unlike Afghanistan, Iraq as a modern state with its extensive infrastructure, provides what U.S. air force pilots like to call "a target rich environment."

Iraq

Now that the Afghan terrorist bases of al Qaeda are effectively eliminated, the next logical step will be for the alliance to demand that Iraq surrender all of the known terrorists that reside in its territory. The West must destroy dozens of Iraqi terrorist training camps used by President Saddam Hussein to train thousands of terrorists from numerous Middle Eastern nations to attack western interests. The United States and the United Nations have demanded that Iraq allow the United Nations' weapons inspectors to enter Iraq by June 2002 to search for and destroy all chemical, nuclear, and biological weapons laboratories, warehouses, and the secret bases used by Iraq's military to store their weapons of mass destruction. There is overwhelming evidence in the hands of America and the United Nations that Iraq has spent billions of dollars over the last two decades in an enormous national program to create weapons to destroy both Israel and the western nations that support the Jewish state's right to exist within secure borders in the Middle East.

The major military challenge problem is that, unlike Afghanistan, the western alliance has no equivalent to the Northern Alliance as an ally to fight the ground war. While the Kurdish rebels in the north of Iraq are capable fighters if supplied with sufficient arms, the defeat of Iraq's military forces on the ground will still require the invasion of a large American army. To that end, President Bush has already transported the first 30,000 soldiers from the American Third Army from Georgia to forward deployment bases in Kuwait and Qatar. Turkey, with its geographical proximity, excellent airbases, and its huge, well equipped army, will be a key to a decisive victory over Iraq. America may also ask Turkey to create a UN sanctioned protectorate over northern Iraq to preserve order to avoid the need for American troops to occupy this area following a victory over Saddam Hussein's regime.

Tragically, in the final days of the 1991 Gulf War, former President Bush agreed to the request of the president of the Soviet Union, Mikhail Gorbachev, that we refrain from completing our victory over Iraq's military forces by destroying Hussein's Republican Guard and eliminating his totalitarian government. In the months that followed the Gulf War, Hussein's brutal forces killed hundreds of thousands of Iraqi citizens who had dared to resist his dictatorship. The failure to decisively defeat all of the military forces of Iraq allowed Saddam Hussein to remain in control of Iraq and its tormented population. For three decades, the people of Iraq have suffered brutal torture and deadly persecution from the sadistic security forces of Hussein and his feared secret police. America's forcing of Iraq's invasion forces back toward Baghdad from their illegal conquest of Kuwait without totally defeating their armored forces and his Republican Guard was a political and military mistake of historic proportions. This would be as bizarre as if the western armies had defeated Hitler's invading army, driven them out of France, Belgium, and

Poland and then stopped General Patton's Third Army at the borders of Germany, leaving Adolf Hitler and the hated Nazi S.S. forces in charge of Germany. Europe would have faced threats and danger thereafter. Germany and Japan became democratic and normal members of the family of nations only after their military and political leadership were decisively defeated. Then, and only then, did these nations come to their senses and ceased to hold aggressive ambitions to conquer their neighbors.

In a bizarre justification of this tragic politically mistaken decision by President Bush Sr., many commentators claimed that the United Nations' resolution authorizing the war against Iraq did not specifically authorize the destruction of the Iraqi army or the military occupation of Iraq. If America's political leadership had only had the wisdom to complete the war they had begun, Iraq's population would have been delivered in 1991 from its tortured existence under Hussein's dictatorial rule and its suffering people would have been given the opportunity, under the protection of United Nations forces, to elect Iraq's first democratic government to replace decades of brutal coups and military dictatorships.

The goal, this time, will be to destroy Iraq's military power and replace the brutal regime of President Saddam Hussein with a new Iraqi government under the temporary supervision of the United Nations. Troops from neighbouring Muslim nations will be the most likely to be asked to provide peacekeeping forces. Hopefully, UN supervised elections and a new U.S. led "Marshall Plan" will assist the Iraqi and Afghan peoples to rebuild their nations and enjoy freedom from brutal tyranny for the first time in decades.

If the combined military forces of the western alliance against terror finally overthrow Iraq's terrorist-supporting regime, it will eliminate one of the greatest sources and supporters of terrorist subversion and violence against both the West and our ally Israel.

Sudan

If the western alliance defeats Iraq's government and the Iraqi people are freed to pursue a normal life, the West will probably demand that Sudan also surrender all identified terrorists that live freely today within its borders and call for the destruction of the terrorist training camps located throughout its territory. Osama bin Laden was exiled from Saudi Arabia early in the 1990s because of his strong threats to the royal family, and he moved his operations to Sudan. In the following years, bin Laden persuaded thousands of young Islamic men to join al Qaeda and dedicate their lives to the destruction of America and Israel. The Sudanese government provided assistance and protection to bin Laden's terrorists.

In addition, the West should demand that the Islamic Arab government of Sudan must immediately stop its evil and murderous attacks upon its population of black Christians living in the south of that country. The population of southern Sudan is composed of black Africans who are primarily Christian with some animists. The extremist Arab Islamic northern population supports the present Muslim government and its decades-long war against the southern population. Over two million Christian civilians have been killed in numerous bombings and other military attacks against defenseless villages.[1] Hundreds of thousand of Christians in the south have been captured in raids by northern Arab groups that have killed and enslaved countless women and children. These Christian slaves are taken far from their Sudanese villages and sold into other nations, including Saudi Arabia and Yemen. This despicable slave trade must be totally destroyed and eliminated by the western nations as part of our war against worldwide terrorism. It would be unthinkable to defeat the worst of the anti-western and anti-Israeli terrorism and leave this curse of slavery intact in our modern world. We must marshal the moral, economic, political, and the military forces of the West to demand that this evil slavery practice cease forever.

Libya

After Sudan, the western forces will likely turn their overwhelming military force against Libya. They will demand that the Libyan government deliver over to western authorities the numerous named terrorists that our intelligence community knows have been training in the terrorist camps in the southern Libyan deserts for many years. In addition, we need to demand that Libya surrender her secret chemical and biological weapons laboratories and bases, where they are attempting to develop weapons of mass destruction. These military facilities should be destroyed under the supervision of the United Nations.

Other Nations

Once the West has achieved these targeted victories against Islamic terror, they will likely turn to the nations of Syria, Yemen, Somalia, and Iran. The western nations will demand that they, too, must surrender the numerous Islamic terrorist groups that live within their nations under the protection of their security services and close their terrorist training camps.

For those who doubt that it is possible to convince these Arab nations to surrender such Islamic terrorist groups, consider the recent history of Syria and Turkey. For many years, Syria provided material assistance, bases, and financial support to a radical Kurdish terrorist group known as PKK (Kurdish Workers' Party), which launched numerous terrorist attacks on Turkey. Despite years of repeated demands that Syria surrender the PKK terrorists to Turkey, Syrian authorities repeatedly ignored Turkey's requests. Finally, Turkey mobilized its large army and moved it up toward the border of Syria in October 1998. Turkey threatened an immediate military invasion unless Syria surrendered the PKK terrorists. Syria expelled the leader of the PKK, Abdullah Ocalan, and his organization from Syria immediately, and he was quickly arrested and imprisoned by Turkey. This history demonstrates that even strong nations can be persuaded by massive military threats to give up their terrorist groups. Since September 11, it is impossible to allow any nation to act as a supporter and supplier of these murderous terror groups that are committed to the destruction of the West and of Israel with weapons of mass destruction.

One of the greatest strategic assets of the West in this major conflict is that most of these terrorist-supporting governments are very vulnerable to both external as well as internal enemies. For example, Iran, though a militarily powerful nation, is led by a narrowly supported extreme Islamic government that is now faced with the democratic popular will of the growing middle class, who desire a free society without religious coercion. Though these terrorist-supporting nations appear to be strong, a judicious application of military, intelligence, political, and economic force may motivate them to relinquish support of these terrorist groups. As long as America and its western allies remain vigilant and relentless in their steadfast determination to destroy both the terrorist fighters as well as their supporters, we will succeed in delivering our nations from the scourge of international Islamic terrorism. Then, we can direct our powerful forces against the remaining non-Islamic terrorists in Ireland, Spain, and South America.

In his September 2001 speech to a joint session of Congress, President George W. Bush declared, 'Tonight, we are a country awakened to danger and called to defend freedom. Our grief has turned to anger and anger to resolution. Whether we bring our enemies to justice or bring justice to our enemies, justice will be done." If our resolution against Islamic terrorism remains firm, we can and will win this war against terror. However, we must be willing to "stay the course," to fight this war to the very end. Then, and only then, will we win the war against terror and free western nations from the scourge of Islamic terror.

Why the West Must Attack the
Terror-Supporting States

Following the September 11 bombing of the World Trade Center and the Pentagon, Osama bin Laden released a prerecorded videotape on *Al-Jazeera*, an Arabic television station in the Middle East, in which he congratulated the terrorist "martyrs" and issued a number of threats to America. "Israeli tanks rampage across Palestine . . . and many other parts of the land of Islam, and we do not hear anyone raise his voice or reacting."

On September 15, 2001, bin Laden's al Qaeda spokesman Suleiman Abu Ghaith declared, "Let America know that the battle will not leave its land until it exits our land, and until it stops supporting the Jews and lifts the unjust sanctions on Iraq." Although bin Laden has never said much about the Palestinian-Israeli conflict in the past, he now tries to obtain wider popularity with the Arab and Islamic population throughout the world by appealing to their hatred of Israel. Behind all of the rhetoric of the Islamic terror groups lies their fundamental and implacable hatred for Israel and the Jewish people's right to exist within secure borders in the Middle East, its ancient homeland. The Islamic terrorists burn with hatred for the United States, the United Kingdom, and other democracies such as Canada and Australia that support Israel's right to exist as a nation in the Middle East.

The media commentators and many western diplomats are now engaged in a dubious moral exercise in situational ethics as they try to differentiate between the terrorist suicide bombers of al Qaeda who killed innocent American office workers on September 11 and the terrorist suicide bombers who kill innocent Jewish men, women, and children in restaurants in Jerusalem. However, such a distinction without a difference is utter intellectual and spiritual nonsense, as well as being morally indefensible. Anyone who purposely plans, supports, and engages in calculated attacks targeted at innocent civilians is a cowardly terrorist, regardless of any perceived political or historical grievance. Those who claim that a legitimate military attack on soldiers and military bases that unfortunately injures or kills several innocent civilians is the moral equivalent of a terrorist attack that purposely aims for the destruction of many civilians are morally blind. Such moral equivalence thinking would see no ethical difference between a murderer who kills an innocent victim and the policeman who kills the murderer who resists arrest.

Many media commentators are now suggesting we should study the root causes of terrorism and look closely at the desperate conditions of the Palestinian refugee camps to find the motivation for the acts of terror directed at Israel and America. However, a careful examination of the nineteen hijackers who killed more than three thousand Americans on September 11 reveals that they were well educated, relatively affluent, and most had families. The stark truth is that the fundamental cause of terrorism is the terrorists themselves, young Muslim men who are so filled with evil hatred of the Jews of Israel and the Christians in the West that they are willing to destroy their own lives to kill those they hate. There is no possibility of negotiation with Islamic terrorists such as Osama bin Laden. You cannot negotiate with someone who wants your death. You have only two choices when faced with the terrorists such as al Qaeda or dictators such as Saddam Hussein or Adolf Hitler: surrender to them and suffer death and the destruction of all you love; or marshal your forces to engage in a just battle to destroy him.

New Technologies to Detect Terrorist Threats

A New Acoustic Gun Can Detect Biological or Chemical Weapons

In free societies, it is extremely difficult to detect and locate every single terrorist attempt to introduce weapons into our nations that can subsequently be used to attack targets in our countries. An enormous difficulty exists due to the huge number of shipments of imports into western nations every day from our various trading partners around the globe. Literally millions of containers as well as barrels of chemicals and oil are shipped into our ports every day.

However, a new sophisticated "acoustical gun" was recently manufactured by the Los Alamos National Laboratory in New Mexico that may make weapons' detection much easier. The acoustic gun can instantly identify up to a hundred different chemicals within a steel barrel from a distance of ten feet. The new miniaturized system is handheld and much less expensive than previous systems. Dipen Sinha, the lead researcher of the Los Alamos team, noted that acoustical resonance of a container depends on whatever is stored inside, the speed of the sound, and the weakening strength of a material in density and viscosity; all of these affect the laser spectrum. Sinha declared, "When all these factors are taken into account, one has a very good idea of the liquid inside." The plan is to miniaturize the chemical detection devices to allow the acoustical gun to be used by biological and chemical weapons security agents to detect dangerous terrorist attacks before they can detonate their weapons.[2]

The new 4-pound acoustic resonance device uses magnets to attach the chemical detector to a metallic drum and then display sound waves on a computer monitor to indicate whether it is solid

América's Counterterror War

or liquid. The machine can also register the acoustical resonance from a missile shell to identify whether or not it is a chemical or biological weapon, as every chemical has a unique pattern.

New Systems to Detect Concealed Weapons

The U.S. National Institute of Justice is now developing an inexpensive handheld device to alert both police and customs security officers to the presence of a concealed weapon at a distance, even though it is concealed within the clothing of a suspect. This device uses acoustic technology to detect both metallic and nonmetallic weapons that may be used in criminal acts.

A new concealed-weapon detector developed at Idaho National Engineering and Environmental Laboratory employs fluxgate magnetometers that detect anomalies in the earth's magnetic field caused by magnetic objects such as guns carried by individuals. It sounds an alarm when it detects a metal object, and indicates the size of the object and where it is located on the suspect. This new sophisticated detection system eliminates the unnecessary delay of numerous airline passengers because it allows security personnel to focus their attention upon the very few individuals who might actually carry weapons that are a threat to the airline and its passengers. The new weapons' detection system, SecureScan 2000, is manufactured by Milestone Technologies and is being acquired by many airports.

Another ultrasound weapon-detection system was developed for remotely detecting and imaging any concealed terrorist weapons. The sensor will detect both metallic and non-metallic weapons concealed on a person, even if the weapon is concealed under heavy clothing up to twenty-five feet away. This system was developed by the Concealed Weapons Detection Technologies program created by the Air Force Materiel Command and the U.S. Defense Advanced Research Projects Agency.

With these new tools at our disposal, the changes to airline security procedures, and the eradication of terrorist training bases around the globe, the West should soon be in a good position to protect itself from further attacks such as the ones on September 11, 2001.

Palestinian Terrorist "Work Accidents"

Have you ever wondered why so many Palestinian terrorist bombers blow themselves up preparing explosives to kill innocent Jewish civilians? More than 100 Palestinian bomb makers have blown themselves up recently. The Israeli military and media call these explosions "work accidents." Recently intelligence and media reports (Arutz 7, April 14, 2001) confirmed what I was told several years ago. Once an Israeli security team detects the presence of explosives (even if they were in a trunk weeks earlier) in a car stopped at a road checkpoint, a micro GPS radio transmitter can be secretly attached to the suspect vehicle. The Israeli teams also have extremely sophisticated electrical devices that enable them to detect explosives such as Semtex at a great distance. The system is called ANAI, Hebrew for "thunderbolt." The powerful focussed pulse of FM radio energy overwhelms the electronic detonator in any bomb in the target area by creating a radio frequency arc of electricity across any open bomb trigger switch, thus detonating any explosives present. Israeli and other security services use a smaller RF system to explode undetected bombs before politicians arrive at a meeting location.

Once explosives are detected, the "Work Accident" team begins a clandestine surveillance on the location or vehicle for 36 hours. Using a nondescript truck filled with advanced radio equipment, the Israeli team observes the target from up to a mile distance. Once they confirm that a bomb is being created—the bomber is on the move toward a target, other Islamic Jihad or Hamas terrorists arrive, or the 36-hour countdown expires—they send an enormously powerful radio signal through a six-foot-long YAGI radio antenna concealed in the truck. If a bomb is present, there will be another "work accident." If not, nothing will happen.

Endnotes

1. Internet web site: http://www.freedomhouse.org/religion/sudan/index.htm.
2. Ian Sample. *The New Scientist.* October 30, 1999. http://www.newscientist.com/ns/19991030/newsstory 4.html.

War on Terror

9

The War Against Terror and the Coming World Government

The global war against international Islamic terrorism requires extraordinary measures. These involve increased government surveillance as well as an unprecedented degree of cooperation by western governments to create a global military and intelligence alliance against the terrorist-supporting nations. The nations of the West must join together in an alliance against global terrorism. However, this war against terror may prove to be one of the key crises that pave the way for the world government that is prophesied to arise in the last days leading to the return of Jesus Christ. The historically unprecedented military, political, and intelligence alliance involving western nations led by America, Russia, and many Arab as well as Central Asian regimes is a major step.

The global political and financial elite who are committed to the creation of a world government realize that the vast majority of the world's citizens are happy to live in their individual nation-states. Although many people are pleased to see the United Nations coordinating global peacekeeping and humanitarian operations that extend international assistance in the event of famines and other disasters, they are not willing to transfer the sovereign powers of their nation state to a new global government. The primary obstacle against the movement toward world government is that most people love their country, their flag, their history, and their democratic ability to choose their own national government that is focused on their practical economic and political issues. Those elite groups who are planning to create a global government realize that the only practical way to achieve their goal is to take advantage of a major economic, political, or military crisis that is so overwhelming that no nation could possibly solve it alone.

David Rockefeller, one of the key leaders of several globalist groups including the Council on Foreign Relations, the Trilateral Commission, and the Bilderberger Group, made a speech in which he clearly outlined their global agenda, as well as their preferred course of action to prepare citizens to accept global government. Rockefeller announced: "We are on the verge of a global transformation. All we need is the right major crisis and the nations will accept the New World Order." (http://www.humanunderground.com/anatomy.html)

America and World Government

Skeptics, who reject warnings against the dangers of a global government, often ask how America could ever relinquish her treasured sovereignty and join the coming world government, in light of the safeguards provided by the U.S. Constitution. However, the U.S. Congress has already given the president powerful executive powers to enable him to exercise total control over the government, the military forces, and the economy in the event of a national emergency. Naturally, it is essential that the president have the full legal authority to direct the military and control the physical resources of the nation to protect its citizens if America is attacked with nuclear, biological, or chemical weapons. A Russian, Chinese, or even a radical Middle Eastern nation's nuclear, chemical, or biological attack against America could obviously wipe out much of the military's command and control system, as well as significant parts of the federal government. Therefore, it is vital that the surviving political leadership of the USA retain the ability to control the remaining government departments and the armed forces through legally authorized presidential Executive Orders.

The almost dictatorial powers available to a U.S. president once he declares a national emergency are virtually equal to the vast legal powers that were held by Adolf Hitler during his Nazi dictatorship. Existing emergency legislation allows a president to suspend the Constitution and exercise emergency powers whenever he determines that the nation faces a "national emergency." Remarkably, the term "national emergency," is not actually defined by the laws themselves. It is left solely to the ruling president to determine when and if a national emergency exists and to exercise his tremendous executive powers. Executive orders are issued solely by the president and have the full force of national law (equivalent to laws normally passed by Congress).

Consequently, these existing executive orders are a "loaded gun" that any president could use to establish a dictatorship and facilitate America joining a world government. A national "emergency" can be declared by a president at any time in the future, providing an excuse to enact laws restricting freedom that Congress would never pass in normal times.

These are some of the *existing* national security Executive Orders that a president could legally exercise during a future declared "national emergency."

Executive Order:

10995: The seizure of all print and electronic communications media in the United States.

10997: The seizure of all electric power, fuels, and minerals, public and private.

10998: The seizure of food supplies and resources, public and private, including farms and equipment.

10999: The seizure of all means of transportation, including cars, trucks, or any other vehicles, including control over highways, harbors, and waterways.

11000: The seizure of all American citizens for civilian labor forces under federal supervision.

11002: The registration of every citizen by the postmaster general for government service.

11003: The seizure of all airports and aircraft.

11004: The seizure of all housing and finance authorities; authority to establish forced relocation designated areas that must be abandoned as "unsafe." The establishment of new locations for population groups.

11005: The seizure of all railroads, inland waterways, and storage warehouses, public and private.

11051: The authorization of the Office of Emergency Planning to put the above orders into effect in times of increased international tension or financial crisis.

Several years ago the conservative writer Howard Ruff commented on the dangers to America's freedom and democracy from the establishment of these extra-constitutional powers. He wrote, "Executive Order 11490 is real, and only the lack of a crisis big enough, a president willing enough, and a public aroused enough to permit it to be invoked, separates us from a possible dictatorship, brought about under current law, waiting to be implemented in the event of circumstances which can be construed as a national emergency." (http://newsandviews.tripod.com/news/fema.html.)

The present national emergency since the terrorist attacks on September 11 certainly creates a situation where the president may invoke at least some of the vast powers conferred on him by this series of executive orders. Despite the obvious need for powerful measures to counter the threat of terror, American freedom could be seriously imperiled in our fight against Islamic terrorism.

In the 1970s, President Gerald Ford signed Executive Order EQ 11921, instructing the Federal Emergency Preparedness Agency (FEPA) to plan for the establishment of total governmental control of the production and distribution of energy, wages, salaries, credit, and currency flow from all American financial institutions during a future national emergency. This remarkable order gives the president almost dictatorial control over the nation. Furthermore, EQ 11921 declares that during the duration of the emergency, Congress cannot reassert political control over these unprecedented presidential powers, nor even review the matter for six months. In 1977, President Jimmy Carter replaced FEPA with the expanded Federal Emergency Management Agency (FEMA). The president can now legally suspend the U.S. Constitution and the Bill of Rights under the McCarran Act with a single phone call, imposing martial law throughout the nation in the event of a national emergency. Most western democracies, including Canada, the United Kingdom, and Australia, have similar national emergency laws.

A Global Government

The prophets Daniel and John warned that a global world government would arise in the last days and would be led by the Antichrist, the world's last dictator. John warned, "And it was given unto him to make war with the saints, and to overcome them: and power was given him over all kindreds, and tongues, and nations. And all that dwell upon the earth shall worship him" (Revelation 13:7–8). John and Daniel reveal that "all that dwell upon the earth" will be under the control of the Antichrist's global government in the last days. This future Antichrist will have power "over all kindreds, and tongues, and nations." There has never been a true world government throughout thousands of years of history, though many ancient empires ruled vast areas of the civilized world. The increasing power of the United Nations, the International Monetary Fund, the World Trade Organization, and the World Court are rapidly destroying traditional national sovereignty, and replacing them with a global political and economic agenda. The elite, who are committed to the concept of global governance, have embarked on a program to subvert and diminish the traditional sovereignty of all nation-states, including America, Britain, and Canada.

In July 1994, a provocative United Nations study entitled *Renewing the United Nations System* was published. This startling report, financed by the Ford Foundation and authored by two former U.N. officials, Sir Brian Urqhart and Erskine Childers, concluded that massive changes are needed in UN operations. This far-reaching proposal expressed their goal of laying the foundation for a one-world government. "While there is no question, *at present*, of the transformation of the U.N. system into a supranational authority, the organization is in a transitional phase, basically shaped and constrained by national sovereignty, but sometimes acting outside and beyond it" [italics added]. Note the phrase "at present." The document repeatedly used terms such as: "gradual limitation of sovereignty"; "notable abridgements of national sovereignty"; "chipping away at the edges of traditional sovereignty"; and "small steps towards an eventual trans-sovereign society." The authors discuss the UN strategy to progressively strip nations of their cherished sovereignty. The plan is to proceed step-by-step to avoid awakening a political backlash by the citizens of the western democracies who will ultimately be forced to surrender their sovereignty.

One example of the shift from national sovereignty toward the coming one-world government is revealed in the 1991 UN General Assembly resolution on humanitarian emergency assistance. Discussing the "emergency-driven temporary cessation of sovereignty," the document notes that for the first time the word *consent* was used instead of *request*, and *country* replaced *government*. The full statement read: "Humanitarian assistance should be provided with the consent of the affected country and in principle on the basis of an appeal by the affected country." In other words, the United Nations no longer feels the need to obtain a request from the political leadership of a national government to intervene inside a nation's borders. As long as the UN believes the country's population will consent to the intervention, then it feels justified in intervening. This is a revolutionary change from the original founding principle of non-intervention in the internal affairs of nations that governed the actions of the United Nations for the first fifty years. Secretary General Boutros-Ghali's 1992 report, *An Agenda for Peace*, contained a significant indication of the new UN thinking: "The time of absolute and exclusive sovereignty, however, has passed, its theory was never matched by reality."

Some of the *Renewing the United Nations System* report's recommendations are very significant steps toward world government. Throughout the document, the authors talk about interim steps that must be taken "until the world is ready for world government." The report suggests that the United Nations should raise funds for its own budget by assessing a global surcharge tax on "all arms sales," on "all transnational movement of currencies," on "all international trade: or on the production of such specific materials as petroleum," or "a United Nations levy on international air and sea travel." Other recommendations include assessing a "one day" income tax on all people of the planet every year. Proposals to have the UN apply a global tax on the citizens of the world are one more indication of the gradual transformation from an international consultative body to the beginnings of a one-world superstate.

The End of Sovereignty

The elite groups that are planning a one-world government have embarked on a conscious program to subvert and diminish the sovereignty of nation states, including America and Canada. There is a continuous struggle for ethnic survival, religious rights, and national sovereignty at the forefront of international affairs today. Wherever these rights or interests are threatened by terrorism, civil war, or other conflict, there is a call for United Nations' intervention. This situation follows a planned political strategy that was developed in the last century by German philosopher Georg Hegel. The Hegelian dialectic theorizes that "conflict brings change, and controlled conflict brings controlled change." Therefore, if you have an agenda to institute massive political change, you must be in a position to trigger or to take advantage of major conflicts and crises. These crises create the necessary political turmoil and focus everyone on the "problem." This will then allow the globalist elite to propose their preplanned "solution" of global government to the anticipated world crisis.

Consider carefully how several recent international crises have developed in Somalia, Rwanda, Haiti, Bosnia, and Kosovo. Why did the United Nations Security Council wait until these crises escalated to the point where human disaster affected millions? Were some of these situations allowed to develop into total catastrophes to provide an excuse for the elite to move us closer to world government? As the existing governments in these Third World trouble spots disintegrated into total anarchy, the United Nations has moved in with their advisors to create a kind of trusteeship, a modern version of colonialism. In a 1993 article in the Council on Foreign Relations journal *Foreign Affairs*, Boutros Boutros-Ghali, the former secretary-general of the UN, declared that he felt the need to "rethink the question of sovereignty."

The historian Arnold Toynbee, who strongly supported world government, argued for global organization. "We are approaching the point at which the only effective scale for operations of any importance will be the global scale. The local states ought to be deprived of their sovereignty and subordinated to the sovereignty of a global world government. I think the world state will still need an armed police [and the] world government will have to command sufficient force to be able to impose peace. . . . The people of each local sovereign state will have to renounce their state's sovereignty and subordinate it to the paramount sovereignty of a literally worldwide world government. . . . I want to see a world government established."[1] These words by Arnold Toynbee are no longer considered revolutionary. His rejection of the nation state is now shared by the financial and political elite who are planning to create a new world government.

The New Colonialism

For a hundred years (1850-1950) the European empires of Britain, Spain, Portugal, France, Italy, and Germany developed their African and Asian colonies to provide raw materials, low-cost labor, and captive markets. However, following the close of World War II, the European powers withdrew quickly from Africa and Asia leaving their former colonies to struggle with few resources or trained people to establish national governments. The intellectual and political elite of Europe wholeheartedly rejected colonialism and were confident that European educated nationals would return to their former colonies to take up the reins of power in their newly liberated countries.

However, with few exceptions, these former colonial nations have failed to develop either representative democratic government or stable administrations. Many of the best-trained personnel chose to remain in Europe due to job opportunities and economic advantages. Vast tracts of Africa such as the Congo (formerly ruled by Belgium), a nation the size of western Europe, are reverting to the wild frontiers with no recognizable government. Any army officer commanding a few soldiers with automatic weapons is a feudal warlord answerable to no one. In many African nations, if you travel a dozen miles outside the capital, the central government is powerless to enforce its will. Many former colonies such as Rwanda, Zimbabwe, and Angola are suffering from the complete breakdown of government functions—anarchy, social disintegration and massive corruption. Appalling levels of famine and disease (AIDS and malaria) are now epidemic in dozens of nations south of the Sahara Desert. Recently, the world witnessed almost one million Tutsi men, women, and children hacked to death by machete by the Hutu majority in Rwanda. Obviously, something must be done to restore some measure of order and good government to these nations. These "failed" nations, including Iraq, Sudan, Afghanistan, et cetera, are now breeding grounds for civil war, epidemics, famine, and the new scourge of fanatical Islamic terrorism.

In the face of this total breakdown of government functions, many Europeans are beginning to think the unthinkable. A number of intellectuals have written editorials and studies calling for the re-introduction of colonialism by individual European nations or the creation of temporary trusteeships under the authority of the United Nations. While these ideas are tempting, especially to those who are pushing for a new world order, none of the European nations would dream of taking on such an onerous burden on its own. The United Nations is broke and cannot get its act together to manage its existing commitments for peacekeeping forces in Bosnia, Kosovo, Cambodia, and dozens of other hot spots around the world. In addition, the UN has proven inept in administrating short-term disaster relief, let alone the long-term commitment of dozens of years required to establish stable governments in Asia or Africa. The kind of instant band-aid solution illustrated by America's short-term military and humanitarian intervention in Somalia will never make a meaningful change in the systemic problems afflicting the former colonies.

A better solution would be to ask the European Union to take on the task of working with these desperate African nations to establish a cooperative UN trusteeship over thirty to fifty years to resurrect these failed nations to rejoin the family of nations as civilized states able to provide peace, order, and good government to their oppressed peoples. Europe possesses ample talented personal who speak the languages and have existing relationships with these nations due to their previous colonial experience. Europe is the natural group to solve this problem because of Europe's past colonial relationships. In addition, Europe has a strong motive to establish some measure of stability in Asia and Africa to prevent tens of millions of illegal immigrants from fleeing the disintegrating states and arriving illegally on the southern shores of the continent. Millions of African immigrants are already fleeing the oppressive situation in the former colonies to seek a better life for their families.

In the council chambers of the European Union, the leaders are looking for long-term political projects that will engage the resources and energies of their citizens. The challenge to join with these African and Asian nations in a long-term project under UN trusteeship to resurrect these desperate nations fits in very well with the globalist agenda of those who are working behind the scenes to establish a world government.

Enlarging United Nations Power

Former British foreign secretary Douglas Hurd claimed in an interview that the United Nations needs to prepare itself to take on an "imperial role." He stated that the UN must usurp national sovereignty and take control as the occupying power when governments collapse, as in Somalia and Cambodia. During an interview held at the UN in New York, Secretary Hurd drew attention to what he called "a new phase in the world's history." There is a need for the UN to intervene in crisis situations earlier to "prevent things getting to the stage where countries are run by corrupt warlords, as in Somalia," he said. Douglas Hurd warned that since the breakup of the former Soviet Union—leaving three or four "crisis areas" itself—the United States was the lone superpower and it had no wish to become the sole "policeman of the world."

One of the key goals of the globalists is to create a militarily capable permanent standing army that would permit the UN Security Council to enforce the will of the world body against any nation or group of nations that opposes its global agenda. The number of UN soldiers serving in operations increased greatly in the last decade with over one hundred thousand civilians and "blue beret" troops deployed in peacekeeping operations worldwide from Bosnia, Kosovo, Haiti, and Afghanistan.

Plans to Build a Permanent UN Army

Despite Washington's reluctance to risk the lives of American soldiers in UN peacekeeping operations in far-off places, the conflict in Afghanistan demonstrated that the U.S. cannot avoid a leadership role in the wars of the future. America and the United Kingdom are the only nations with highly trained troops, huge transport planes, a sea-lift capacity, spy satellites, and technical intelligence facilities to make such military global interventions both practical and relatively safe. In Bosnia, with NATO's coordination, America provided logistical air- and sea-lift support while France, Britain, and other nations supplied troops on the ground. Until 1999, NATO was unwilling to act outside Europe and the Mediterranean basin. Meanwhile, the United Nations has a worldwide membership and the political, legal, and moral authority to order military "peacemaking" interventions.

Significantly, a September 26, 1994, article in *Newsweek* called for the creation of a standing army for the New World Order to respond to future crises anywhere in the world. "The United Nations needs its own army, accountable not to national governments but to the United Nations itself. The rich nations would have to donate equipment to such an army; real live soldiers would be recruited from volunteers. Some would be trained mercenaries, like the Nepalese Gurkhas; others would be units from the armies of the western world."

The August 1994 issue of the *Economist* magazine wrote about the 1990s disasters in Somalia and Rwanda as the UN tried and failed to create a professional army assembled from the different units of dozens of military forces provided by its member states. Often the ammunition did not match the weapons, the troops were not trained for the equipment they had to use, and the soldiers were commanded by foreign officers who could not speak the languages of the troops they led. The *Economist* argued, "A standing force would respond to emergencies only when the Security Council told it to . . . it would be ready to try at once, not after UN officials had gone cap in hand to umpteen governments. The idea bristles with tricky questions: command, recruitment, training, pay, nationality, transport, supply, and support backup. But it should be possible to create a brigade-sized force of this kind. And it is what the UN needs if it is to be a peacekeeper worthy of its name."

The leadership of the UN has called repeatedly for the creation of a special UN rapid-deployment military force of sufficient size to defeat any potential opponent. The UN wants member states to provide trained soldiers, equipment, and necessary funding on a permanent basis, supported by each member state's defense budget. The creation of a permanent UN armed force will be one of the key milestones on the road to world government.

NATO and the Coming World Government

America, Britain, and Canada strongly supported the creation of the North Atlantic Treaty Organization (NATO) in 1948 to prepare a powerful defensive alliance against the huge armies of the Soviet Union and the Warsaw Pact nations. Analysts and historians agree that NATO is the most successful military and strategic alliance in history.

NATO's New Strategic Doctrine

The representatives of the member states of NATO met in Washington on April 23-24, 1999, to celebrate the fiftieth anniversary of the military alliance and to negotiate the basis for continuation and expansion of the alliance in the new millennium. Many members of NATO raised concerns over the necessity for the continued existence of the military alliance since the former Soviet Union and communist Eastern European nations were no longer considered a serious military threat to western Europe.

The most serious issue involved the role of NATO military forces in future conflicts outside Europe. Prior to the 1998 Kosovo conflict, for example, NATO had absolutely refused to become involved in any military operations outside the territory of its member states. The NATO treaty specifically limited its role to defense of the national territory of its member states. For example, NATO played no role in the British war to regain the Falkland Islands from Argentina or America's military action in Grenada. Even though members of NATO such as Britain, Canada, Italy, and Turkey contributed significantly in the Gulf War response to Iraq's 1990 invasion of Kuwait, they did so as individual nations and not under the direction of NATO. However, human rights abuses in Kosovo and the obvious danger to European stability in the Balkans caused by Serbia's military actions forced NATO to break its rules and intervene decisively with a three-month bombing campaign that defeated Serbia and ended the Kosovo conflict. The proximity of Kosovo to NATO's member states in western Europe and its location between the member states of Greece and Hungary provided some justification for this intervention outside of NATO's territory.

However, the Washington NATO summit of 1999 announced a massive change in the role and purpose of the alliance. Despite the huge implications of this policy change, this decision received little media scrutiny and less political debate. The summit announced that NATO will no longer be a defensive-only alliance for the protection of the territory and sovereignty of its member states. This new strategic concept for the NATO alliance is a complete reversal of the defensive strategy that effectively preserved the peace in Europe for fifty years. The president of the United States and prime minister of the United Kingdom endorsed this revolutionary change in military doctrine that may set the stage for the coming world government.

Joe de Courcy, the former editor of *Intelligence Digest*, the most important private intelligence analysis agency in the world, alerted me to the political significance of this new NATO strategic doctrine. *Intelligence Digest* has provided very accurate as well as timely intelligence information and analysis of critical situations throughout the world since 1938. Many heads of state and executives of multinational corporations throughout the world read its reports.[2]

This new strategic doctrine declares that NATO's "essential and enduring purpose . . . is to safeguard the freedom and security of all its members by political and military means." While this language appears innocent, the phrase "by political and military means" opens the door for NATO to move into areas and activities far beyond its traditional role of military defense of its member states. The word "political" allows espionage activities, political pressure, and many other previously prohibited activities.

The document also defines the new strategic doctrine that will govern future military or political intervention by NATO as follows:

> The security of the Alliance remains subject to a wide variety of military and non-military risks. . . . These risks include *uncertainty and instability in and around the Euro-Atlantic area* and the possibility of *regional crises at the periphery of the Alliance* which could evolve rapidly. Some countries in and around the Euro-Atlantic area face serious economic, social and political difficulties. *Ethnic and religious rivalries*, territorial disputes, inadequate or failed efforts at reform, the *abuse of human rights*, and the dissolution of states can lead to *local and even regional instability*. The resulting tensions could lead to crises affecting Euro-Atlantic stability, to human suffering, and to armed conflicts. Such conflicts could affect the security of the Alliance by spilling over into neighbouring countries, including NATO countries, or in other ways, and could also affect the security of other states.[3]

This alliance's new definition of military and non-military situations that could provoke NATO military intervention is astonishing in its length and variety. During its first fifty years,

NATO refused to intervene unless a member's territory was attacked. Now the Western Alliance declares to other nations that *"uncertainty and instability in and around the Euro-Atlantic area"* or even *"at the periphery of the Alliance"* justifies NATO's military or political intervention in a future crisis. Situations that could provoke a NATO invasion include: *"ethnic and religious rivalries," "abuse of human rights,"* or *"local and even regional instability."* NATO's new strategic doctrine justifies its right to intervene militarily or politically in virtually any surrounding nation or territory if the leaders of NATO conclude that any of the above conditions exist.

In light of the new war on terrorism that America and Britain are now waging, it is noteworthy that the new strategic concept adds terrorism as a reason for NATO to justify an invasion of another nation and the violation of its sovereignty: "Alliance security interests can be affected by other risks of a wider nature, including *acts of terrorism, sabotage and organized crime, and by the disruption of the flow of vital resources.* The uncontrolled movement of large numbers of people, particularly as a consequence of armed conflicts, can also pose problems for security and stability affecting the Alliance."[4]

Western nations now believe they have the right to invade another sovereign nation because of the existence in that country of *"acts of terrorism, sabotage and organized crime, and by the disruption of the flow of vital resources."* This same NATO document declares another justification for the alliance's military intervention would include even the *attempt* by another nation within its declared security zone to acquire nuclear, biological, and chemical weapons and the means to deliver such weapons that "can pose a direct military threat to the Allies' populations, territory and forces." This NATO document takes on new importance in light of President Bush's declaration in late November 2001 that Iraq's possession of labs and secret plants making nuclear, biological, and chemical weapons would be justification to attack that nation.

General Klaus Naumann, chairman of the NATO military committee, in April 1999 defined the regions that NATO considered to be within her security zone as "the nations resting on its periphery from Morocco to the Indian Ocean."[5] In other words,

NATO declared that it is now willing to intervene anywhere from Morocco across North Africa through the Middle East, including the Arabian Peninsula, and extending to the east as far as Iran. This new NATO doctrine helps explain the commitment by Britain, Canada, Germany, France, Italy, and Turkey to join the war against terror and the Taliban government in Afghanistan, which supported al Qaeda.

This remarkable new strategy of NATO may set the stage for the end-time wars and the coming world government that will rise to power in the last days as described in the book of Revelation. The aggressive strategy of NATO is an attack on the national sovereignty of all states, both those within the NATO alliance and those states that oppose it. These developments may lead to the fulfillment of Daniel and John's prophecies about the ten-nation superstate, the kingdom of Antichrist, that will be based on the territory of the ancient Roman Empire and become the power base for the coming world dictator.

Consider the tragic and horrendous failures of the previous UN peacekeeping missions in Somalia, Rwanda, and Sierra Leone in comparison to the highly effective and successful military campaigns of the western-led armies and air forces during the Gulf War, the Kosovo bombing campaign, and the recent attack on bin Laden's al Qaeda terrorists and the Taliban. This comparison suggests that the only way the UN will achieve the military power necessary to enforce the will of the Security Council is to utilize the existing professional and modern integrated military forces of NATO.

Under the original NATO doctrine, which called only for the defense of the territory of its member states, it was difficult to conceive of NATO forces being used outside of western Europe to support the UN's mission to achieve world government. However, the new aggressive strategic doctrine of NATO will allow the powerful military alliance to support the globalists' plans.

The Threat to National Sovereignty

During the debates in the United Nations' Security Council regarding NATO's Kosovo intervention, Russia, China, and many Third World nations strongly objected. Their objection was that

NATO's action against Serbia was a dangerous precedent and a very real threat to their own sovereignty. Therefore, it is not surprising that Russia, China, India, and many Third World nations issued statements denouncing NATO's declaration of intervention. One example is a thought-provoking article in the *Jordan Times* in early 1999 stating:

> But the most important issue raised by the NATO Yugoslavia confrontation is the inviolability of a country's sovereignty, or more specifically under what circumstances is intervention in an independent state's internal affairs permissible and who should be allowed to intervene. Many of the states opposing the NATO action fear it will set a precedent of support for separatist movements which could be used against China in Tibet, against Russia in Chechnya, and against India in Kashmir. Another concern is the bypassing of the UN by NATO. NATO is viewed as simply promoting US interests and in effect making the US a sort of world policeman.[6]

If even an Arab nation such as Jordan, which is friendly to the West, expresses deep concerns about the threats to national sovereignty from the implications of NATO's new policies, you can imagine the concerns felt by Russia and China toward the perceived threat from NATO's new strategy to intervene wherever they desire "from Morocco to the Indian Ocean." It seems that the inevitable response to NATO's new aggressive doctrine will be the creation of an anti-NATO military alliance that may form over the next few years, composed of Russia, China, India, and many nations of the Third World. They naturally believe they have good reason to fear a new wave of imperialism and neo-colonialism from the western powers led by America and Britain.

Daniel and John foretold that an extremely powerful military, economic, and political power will arise in the last days, led by a revival of the ancient Roman Empire in Europe. The Scriptures describe the growing power of the revived Roman Empire, ultimately encompassing the nations of the entire world for seven years during the Tribulation Period described in Daniel 2 and Revelation 13. However, the prophet Daniel clearly prophesied that the nations of the East will rebel against the worldwide domination of the western alliance of the Antichrist toward the end of the seven year Tribulation period: "And the sixth angel poured out his vial upon the great river Euphrates; and the water thereof was dried up, that the way of the kings of the east might be prepared" (Revelation 16:12). The nations of the East will mobilize with an enormous army of two hundred million men from "the kings of the East" to go to war against the western nations under the military leadership of the Antichrist: "And the number of the army of the horsemen were two hundred thousand thousand: and I heard the number of them" (Revelation 9:16). The new political and military developments in NATO and the natural defensive response of the nations of the East and their Third World allies may be setting the stage for the prophetic events described in the Scriptures that will occur just before the return of the Messiah to establish His kingdom.

Endnotes

1. Toynbee, Arnold. *Surviving the Future*. London: Oxford Univ. Press. 1971.
2. Joe de Courcy. "NATO's Recipe for War." *Intelligence Digest*, 30 April 1999.
3. Joe de Courcy. "NATO's Recipe for War." *Intelligence Digest*, 30 April 1999.
4. Joe de Courcy. "NATO's Recipe for War." *Intelligence Digest*, 30 April 1999.
5. Joe de Courcy. "NATO's Recipe for War." *Intelligence Digest*, 30 April 1999.
6. *Jordan Times*, April 1999.

10

The Need for Surveillance Versus the Loss of Privacy and Freedom

The extended war against the global Islamic terrorism threat will produce many casualties, including the three thousand plus victims of September 11, the Taliban soldiers, al Qaeda terrorists, and innocent civilians in Afghanistan as well as in other terrorist-supporting nations. Inevitably, the war on terror required western governments to introduce massive global surveillance of the electronic communications of the world's population to detect and arrest the Islamic terrorists that want to destroy our freedom and way of life. One of the first casualties in this historically unprecedented war on terror is our normal democratic expectation of personal privacy and freedom from surveillance. One of our most cherished freedoms and human rights—"the freedom to be let alone"—is being rapidly eroded by the new technological developments in surveillance and by the need for western governments to respond to the growing threat of Islamic terrorism.

A 1998 Harris poll, completed by Louis Harris and Associates for the *Privacy & American Business* publication, found that 88 percent of U.S. citizens were very concerned about threats to their personal privacy.

The growing use of the Internet, the sophisticated analysis of computer data in both corporate and government databases, and the lack of meaningful privacy legislation has resulted in the erosion of our personal privacy, according to New Media Summit '99: A Deeper View, held in New York City. A staggering amount of sensitive personal data is now available on the Internet as well as data contained in thousands of computer databases established by consumer reporting agencies, government, and businesses. Thomas Evans, the president of GeoCities, cynically but accurately summed up our current privacy situation as follows: "You already have no privacy. Get over it."[1]

Very few Internet users are aware that everything we do on the Internet—from visiting particular Web sites, visiting chat rooms, sending or receiving e-mail, and our shopping—is permanently recorded in computer databases. Who hesitates to consider the possible consequences that could result from researching a topic on the Internet? For example, an innocent search to gain information about a particular disease could be accessed years later during a background check by a future employer. Even the possibility of a link between the prospective employee and a dangerous disease may be sufficient to motivate a company to reject an employment application. There is currently no legal protection in North America from such possible misuse of information regarding a citizen's Internet activity.

Big Brother Is Watching You

The recent increase in government surveillance of virtually every aspect of our society since the horrific September 11, 2001 terrorist attack has fundamentally altered our way of life. Throughout history, people have conducted their daily lives under the natural assumption that their personal activities were no one else's business. However, the totalitarian governments of Germany, Russia, and China in the last century introduced secret police surveillance of their total populations for the first time in history. Sophisticated surveillance technologies now enable our governments to gather enormous amounts of information on the communications, assets, activities, financial transactions, health, political, and religious activities of every citizen within their control.

Our highways, streets, parking lots, and buildings are now monitored 24 hours a day with millions of hidden closed-circuit surveillance television cameras, in the interest of public safety, crime control, and national security. These intrusive surveillance cameras are eliminating the fundamental right of privacy that all citizens of democracies have previously taken for granted. Our privacy is being eroded by new sophisticated audio, visual, and identification technology. The development of miniature security cameras to promote personal safety and assist in crime control has recently expanded to include surveillance of employees at their desks, in the washrooms, and throughout a building. The new and growing threat from Islamic terrorism, employee theft, drug use, and industrial espionage provides a powerful argument for the necessity of this intrusive surveillance on the daily life of millions of western citizens.

Constant monitoring of employees and background checks are now routinely used by corporations and governments. In effect, since September 11, 2001, we are living in a total-surveillance environment resembling the horror described by English author George Orwell in his frightening futuristic novel *1984* about the growing threat of totalitarian government. In fact, the remarkable technology developed during the last decade has produced surveillance possibilities far more pervasive and threatening than any faced by his fictional character, Winston, in Orwell's prophetic novel.

Many government agencies and corporations have introduced security systems requiring all of their workers to wear an employee badge containing a radio frequency microchip. This enables organizations to monitor the location and precise activity of each worker. When an employee enters the office, the computer records the exact time and quietly monitors his or her every move throughout the day. Security sensors placed at strategic locations throughout the building record the location and duration of all activities of the employee wearing the badge.

Many employees are blissfully unaware of the fact that many office phone systems now secretly monitor their personal phone calls. Computerized office phone systems often contain a record of all possible legitimate business phone numbers. If an employee places a personal call to a friend, the office phone system will record the unauthorized number and produce a report of the employee's private calls and their duration to be presented at the employee's next evaluation interview.

"Workers in industrialized countries are losing privacy in the workplace as technological advances allow employers to monitor nearly every facet of time on the job," according to the International Labor Organization in Geneva, Switzerland. American corporations use secret employee surveillance systems more than any other nation. The American Civil Liberties Union (ACLU) warned, "Criminals have more privacy rights than employees. Police have to get a court order, whereas in the workplace, surveillance can be conducted without safeguards."[2] Computer network security supervisors in many companies secretly monitor the actual keystrokes and productivity of every employee who uses a computer. Employees often complain about the intense stress they experience in the knowledge that they are being secretly monitored every minute of the day. In many companies, random drug testing, secret cameras, and intrusive psychological questionnaires can create an unhealthy psychological environment.

The police, intelligence agencies, government officials, business competitors and even your inquisitive neighbor can now acquire virtually any private detail of your personal life and private business. Your travel destinations, the newspapers and books you read, the video rentals you make, the pay TV choices you subscribe to, traffic tickets you incur, your medical tests, and any purchases you make are all recorded and are now permanently "on file" for anyone who can acquire access to the information database. There is growing public awareness and concern about the issue of privacy for our personal computer records, especially regarding our health, criminal, and financial records. Despite these growing concerns, the U.S. Congress and the Canadian Parliament have failed, to date, to enact serious laws to protect the privacy of our citizens. The deadly terrorist attacks on September 11 together with the anthrax attacks that followed naturally resulted in demands for even greater surveillance and new anti-terror legislation introduced in all western democracies.

Security companies have recently made remarkable technical advances in creating sophisticated surveillance devices. New pinhole cameras can be placed behind a wall to audibly and visually monitor the next room. The tiny lens (the size of the head of a pin) is virtually impossible to detect unless you examine every wall, floor, and ceiling surface with a magnifying glass. New infrared surveillance cameras can photograph silently and in almost total darkness. A new surveillance camera can be secretly concealed in a small mobile telephone with the camera lens recording through the tiny hole normally used for the microphone.

Surveillance devices that enable anyone to monitor activities occurring in your home or office while you are away are now widely available. A new remote telephone and room monitoring device, the XPS-1000, allows you to activate it from anywhere in the world by dialing your phone with a special activation code. The device will not cause your phone to ring, but you can now monitor every sound in the building. Another tiny device, a micro-transmitter surveillance bug powered for three months by a miniature battery, can be secretly left in any room and will broadcast up to one thousand yards to a radio receiver on an FM frequency. The truth is that personal privacy has now become an illusion. If someone is determined to secretly monitor your activities and communications, he can do it. There is very little you can do to stop him Even if you adopt various available encryption devices for your phone or computer communication you will only attract much greater surveillance attention because the security agencies will wonder why you are trying to hide your communications.

It is impossible to contemplate the growing surveillance capabilities of governments throughout the world without being reminded of the ancient biblical prophecy from the book of Revelation about an unprecedented totalitarian police system arising in the final global dictatorship of the Antichrist in the last days. The prophet John warned, "No man might buy or sell, save he that had the mark, or the name of the beast, or the number of his name" (Revelation 13:17). This remarkable prophecy predicts the total control of the future Antichrist over the activities of every person throughout the globe. This prophecy can only be fulfilled in a society that can monitor everyone all the time. Modern surveillance technology has made this possible for the first time in history.

Government officials and national security agencies are constantly seeking personal information about the details of our daily lives, our finances, and our communications. Government agencies naturally now raise the threat of Islamic terrorism to justify the surveillance. National security agencies now collect and permanently record vast amounts of information on every citizen in sophisticated computer databases capable of storing millions of detailed records such as health status, medical treatments, employment record, vehicle ownership, driving records, communications, criminal records, and real estate ownership. In addition, all of your credit records, banking and financial transactions, credit ratings, educational transcripts, and travel records are included in these databases and are available to the government agencies, allied nations policy agencies, and to key research institutes. Governments throughout the world now share enormous computer databases containing literally thousands of facts about millions of citizens. The massive Interpol computer network and its instantaneous exchange of intelligence, criminal, and immigration records by over eighty nations committed to the war against terror means that the details of your life are now available to national security and police forces throughout the globe.

Growing Threats to Your Freedom and Privacy

The public is finally awakening to the dangers posed by these new surveillance technologies and the necessary but very dangerous counterterrorism laws. When the U.S. Congress passed legislation in 1996 to allow individual states to utilize Social Security numbers for drivers' licenses, there was so much public opposition that

Congress voted to hold a moratorium on implementing this intrusive practice. It was recently revealed that Intel Corporation included a secret serial number hidden within each Pentium III chip that would allow the identification of the communications of the individual computer user. Naturally, computer users and privacy groups protested this potential infringement of their privacy. According to reports on the Internet, Microsoft allegedly secretly embedded a hidden identification number in all documents produced by any PC computer using their Microsoft software. The huge protests against Microsoft's alleged abuse of privacy forced the company to offer a free software program on the Internet that would allow a user to eliminate the identifying number. However, the vast majority of existing Microsoft software customers are either unaware of the problem or lack the necessary computer expertise to use the downloadable software program to fix it.

Although the vast majority of Internet uses are unaware of it, every e-mail message or electronic file they send carries hidden numbers that identify the sender. If we are to protect what little privacy we have left, we need to encourage citizens in all nations to become aware of the growing surveillance they are subjected to. We should encourage a healthy debate in our democracies about the relative advantages and disadvantages to society of each new surveillance technique. In addition, citizens and businesses who value their privacy should seriously consider using widely available encryption programs that would make it difficult, though not impossible, for the intelligence agencies to monitor all of their computer communications.

The greatest argument in favor of increasing national security surveillance as we wage war against terrorism is that each new technology provides significant protection against Islamic and other terrorists. While I believe that citizen involvement and thoughtful protest against government abuse of our privacy may slow the relentless attack on our privacy and freedom, the Islamic terrorist attacks on western society and the technological advances in surveillance devices are moving us relentlessly toward the surveillance society of the coming Antichrist described in the ancient prophecies in John's book of Revelation. In light of the Islamic al Qaeda terrorists' Declaration of War and the obvious need to increase surveillance to protect our national security, we will continue step by step toward a total surveillance society in which our right to privacy will be only a distant memory.

The Dangers From Islamic Terrorists

Despite the fact that America spends over $30 billion annually on counterterror activities, the true level of national security in the United States, Canada, and Europe against terrorist attacks has been abysmal. Most anti-terrorist security measures before September 11 were nothing more than "smoke and mirrors" designed to create the illusion of security. The only reason the terrorists did not hijack planes and attack office towers before September 11 is that the terrorists did not try. The truth is that prior to September 11, airline security was so lax that a group of determined boy scouts could probably have hijacked most U.S. airplanes.

For example, an article in *The New York Times* in October 2001 revealed that the U.S. military has less security and control over its shipments of deadly armaments and offensive weapons than do commercial courier companies such as FedEx. The *New York Times* article stated, "Security for domestic shipments of surface-to-air missiles, cruise missiles and other explosives has been so poor that terrorists could easily obtain them for use in an attack in this country, according to a classified government report and other confidential records." The U.S. General Accounting Office (GAO) discovered astonishing security lapses in the system controlling truck shipments of military explosives throughout the U.S. The GAO July 2001 report to Congress declared that these lapses posed "substantial national security or public safety risks." Following the terrible national security wake-up call after the devastating September 11, 2001, terrorist attacks on the World Trade Center and the Pentagon, the conclusions of the GAO report are alarming in their implications for possible future devastating terrorist attacks on American citizens. The GAO report declared:

- Terrorists could obtain U.S. military weapons as they are moved and temporarily stored in private trucks.
- The U.S. military often cannot identify where weapons and explosives are located while they are being shipped.

- A shipment of 192 Stinger missiles was left in a civilian storage area without the knowledge of the military or the contractor that shipped them.
- Trucking companies transporting weapons are allowed to leave trucks in commercial-carrier terminals with few safeguards from intruders.
- Security investigators gained access to missiles and rockets in storage terminals by presenting phony Defense Department credentials.
- Gates protecting dangerous military U.S. weapons were often left unlocked.
- None of the weapons storage facilities had proper alarms to detect terrorist intrusions.
- One site that stored Hawk surface-to-air missiles left its garage door open.
- Five storage sites with an arsenal of cruise missiles, SAMs, anti-tank rockets, bombs, 14,000 rounds for howitzers and other munitions were accessible to an attack by terrorists.[3]

This obvious negligence and gross incompetence demonstrated by the U.S. military is cause for a major Congressional investigation and the leveling of numerous security violation charges against the officials responsible for such a dangerous dereliction of duty to protect the national security of the United States of America.

The FBI's DNA Database

The FBI has opened a secret national DNA database for criminals and terrorists at a secret location in New York City that will provide investigators with additional evidence that will assist them in tracking down the elusive Islamic terrorists who are committed to our destruction. The FBI criminal DNA database, using a new generation of forensic genetic techniques and powerful new supercomputers, promises to efficiently detect criminals and terrorists who have left identifiable DNA genetic evidence at the scene of some previous crime scene or terrorist attack.

Many civil libertarians are concerned that the DNA database of criminals will inevitably be expanded from terrorists and criminals to include virtually every citizen, thereby providing our government's national security agencies with truly staggering investigative powers over our lives in the future. After a decade of testing and negotiation with the individual states, the new FBI national DNA genetic database will incorporate all fifty of the existing state-controlled computer criminal databases. The new national FBI database will ultimately unify the DNA data through common test procedures and computer software distributed to the individual states by the FBI.

Echelon

Following World War II, the most ambitious intelligence effort in history was launched by the U.S.A.'s National Security Agency (NSA), the largest intelligence agency in America (with a budget 13 times larger than the CIA). Created in 1948 by the U.S., United Kingdom, Canada, Australia, and New Zealand, Echelon was designed to spy on Russia and its Warsaw Pact allies during the Cold War. This extraordinary global spy system can intercept and analyze every phone call, fax, e-mail, Internet, radio, and telex message throughout the world. Echelon is unique in that its primary espionage focus involves civilian targets including the messages of governments, corporations, and individuals in every nation across the globe.

How Does Echelon Work?

Unlike military intelligence activities that seek to acquire specific communications from a targeted military base or agency, Echelon is like a giant electronic vacuum cleaner, acquiring virtually all electronic communications. It utilizes advanced spy satellites, global phone intercepts, massive Internet surveillance, and the fastest supercomputers in the world. Surveillance targets include all local, cellular, and long-distance phone calls; fax and telex transmissions; Internet communications including Web surfing, newsgroups, chat rooms, and e-mails; and all radio traffic throughout the world. Echelon also collects messages from downlinked satellite, microwave, cellular, and ground-based fiber-optic communications traffic. One of the primary targets is the interception of data from twenty international telecommunications satellites (Intelsat) that circle the globe above the Equator, relaying most of the planet's most critical daily e-mail, Internet, fax, and telex communications.

The interception function of Echelon depends upon a global communications monitoring system. The analysis function of Echelon is completed in "real time" at NSA headquarters in Fort Mead, Maryland, utilizing an enormous number of advanced supercomputers (far faster than anything available commercially) and tens of thousands of brilliant and well-paid human analysts. The transmissions are instantly searched for messages containing certain key words identified by the five member states' intelligence agencies in Echelon "dictionaries." The reporting function involves a remarkably complex system that transmits the relevant intelligence data and analysis to the various intelligence agencies in the respective nations and their political masters. The five governments use their sophisticated surveillance technology cooperatively, secretly spying on the communications of each other's citizens in order to escape the legal prohibition against spying on the private communications of their own citizens. For example, two Canadian intelligence officers are technically in charge of the Echelon systems' monitoring of all American communications. The Canadian officers then immediately forward the relevant intelligence intercepts to the U.S.'s NSA intelligence community. This arrangement enables the U.S. to technically deny that its people are illegally intercepting the electronic communications of American citizens. The same system is in place for Echelon to monitor all Canadian communications.

Echelon processes the acquired information utilizing NSA's sophisticated computer analysis, including advanced voice recognition systems, artificial intelligence, neural networks, and optical character recognition (OCR) programs that can read and analyze enormous numbers of text files. At Echelon's Menwith Hill station in Britain, an extremely sophisticated voice recognition program called Voicecast can actually target a particular person's voice pattern, such as the recorded voice of Osama bin Laden. The computer programs search for key words or special phrases listed in the Echelon dictionary, such as key Arabic words connected to Islamic terror attacks and alerts the computers to flag any targeted message for detailed analysis. The targeted message is recorded and transcribed for future analysis by an intelligence specialist dealing with that language, nation, or terror group. Any useful information collected by Echelon is forwarded to the intelligence agency that originally requested the intelligence intercept. Obviously, the vast majority of intercepts are communications that contain no relevant names, key words, or phone numbers. Therefore, 99.999 percent of the millions of messages every hour are immediately erased by the Echelon computers and are never listened to or analyzed by a human intelligence specialist.

The western governments' new justification for Echelon's universal surveillance program is that our society must be protected against the so-called "Four Horsemen of the Infocalypse": Islamic terrorists, drug dealers, sexual predators, and organized crime. However, the unprecedented increase in the monitoring of our private and business conversations since September 11, 2001, is a dangerous assault on our fundamental human right to freedom and privacy—"the right to be left alone". While this system is now being used for valid purposes of espionage against Islamic terrorists such as al Qaeda and terror-supporting states such as Iraq and Syria, these powerful surveillance technologies could be used by authorities in the future as a powerful tool of political or religious surveillance against ordinary citizens.

Sample Echelon Dictionary Key Words

A short list of a few key words used by the Echelon dictionary program provides an example of the topics an intelligence agency may consider worthwhile. The complete secret list of key words would include thousands of possible names and terms that are updated continually by Echelon's five national dictionary managers. If a voice or e-mail message contains several of these key words, then Echelon operatives examine all subsequent messages connected to that person to determine if they are communications of a criminal or terrorist.

Examples of the key words include: explosives, chemical, anthrax, smallpox, al Qaeda, guns, assassination, conspiracy, primers, detonators, nuclear, ambush, motorcade, IRS, CIA, hostages, munitions, weapons, FBI, presidential motorcade, grenades, rockets, fuses, mortars, incendiary, security forces, intelligence, infiltration, assault team, evasion, detection, mission, charges, timing devices, booby traps, silencers.[4]

Recent reports indicate that Echelon's Oratory voice recognition program that analyzes thousands of simultaneous communications now tracks targeted individuals. Our voices are as unique as our fingerprints or our irises. Within seconds of making a phone call anywhere in the world, a fugitive, a terrorist, for example, can be instantly identified and his exact location targeted through his unique voiceprint. Once, the Echelon system intercepts the terrorist's calls, they can be monitored or redirected to one of his enemies to create chaos in the terrorist group. Within seconds, the physical location of the phone call can be precisely identified. Don't believe what you see in the movies, where someone hangs up the phone in less than thirty seconds and thereby foils the ability of the FBI or NSA to accurately trace his call. In reality, only four seconds are needed to determine a target's phone number and location.

Warnings about Echelon

When Congressman Bob Barr of Georgia spoke to the U.S. Congress and publicly called for Congressional hearings in 1999, it was the first time in history that the threat Echelon posed to the freedom and privacy of Americans was publicly raised in the U.S. Congress. Barr stated:

> As a former intelligence officer, I support legitimate intelligence activities. However, I also believe Congress has a duty to make absolutely certain the massive capabilities our intelligence agencies have developed, are allowed to be used only with adequate safeguards against abuse. The massive technological changes that have occurred since the last significant update of our foreign intelligence surveillance laws mean our existing legal structure is not adequately protecting the privacy rights of Americans. My concerns in this area are heightened by the reluctance of intelligence agencies to fully cooperate with congressional oversight. This acknowledgment underscores the need for

open public hearings on the legal standards intelligence agencies use when they intercept the communications of American citizens. If these reports are accurate, the sheer power and potential for abuse created by Project Echelon demands congressional attention.[5]

During recent hearings about the dangers of Echelon's global electronic surveillance, Congressman Barr warned about the growing dangers to our freedom and privacy:

Under current law, electronic communications receive less legal protection than traditional mail, or even telephone conversations. Furthermore, the rules for electronic surveillance and foreign intelligence gathering that do exist are so vague and inconsistent that they simultaneously threaten privacy and impede law enforcement. . . . Federal agencies, from the Securities and Exchange Commission to the Department of Justice, have recently shown a disturbing tendency to apply a vacuum cleaner surveillance approach to the Internet, sucking in all kinds of irrelevant data, then isolating, storing and manipulating items of interest. . . . This approach rejects time-honored principles that have done a remarkably good job of balancing privacy and law enforcement. These principles include the Fourth Amendment's particularity requirement and statutory provisions, such as the Privacy Act.[6]

In April 1999, the American Civil Liberties Union wrote to members of Congress about the dangers of Echelon. When the official spokeswoman of the NSA was asked about the existence of Echelon, she replied, "We don't confirm or deny the existence of Echelon."[7]

The U.S. National Security Council proposed in July 1998, that American intelligence agencies should constantly monitor the computer networks of banks, telecommunications corporations, transportation companies, and non-military government operations in an attempt to protect America's important communication data networks from hackers and terrorists. Only one month later,

Attorney General Janet Reno proposed legislation to give the Justice Department and the FBI legal authority to place hidden encryption-breaking devices and secret surveillance software programs in American citizen's computers in their homes and offices during criminal investigations. At the same time, the FBI is publicly supporting a proposal for new technical standards in the design of the Internet infrastructure to enable their agents to secretly set up court-authorized wiretaps on personal computers without anyone becoming aware of it.[8]

Some in the media deny that our communications are constantly being intercepted by the national security and intelligence agencies of the West. However, major news sources are finally investigating the Echelon system, confirming its existence and its pervasive intrusion into our lives. The *London Times*, the *New York Times*, *La Monde*, and the BBC have recently reported on the mounting European public and governmental outrage at the intrusive surveillance by Echelon. However, the U.S., Canada, Australia, New Zealand, and fifteen European nations are now establishing a global surveillance system targeting all international communications, especially on the Internet. The deadly threat from terrorists has strongly increased the government's argument that global surveillance is absolutely vital to our national security.

In 1975, during the famous Church Senate hearings on the misuse of intelligence agencies' resources by President Nixon's Watergate team, Senator Frank Church warned of the possible danger to American freedom and privacy if our intelligence agencies and powerful surveillance capabilities were ever unleashed against our own citizens. Senator Church warned about the dangers from the technology of surveillance now used by the National Security Agency:

That capability at any time could be turned around on the American people and no American would have any privacy left. There would be no place to hide. If this government ever became a tyranny, the technological capacity that the intelligence community has given the government could enable it to impose total tyranny. There would be no way to fight back because the most careful effort to join together in resistance to the government, no matter how privately it was done, is within the reach of the government to know. Such is the capacity of this technology.[9]

The danger to democracy and individual freedom is far greater today than it was when Senator Church raised his first warning in 1975. Unless the intelligence agencies that operate Echelon and related global and national surveillance systems are placed under the direct political control of the U.S. Congress and Senate, our fundamental freedoms might easily be eliminated forever in the interests of a campaign to defeat terrorism, organized crime, drug lords, and foreign enemies.

Echelon was designed and built during the Cold War, when we faced the danger of a massive Soviet invasion in Europe. We are now in a period when the number of Islamic terrorists and terror-supporting rogue states who would attack our western nations is growing exponentially. As the cost and difficulty of producing devastating biological, chemical, and even nuclear weapons is dropping rapidly, the number of terrorist and ethnic hate groups willing to use these weapons of mass destruction against America, Israel, and the West is growing as quickly. While I hate the thought of government intelligence agencies monitoring all of our private and business communications, I believe our governments would abandon their national security responsibilities to defend the safety of our citizens if they failed to utilize the sophisticated Echelon communications intelligence capabilities to monitor terrorists. Since September 11, 2001, we are all painfully aware of our vulnerability to sudden terrorist attacks. The citizens of the West now realize we are living in a very tough neighborhood. Therefore, it is essential that our intelligence agencies and national security forces use the best intelligence and sophisticated surveillance technologies to detect, deter, and defeat these Islamic terrorist attacks by those extremists who have dedicated themselves to our destruction.

History reveals that almost every technological advance was initially abused by the political and police authorities that ruled the nation-states. The first use of technology by political authorities tends to be in the areas of communications control, security, policing, and the military. However, history also reveals that new technologies are eventually used by democratic citizens to further their desires for free communication, privacy, and political as well as religious freedom.

The introduction of the printing press in Europe was immediately monopolized under exclusive license by the authorities of that day. However, free men begin to use the printing press to print democratic political pamphlets and Bibles. This new printing technology facilitated the Protestant Reformation, the Enlightenment, and the greatest advance in political and religious freedom in human history. The computer and the Internet are the latest technologies that present new dangers to our political and religious freedoms. However, this new computer technology is a double-edged sword. It will also allow determined men and women to develop sophisticated encryption techniques that will make it very difficult or impossible for authoritative governments to keep all communications under total surveillance.

The lesson of history, as illustrated by England's Lord Acton's wise statement nearly a century ago, was that "power corrupts, and absolute power corrupts absolutely." No government has ever held such potential political security and police power as the Echelon system provides to the intelligence and security agencies of the West. In light of the overwhelming evidence that the western powers, as well as that of Russia and China, are now using these powerful surveillance technologies to examine every communication of private citizens, corporations, and governments, our political and religious liberties now stand in the greatest peril in history.

Echelon has known about you for many years. Now you know about Echelon. Our only hope is to make certain that this powerful surveillance technology remains a servant of democratic government and not its master. We must encourage our elected governments to ensure that there is a powerful system of democratic oversight to "watch over the watchers." It is my hope that the U.S. Congress, as well as the British and Canadian Parliaments, will demand democratic accountability of these very necessary but inherently dangerous surveillance technologies.

In the past, many students of the Bible's prophecies wondered about how the prophet John's prediction about the Antichrist's future global monitoring of citizens' activities could ever be fulfilled literally. Until this last decade, it was impossible for any government to provide continuous monitoring of every citizen, no matter how many informers or secret police were employed. However, the Echelon surveillance system and parallel systems developed by Russia, China, and the European Union demonstrate how a future world dictator may exercise total surveillance control over the world's population. Humanity would suffer under a global totalitarian state that would extinguish freedom and the hope of liberty forever because the total surveillance system would make a political revolution virtually impossible. Mankind's only hope for freedom is found in the certain promise of the Word of God that Jesus Christ will return soon and liberate humanity from the satanic oppression of the global dictatorship of the coming Antichrist.

Endnotes

1. "Panel: Privacy Doesn't Exist Anymore." *Direct Marketing News.* July 5, 1999.

2. http://www.fecl.org/circular/2807.htm.

3. *The New York Times.* October 2001.

4. Michael Owens. Echelon Code Word List. http://www.internetofficenews.com.

5. Joseph Farah. "Echelon: See, I Told You So." *World Net Daily.* November 4, 1999.

6. Charles Smith. "The Information Vacuum Cleaner." April 9, 2000. WorldNetDaily.com.

7. Kathryn Balint. "Spy in the Sky? That Could Be Echelon." *San Diego Union-Tribune.* October 17, 1999.

8. Kathryn Balint. "Spy in the Sky? That Could Be Echelon." *San Diego Union-Tribune.* October 17, 1999.

9. Frank Church, U.S. Senate Hearings, 1975.

11

Practical and Spiritual Strategies for the War on Terror

How Do I Protect My Family From the Dangers of Terrorism?

It is vital that we respond to the war on terrorism with a well-planned strategy of practical and spiritual actions. In this chapter I will recommend a practical, balanced, and reasonable strategy that will provide protection to your loved ones without disrupting your normal life. It is vital that we protect ourselves and our loved ones from the possible effects of this crisis. An excellent motto for these last days is "Pray for the best and prepare for the worst."

The concept of personal preparedness in the global crisis of worldwide terrorism must be based on a mental and spiritual attitude of being aware of the possible dangers and having the resolve to respond to these terrorist threats with appropriate plans and actions. Since these terrorists believe that all Christians and Jews in the West or in Israel are legitimate targets for their murderous attacks (see appendix A, al Qaeda's Declaration of War) and since they see no moral difference between attacking a soldier or killing an innocent housewife and child, we must protect our loved ones from the continuing terrorism crisis and establish a plan to minimize these risks to our families.

There are three aspects to this serious terrorism problem:

1. *Spiritual preparations.* This involves becoming aware of the spiritual principles that instruct us to prepare for the dangers that lie ahead while ultimately depending on God for His guidance and protection. The Lord does not want us to experience a "spirit of fear" but that we should adopt a spirit of confidence that God will empower us and protect us to destroy the terrorist enemies that seek to destroy innocent civilians throughout the western world.

2. *A practical home storage plan.* This plan involves a reasonable and balanced plan to accumulate the necessary supplies of essential goods and foods that will enable our families to live comfortably for several weeks despite possible disruptions of food, water, and power that might result from possible terrorist attacks. The Red Cross and the Federal Emergency Management Agency recommend that all families should have enough food and water to withstand up to two weeks of disruptions of supplies.

3. *Personal protection against the threat of biological or chemical weapons.* Later in this chapter we will examine several practical preparations you can take to protect your family and loved ones against the possibility of biological and chemical weapons in our country.

Our modern generation has not needed to think about the need to plan for emergencies, as our parents and grandparents did. Before September 11, 2001, our generation did not feel the need to protect ourselves from the dangers of war, famine, terrorism, plague, and earthquakes. In past centuries, people believed that it was normal to plan and prepare for the occasional disasters that would interfere with the normal functioning of society. The astonishing technological advancements and the apparent stability of modern life caused many in North America to feel that we were virtually immune to disasters, disruptions, and terrorist attacks. We felt that terrorism was something that happened "over there" in Israel and the Middle East, but not here at home in North America.

However, the unprecedented terrorist attacks on the World Trade Center and the Pentagon on September 11, 2001, and the frightening anthrax attacks against dozens of citizens have awakened North Americans to the very real dangers of bombs, chemicals, and biological weapons released by desperate suicide terrorists bent on the destruction of America and the lives of its innocent citizens. The prospect of major disruptions directly caused by terrorist attacks or disruptions caused by the government's security response to a major terrorist attack have caused many citizens to reconsider their family's situation and begin planning to protect themselves from future temporary loss of either services or supplies. Americans have become used to acquiring whatever their family needs with a quick trip to the local grocery or hardware store. However, the possibility of severe disruptions and delays affecting normal services or supplies has now awakened many citizens to consider the needs of their family and to begin to carefully provide for at least a few weeks of necessary supplies.

We take for granted the multitude of automated services and computers that make our modern world very comfortable. We rely on twenty-four-hour automated banking machines, late-night supermarkets, convenience stores, and debit cards that enable us to purchase whatever we need in almost any city across the globe. Another factor that causes many to live in denial of the possibility of disaster is the fact that many North Americans live so close to the edge financially that they have almost no savings available to enable them to acquire necessary survival foods and other materials required to protect their family from possible future disruptions.

Spiritual Preparations

Throughout the Word of God, the Lord commands us to take active preparations to protect ourselves and our families from the possibilities of danger. The Bible does not suggest that Christians can simply ignore trouble ahead, expecting the Lord to supernaturally provide for us if we fail to take reasonable precautions.

The Scriptures record God's command to His servant Joseph to advise the pharaoh of Egypt to take advantage of the seven years of plenty to store precious grain foods for the approaching seven years of famine. The Bible clearly teaches us the principle of preparing for future disasters while maintaining our unshakable trust in God. However, as confident followers of Christ, we should not allow ourselves to become victims of worry or anxiety about the future.

God commands us to exercise prudence and foresight in avoiding dangers. In the book of Proverbs, King Solomon, the wisest man in history, suggested the following advice: "A prudent man foreseeth the evil, and hideth himself: but the simple pass on, and are punished" (Proverbs 22:3; 27:12).

A Practical Home Storage Plan

Medical Emergencies

If you or some member of your family has serious medical problems that necessitate the regular taking of prescription medicine, it might be wise to discuss this need with your family doctor and pharmacist. You might suggest to your doctor that he write an emergency supply of any essential prescription. Also make sure you have a first-aid kit stocked.

Home Security Systems

Provide additional backup batteries to provide continuous power to your security system, even if the electrical power system is disrupted temporarily in a future crisis.

Food Supplies

We should consider the possibility that a major biological or chemical attack on our nation might seriously disrupt our food distribution system. Our situation may depend on the country, county, or city we live in. We should anticipate a certain amount of disruptions to the normal delivery of food to the millions of supermarkets, corner grocery stores, and restaurants if there are further additional serious terrorist attacks. You might consider acquiring a one-month supply of freeze-dried food and various appropriate canned foods that will be edible for months. There are many reliable suppliers of such products.

Survival supplies

It would be worthwhile to acquire the necessary skills and tools that would enable you to survive with your family for a period of up to a month, or more, if electrical power, water supplies, and sewage service were disrupted. In the event of the failure of utilities in your area for a few weeks due to a terrorist attack, a supply of stored potable water and a chemical toilet would be useful. If there is a disruption of electrical power, a supply of several cords of hardwood that can be burned in a wood-burning stove or a fireplace would provide the heat necessary to protect your family if you live in the north.

Personal Protection against Biological or Chemical Weapons

The best way to deal with this complex issue is to address a series of questions that I believe readers may have considered because of the recent anthrax attacks in various parts of America. There have been repeated security warnings that terrorists have worked for years with Iraq and other enemy states to develop biological agents such as anthrax, small pox, and bubonic plague as well as chemical weapons including VX, sarin, tabum, and other nerve gases.

Signs That a Poison Gas Attack Might Have Occurred

First, we should realize that a single person lying on the ground is most likely to be suffering from a medical condition such as a heart attack. On the other hand, if you observe several people collapsed or suffering from symptoms, then it is possible that they are suffering from a biological or chemical attack. Leave the area immediately and contact 911. If you feel you may have been exposed to some dangerous agent, removing your outer clothes can eliminate up to 80 percent of the danger of contamination. If water is available, immediately wash your body, as water is a very effective decontamination agent. When firefighters arrive, they will immediately decontaminate civilians using water sprays to wash people down.

If you observe birds and small animals dropping to the ground, then it is possible that a toxic substance is present. You should immediately remove yourself from the area, enter a building where you can seal yourself in a closed room, or lock yourself in a car (closing the air conditioning vents and windows). Call 911 and advise that a toxic substance may be present. When you can, place your clothes inside a plastic bag and take a long shower to wash any possible contamination from your body.

If you receive a report of the possibility of an attack of biological or chemical weapons in your area, immediately shut down your air conditioning and make sure all windows and vents are closed. If you observe the unusual spraying of a substance from a plane or helicopter in your area, you should check with media or the police to verify that it is a legitimate spraying of insecticides.

Dangers from Anthrax or other Chemical Agents in the Mail

We need to be aware of the various practical steps we should take if a suspect package arrives at your home or office or you come into contact with a biological or chemical substance such as anthrax. While terrorist attacks using anthrax are extremely rare, we need to be aware of the steps to take if you believe that you may have received a package contaminated with anthrax. The first thing is to remember to keep calm. Remember, anthrax can be treated effectively with antibiotics such as penicillin or Cipro.

What indications suggest a suspicious letter or package may be dangerous?

- A letter with no return address
- Discoloration, strange odors, oil stains, or a powder-like residue
- Excessive tape or postage
- An oddly shaped package of unusual size or weight
- A postmark that does not match the return address or a letter to a former employee
- Restrictive endorsements including "Personal" or "Confidential"

- Handwritten, block-printed, or poorly typed addresses with possibly incorrect titles
- Misspellings of common words.

If you encounter a suspicious letter or package:
- Carefully open the mail with a letter opener
- Don't shake, pour, or blow into envelopes
- Keep your hands away from your nose and mouth while opening suspicious mail
- Wash your hands after handling mail
- If in doubt, don't touch, open, or move it. Call the police at 911.

If you believe you have received a contaminated package:
- Don't touch the package or move it to another location
- Shut windows and doors and leave the room, making sure the air conditioning is shut off
- Immediately ask for a medical examination.

If you believe you were exposed to biological/chemical agents:
- Remain calm; do not touch your eyes, nose, or any other part of your body
- Wash your hands with soap thoroughly
- Notify police immediately by calling 911
- Keep separate from others and wait for medical attention

The government emergency health authorities are storing vast amounts of antibiotics, vaccines, and sophisticated air filters to protect the population from chemical or biological terrorist attacks. The chances of dying from any of these types of attacks is very small, especially if you follow the procedures outlined above and are alert to the possible dangers.

Recommended Sources:

A. "Bioterror: The Hunt for the Anthrax Killers." *Time*, November 5, 2001.

B. Web site: www.cnn.com/2001/HEALTH/conditions/10/12/anthrax.qanda/

CNN.com/Health, October 29, 2001. "10 things you need to know about anthrax."

12

Our Spiritual Response to the War on Terror

The prophet Ezekiel recorded God's command to His faithful followers to be prepared to give warning to their neighbors when they perceived that a danger was approaching their community:

> Son of man, I have made thee a watchman unto the House of Israel: therefore hear the word at my mouth, and give them warning from me. When I say unto the wicked, Thou shalt surely die; and thou givest him not warning, nor speakest to warn the wicked from his wicked way, to save his life; the same wicked man shall die in his iniquity; but his blood will I require at thine hand. Yet if thou warn the wicked, and he turn not from his wickedness, nor from his wicked way, he shall die in his iniquity; but thou hast delivered thy soul. . . .

> Nevertheless if thou warn the righteous man, that the righteous sin not, and he doth not sin, he shall surely

live, because he is warned; also thou hast delivered thy soul. (Ezekiel 3:17–21)

My purpose in writing *The War on Terror* is to examine the fulfillment of prophecies in our generation concerning the conflict in the Middle East that point to the soon return of Jesus Christ. Additionally, my hope is that this information will help you to understand the significance of the terrible Islamic terrorist attacks that have recently occurred. The western nations must launch a powerful counterterrorism war against fundamentalist Islamic terrorism to decisively defeat the evil forces that are dedicated to the destruction of the Christians of the West, the Jews in Israel, and our allies in the moderate Islamic governments of the Middle East. The prophecies of the Bible clearly predict that the armed forces of the northern alliance of nations will destroy the military forces of Babylon, the modern nation of Iraq (Jeremiah 50–51).

Jesus Christ commanded His followers to share their faith with everyone we encounter. If we truly believe that Jesus Christ is the only way to find salvation with God, then we have a profound spiritual responsibility to intelligently and compassionately share our faith with our neighbors and loved ones. If we believe the Bible's prophecies about Jesus' Second Coming, we should be motivated to share our hope in Christ with those who seek to understand the prophetic events that are unfolding in our generation, especially since the tragic events of September 11, 2001.

Developing a Personal Perspective on the War on Terror

The war against terror will certainly be a very expensive and long term global effort to destroy bin Laden's extensive al Qaeda and allied terrorist groups. In addition, the terrorist-supporting states such as Iraq that threaten the peace and freedom of the western nations must be militarily forced to expel the terrorist groups they have supported for decades. It will take several years—possibly decades—to accomplish this dangerous but vital goal. However, there is no substitute for victory in this war with Islamic terrorism. Tens of thousands of Islamic terrorists were trained in bin Laden's camps and are now hiding in over eighty nations throughout the world. These Islamic terrorists have declared war to the death against the governments and populations of Israel and the western democracies. These terror groups have dedicated themselves to the acquisition of nuclear, biological, and chemical weapons of mass destruction. If they don't possess devastating nuclear, biological, or chemical weapons that can destroy our cities yet, they will soon acquire them. It's only a matter of time. Therefore, we have no choice. We must stay the course in this long-term war to destroy the terrorist groups before they succeed in destroying our freedoms and our cities.

As we marshal the tremendous strength of the western world—our powerful spiritual, political, financial, intelligence, and military forces—we shall prevail against our enemies. The spiritual dimension of this crisis is very important. King Solomon recorded God's promise to His people: "If my people, which are called by my name, shall humble themselves, and pray, and seek my face, and turn from their wicked ways; then will I hear from heaven, and will forgive their sin, and will heal their land" (2 Chronicles 7:14).

It is vital that we pray that God will give our leaders the wisdom to understand this complex situation and make the right decisions. It would be easy to let this terrorist crisis overwhelm us to the point that we become paralyzed with fear. Some have already succumbed to a passive approach, saying, "What can I do? This is too large a problem for me to deal with."

However, this book has illustrated several practical and spiritual strategies that you can follow in the months ahead that will make a real difference to your peace of mind and to the quality of your life, despite the continuing threat of terrorist attacks on the West. Those who are forewarned about the dangers of the coming terrorist crisis are forearmed to protect their families and friends. Practical preparations made today will make a tremendous difference to your family's security and peace of mind in the years ahead.

The apostle Paul reminds us, "For God hath not given us the spirit of fear; but of power, and of love, and of a sound mind" (2 Timothy 1:7). Those who have a personal relationship with Jesus Christ can trust in Him to give them "a sound mind" as they make spiritual and practical preparations to meet this unprecedented challenge. King David declared his faith in the Lord to guide and provide for him in these words: "This poor man cried, and the Lord heard him, and saved him out of all his troubles. The angel of the Lord encampeth round about them that fear him, and delivereth them. O taste and see that the Lord is good: blessed is the man that trusteth in him. O fear the Lord, ye his saints: for there is no want to them that fear him" (Psalm 34:6–9). David experienced a life filled with disasters, challenges, betrayals, as well as triumphs. He also taught us to believe and trust in God's mercy and supernatural provision. David wrote, "I have been young, and now am old; yet have I not seen the righteous forsaken, nor his seed begging bread" (Psalm 37:25).

However, if you have never yet trusted Jesus Christ as your personal Lord and Savior, you need to carefully consider this vital issue today. The Bible makes it clear that every one of us must decide whom we will follow. Either we will give allegiance to the true God or to the false gods of this world. Who will be the god of your life? Will it be Jesus Christ or yourself? Either you will admit you are a rebellious sinner in need of God's pardon and accept Jesus as your Lord, or you will insist on remaining the "god" of your life, at the final cost of an eternity without God. The Scriptures warn us that our spiritual pride is our first and greatest sin. Our sinful pride is revealed in the stubborn attitude of many who insist on having their own way, even at the cost of an eternity without God. The great English poet John Milton wrote about this fundamental choice that confronts every human in his epic poem *Paradise Lost*. Milton wrote that in the end, either you will say to God, "Thy will be done" or, in the end, God will say to you, "Thy will be done."

In the end, it is your personal choice. Ultimately, you must either choose either heaven or hell as your eternal destiny. If you choose to ask God to forgive your sins and commit your life to Jesus Christ, the Scriptures assure us that you will meet Him at the Resurrection as your Lord and Savior. If you choose to reject Jesus Christ's claims to be the Lord of your life, you have chosen to meet Him as your final judge at the end of your life. The apostle Paul quoted the prophet Isaiah when he said, "Every knee shall bow to me, and every tongue shall confess to God" (Romans 14:11; Isaiah 45:23). The Scriptures tell us that every one of us will someday bow our knee in acknowledgement of Christ's glory as Lord God. The only question is this: Will you repent of your rebellion and bow your knee today to Christ as your Lord and Savior, or will you reject His offer of salvation now and be forced to finally bow to Him in heaven as your final judge?

Every one of us will meet Jesus Christ face to face at the end of our life. The writer of the book of Hebrews declared: "It is appointed unto men once to die, but after this the judgment" (Hebrews 9:27). God warns us, "For all have sinned, and come short of the glory of God" (Romans 3:23). In light of the many prophetic signs that point to His imminent return, including the conflict in the Middle East, the rush toward world government, and the growing surveillance society as described in Revelation, each of us must make our final choice. Every day their sinful rebellion is leading men and women inexorably toward hell and an eternity without God. "For the wages of sin is death; but the gift of God is eternal life through Jesus Christ our Lord" (Romans 6:23). However, God loves every one of us so much that He sent His Son Jesus to suffer the punishment due to our sins for any one who will confess his sin and ask for God's forgiveness. In the Gospel of John, the prophet declared: "But as many as received him, to them gave he power to become the sons of God, even to them that believe on his name" (John 1:12).

The only basis by which we will be allowed to enter heaven will be our relationship to Jesus Christ. God demands perfect holiness and righteousness. Therefore, since we are all sinners, no one has the right to enter heaven on his or her own merits. Every one of us has been a rebel against God from the day we were born. It is impossible for a holy God to allow an unrepentant sinner into a sinless heaven. Since God cannot ignore the fact that we have all sinned against Him, it was necessary that someone who was perfectly sinless should pay the penalty of physical and spiritual death as a substitute for us. The only one who could qualify was Jesus Christ, the holy, sinless Son of God.

Christ's sacrificial death on the Cross paid the full price for our sins. By accepting His pardon, we will be able to stand before the Judgment Seat of God saved by Christ's righteousness: "For he hath made him [Jesus] to be sin for us, who knew no sin; that we might be made the righteousness of God in him" (2 Corinthians 5:21).

Jesus Christ's atonement for our sins is perhaps the greatest mystery in creation. Jesus is the only one in history who, by His sinless life, was qualified to enter heaven. Yet He loved every one of us so much that He chose to die upon that Cross to pay the sacrificial price for our salvation. In a marvelous demonstration of God's mercy, the perfect righteousness of Jesus is placed to our personal account with God when we choose to repent of our sins and follow Him the rest of our lives.

Nicodemus was a righteous religious leader in ancient Israel. After listening to Christ's teaching, he visited Jesus secretly one night and asked Him about the way of salvation. Jesus answered in these words, "Verily, verily, I say unto thee, Except a man be born again, he cannot see the kingdom of God" (John 3:3). It isn't enough that you intellectually accept the historical truth about Christ's death and resurrection. To be truly "born again," you must sincerely repent of your sinful life, asking Him to forgive you and to wholeheartedly place your faith and trust in Jesus Christ for the rest of your life. This decision will transform your life forever. God will give you a new purpose and meaning to your life. The Lord promises believers eternal life in heaven: "This is the will of him who sent me, that everyone which seeth the Son, and believeth on him, may have everlasting life: and I will raise him up at the last day" (John 6:40). The moment you commit your life to Christ, you will receive eternal life. Though our body will someday die, He has promised us that we will live forever with Christ in heaven. Jesus explained to Nicodemus, "For God so loved the world, that he gave his only begotten Son, that whosoever believeth in him should not perish, but have everlasting life" (John 3:16).

Your decision to accept or reject Jesus Christ as your personal Savior is the most important decision you will ever make. However, this decision to follow Christ is only the beginning. Jesus Christ commands His disciples, "Follow Me." This spiritual decision will change your life forever. Your commitment to Christ will transform your previously purposeless life into a new life filled with joy, peace, and spiritual purpose beyond anything you have ever known. Jesus challenges you to consider your choice in terms of eternity, "For what shall it profit a man, if he shall gain the whole world, and lose his own soul?" (Mark 8:36). While you will certainly be confronted with many spiritual challenges after you accept Christ as your Lord and Savior, God will never abandon you. Jesus promises to send you His Holy Spirit to empower you and give comfort to face the spiritual challenges that lie ahead.

I encourage you to give this book *War on Terror* to your friends, family, and neighbors who have not yet experienced personal faith in Jesus Christ. My goal is to equip believers with books that will share my research on the prophecies unfolding in our generation that point to Christ's near return as well as strengthen your faith in Christ and help you to witness effectively. The incredible events that will occur as the western nations launch overwhelming attacks upon the nations supporting global terrorist groups will cause many to ask what lies ahead for our world. There is a growing fascination with the prophecies of the Bible regarding the events that will transpire in the last days. There is tremendous interest and concern in our fellow citizens regarding the growing political-military crisis in the Middle East. This provides Christians with an unprecedented opportunity to discuss practical strategies to protect our families as well as a unique opportunity to share our personal faith in Jesus Christ as our only certain security in an uncertain world. I trust this book will provide you with the knowledge to better understand this crisis and the confidence to share your faith with your family and friends during the challenging days that lie ahead.

APPENDIX A

Osama bin Laden's Declaration of War Against America

These are excerpts from the fatwa (a legal decree announced by an Islamic scholar) announced in February 1998 by the Islamic terrorist leader Osama bin Laden. The document was translated from the Arabic by the Central Intelligence Agency.

> Praise be to God, who revealed the Book, controls the clouds, defeats factionalism, and says in His Book: "But when the forbidden months are past, then fight and slay the pagans wherever ye find them, seize them, beleaguer them, and lie in wait for them in every stratagem (of war)."

> The Arabian Peninsula has never—since God made it flat, created its desert, and encircled it with seas—been stormed by any forces like the crusader armies spreading in it like locusts, eating its riches and wiping out its plantations. All

this is happening at a time in which nations are attacking Muslims. In the light of the grave situation and the lack of support, we are obliged to discuss current events, and we should all agree on how to settle the matter.

No one argues today about three facts that are known to everyone:

First, for over seven years the United States has been occupying the lands of Islam in the holiest of places, the Arabian Peninsula, plundering its riches, dictating to its rulers, humiliating its people, terrorizing its neighbors, and turning its bases in the Peninsula into a spearhead through which to fight the neighboring Muslim peoples.

Second, despite the great devastation inflicted on the Iraqi people by the crusader-Zionist alliance, and despite the huge number of those killed, which has exceeded 1 million . . . despite all this, the Americans are once again trying to repeat the horrific massacres, as though they are not content with the protracted blockade imposed after the ferocious war or the fragmentation and devastation.

Third, if the Americans' aims behind these wars are religious and economic, the aim is also to serve the Jews' petty state and divert attention from its occupation of Jerusalem and murder of Muslims there.

All these crimes and sins committed by the Americans are a clear declaration of war on God, his messenger, and Muslims. On that basis, and in compliance with God's order, we issue the following fatwa to all Muslims:

The ruling to kill the Americans and their allies—civilians and military—is an individual duty for every Muslim who can do it in any country in which it is possible to do it, in order to liberate the al-Aqsa Mosque and the holy mosque [Mecca] from their grip, and in order for their armies to move out of all the lands of Islam, defeated and unable to threaten any Muslim. This is in accordance with the words of Almighty God.

We—with God's help—call on every Muslim who believes in God and wishes to be rewarded to comply with God's order to kill the Americans and plunder their money wherever and whenever they find it. We also call on Muslim ulema [a group of official Muslim scholars], leaders, youths, and soldiers to launch the raid on Satan's U.S. troops and the devil's supporters allying with them, and to displace those who are behind them so that they may learn a lesson.

Almighty God also says: "o ye who believe, what is the matter with you, that when ye are asked to go forth in the cause of God, ye cling so heavily to the earth! Do you prefer the life of this world to the hereafter? But little is the comfort of this life, as compared with the hereafter. Unless ye go forth, He will punish you with a grievous penalty, and put others in your place; but Him ye would not harm in the least. For God hath power over all things."

A Rebuttal to bin Laden's Claims
in his Declaration of War

1. Osama bin Laden is not trained as an Islamic scholar and has no officially accepted authority in the Islamic religion to issue a "fatwa" regarding religious doctrine or duties for Muslims.

2. Bin Laden's accusations against America are false. A small number of U.S. forces (6,000 troops) are in the deep deserts of Saudia Arabia many miles from either cities or Islamic holy places. They are in Saudi Arabia to protect that nation, its government, and Islamic population from the aggressive designs of the armies of the secular Iraqi dictator, Saddam Hussein. Far from "dictating to its rulers" or "humiliating its people" the U.S. troops are there at the pleasure of Saudi Arabia's leaders and barely contact its population because of the remote location of their bases. The reason that American forces still remain in the desert kingdom a decade after the conclusion of the War in the Gulf is due to the need to protect

Saudi Arabia against the continued Iraqi threats of aggression against its neighbours.

3. The reason for the devastation inflicted on Iraq's people is solely due to the evil aggression of Saddam Hussein and his continuing committment to the development of weapons of mass destruction in his attempt to ultimately destroy Israel and America. At the conclusion of the War in the Gulf in 1991 Iraq signed United Nation's resolutions that committed its government to allow UN weapons inspectors to examine all facilities and destroy any labs or plants making such deadly weapons. Hussein's rejection of his committments is the reason for the UN economic sanctions that have caused hardship in Iraq. However, the UN allowed Iraq to sell enough oil to provide billions in revenue annually to purchase essential food and medicine for their people. Tragically, Hussein has spent little of these oil revenues on medicine or food, but has chosen to invest these billions in building weapons of mass destruction and for payments to his Revolutionary Guard. Hussein's expulsion of the UN weapons inspectors in 1998 violated his written treaty obligations with the United Nations.

4. One of the strongest reasons for Osama's overwhelming hatred for Americans is that the United States supports Israel, a legal member of the United Nations, and supports Israel's right to exist within secure borders. His hatred of the Jews and the U.S.A. for supporting them is a fundamental motivation for his al Qaeda terrorist assaults on a variety of American targets over the last decade including the latest, the September 11, 2001 bombing of the World Trade Center twin towers in New York City and the Pentagon.

5. Osama bin Laden's tens of thousands of al Qaeda terrorists have declared war on America and Israel. They launched their most deadly attack against the West on September 11, 2001. However, America and its allies will destroy this dangerous threat to our freedom and our way of life. While it will take several years to complete this war, we will win it because there is no alternative. Our enemies are totally committed to our destruction with weapons of mass destruction when and

if they can obtain them. We can and must defeat this deadly terrorist threat to our freedom. If we have the resolve to "stay the course," our military skill, resources, technology, and the commitment of our professional armed forces to our freedom provide the means to win this war. Ultimately, we need to rely on the wisdom and providence of God to direct our leaders and our nation's efforts to preserve our treasured freedom from its deadly enemies.

APPENDIX B

The Case Against Osama bin Laden and his Al Qaeda Terror Network As Established by British Intelligence

[Released by Prime Minister Tony Blair of the United Kingdom]

This document does not purport to provide a prosecutable case against Usama Bin Laden in a court of law. Intelligence often cannot be used evidentially, due both to the strict rules of admissibility and to the need to protect the safety of sources. But on the basis of all the information available Her Majesty's Government is confident of its conclusions as expressed in this document.

[Note: this UK government document spells Osama bin Laden as Usama Bin Laden and al Qaeda as Al Qaida.]

RESPONSIBILITY FOR THE TERRORIST ATROCITIES
IN THE UNITED STATES, 11 SEPTEMBER 2001

INTRODUCTION

1. The clear conclusions reached by the government are:
   - Usama Bin Laden and Al Qaida, the terrorist network which he heads, planned and carried out the atrocities on 11 September 2001;
   - Usama Bin Laden and Al Qaida retain the will and resources to carry out further atrocities;
   - the United Kingdom, and United Kingdom nationals are potential targets; and
   - Usama Bin Laden and Al Qaida were able to commit these atrocities because of their close alliance with the Taleban régime, which allowed them to operate with impunity in pursuing their terrorist activity.
2. The material in respect of 1998 and the USS *Cole* comes from indictments and intelligence sources. The material in respect of 11 September comes from intelligence and the criminal investigation to date. The details of some aspects cannot be given, but the facts are clear from the intelligence.
3. The document does not contain the totality of the material known to HMG, given the continuing and absolute need to protect intelligence sources.

SUMMARY

4. The relevant facts show:

Background

   - Al Qaida is a terrorist organisation with ties to a global network, which has been in existence for over 10 years. It was founded, and has been led at all times, by Usama Bin Laden.
   - Usama Bin Laden and Al Qaida have been engaged in a jihad against the United States, and its allies. One of their stated aims is the murder of US citizens, and attacks on America's allies.
   - Usama Bin Laden and Al Qaida have been based in Afghanistan since 1996, but have a network of operations throughout

the world. The network includes training camps, warehouses, communication facilities and commercial operations able to raise significant sums of money to support its activity. That activity includes substantial exploitation of the illegal drugs trade from Afghanistan.

- Usama Bin Laden's Al Qaida and the Taleban régime have a close and mutually dependent alliance. Usama Bin Laden and Al Qaida provide the Taleban régime with material, financial and military support. They jointly exploit the drugs trade. The Taleban régime allows Bin Laden to operate his terrorist training camps and activities from Afghanistan, protects him from attacks from outside, and protects the drugs stockpiles. Usama Bin Laden could not operate his terrorist activities without the alliance and support of the Taleban régime. The Taleban's strength would be seriously weakened without Usama Bin Laden's military and financial support.
- Usama Bin Laden and Al Qaida have the capability to execute major terrorist attacks.
- Usama Bin Laden has claimed credit for the attack on US soldiers in Somalia in October 1993, which killed 18; for the attack on the US Embassies in Kenya and Tanzania in August 1998 which killed 224 and injured nearly 5000; and were linked to the attack on the USS *Cole* on 12 October 2000, in which 17 crew members were killed and 40 others injured.
- They have sought to acquire nuclear and chemical materials for use as terrorist weapons.

In relation to the terrorist attacks on 11 September

5. After 11 September we learned that, not long before, Bin Laden had indicated he was about to launch a major attack on America. The detailed planning for the terrorist attacks of 11 September was carried out by one of UBL's close associates. Of the 19 hijackers involved in 11 September 2001, it has already been established that at least three had links with Al Qaida. The attacks on 11 September 2001 were similar in both their ambition and intended impact to previous attacks undertaken by Usama Bin laden and Al Qaida, and also had features in common. In particular:
   - Suicide attackers

- Co-ordinated attacks on the same day
- The aim to cause maximum American casualties
- Total disregard for other casualties, including Muslim
- Meticulous long-term planning
- Absence of warning.
6. Al Qaida retains the capability and the will to make further attacks on the US and its allies, including the United Kingdom.
7. Al Qaida gives no warning of terrorist attacks.

THE FACTS

Usama Bin Laden and Al Qaida

8. In 1989 Usama Bin Laden, and others, founded an international terrorist group known as "Al Qaida" (the Base). At all times he has been the leader of Al Qaida.
9. From 1989 until 1991 Usama Bin Laden was based in Afghanistan and Peshawar, Pakistan. In 1991 he moved to Sudan, where he stayed until 1996. In that year he returned to Afghanistan, where he remains.

The Taleban Regime

10. The Taleban emerged from the Afghan refugee camps in Pakistan in the early 1990s. By 1996 they had captured Kabul. They are still engaged in a bloody civil war to control the whole of Afghanistan. They are led by Mullah Omar.
11. In 1996 Usama Bin Laden moved back to Afghanistan. He established a close relationship with Mullah Omar, and threw his support behind the Taleban. Usama Bin Laden and the Taleban régime have a close alliance on which both depend for their continued existence. They also share the same religious values and vision.
12. Usama Bin Laden has provided the Taleban régime with troops, arms, and money to fight the Northern Alliance. He is closely involved with Taleban military training, planning and operations. He has representatives in the Taleban military command structure. He has also given infrastruture assistance and humanitarian aid. Forces under the control of Usama Bin Laden have fought alongside the Taleban in the civil war in Afghanistan.
13. Omar has provided Bin Laden with a safe haven in which to

operate, and has allowed him to establish terrorist training camps in Afghanistan. They jointly exploit the Afghan drugs trade. In return for active Al Qaida support, the Taleban allow Al Qaida to operate freely, including planning, training and preparing for terrorist activity. In addition the Taleban provide security for the stockpiles of drugs.

14. Since 1996, when the Taleban captured Kabul, the United States government has consistently raised with them a whole range of issues, including humanitarian aid and terrorism. Well before 11 September 2001 they had provided evidence to the Taleban of the responsibility of Al Qaida for the terrorist attacks in East Africa. This evidence had been provided to senior leaders of the Taleban at their request.

15. The United States government had made it clear to the Taleban regime that Al Qaida had murdered US citizens, and planned to murder more. The US offered to work with the Taleban to expel the terrorists from Afghanistan. These talks, which have been continuing since 1996, have failed to produce any results.

16. In June 2001, in the face of mounting evidence of the Al Qaida threat, the United States warned the Taleban that it had the right to defend itself and that it would hold the régime responsible for attacks against US citizens by terrorists sheltered in Afghanistan.

17. In this, the United States had the support of the United Nations. The Security Council, in Resolution 1267, condemned Usama Bin Laden for sponsoring international terrorism and operating a network of terrorist camps, and demanded that the Taleban surrender Usama Bin Laden without further delay so that he could be brought to justice.

18. Despite the evidence provided by the US of the responsibility of Usama Bin Laden and Al Qaida for the 1998 East Africa bombings, despite the accurately perceived threats of further atrocities, and despite the demands of the United Nations, the Taleban régime responded by saying no evidence existed against Usama Bin Laden, and that neither he nor his network would be expelled.

19. A former Government official in Afghanistan has described the Taleban and Usama Bin Laden as "two sides of the same coin:

Usama cannot exist in Afghanistan without the Taleban and the Taleban cannot exist without Usama."

Al Qaida

20. Al Qaida is dedicated to opposing 'un-Islamic' governments in Muslim countries with force and violence.

21. Al Qaida virulently opposes the United States. Usama Bin Laden has urged and incited his followers to kill American citizens, in the most unequivocal terms.

22. On 12 October 1996 he issued a declaration of jihad as follows:
"The people of Islam have suffered from aggression, iniquity and injustice imposed by the Zionist-Crusader alliance and their collaborators . . .
It is the duty now on every tribe in the Arabian peninsula to fight jihad and cleanse the land from these Crusader occupiers. Their wealth is booty to those who kill them.
My Muslim brothers: your brothers in Palestine and in the land of the two Holy Places [i.e. Saudi Arabia] *are calling upon your help and asking you to take part in fighting against the enemy – the Americans and the Israelis. They are asking you to do whatever you can to expel the enemies out of the sanctities of Islam."*
Later in the same year he said that
"terrorising the American occupiers [of Islamic Holy Places] *is a religious and logical obligation."*
In February 1998 he issued and signed a 'fatwa' which included a decree to all Muslims:
". . . the killing of Americans and their civilian and military allies is a religious duty for each and every Muslim to be carried out in whichever country they are until Al Aqsa mosque has been liberated from their grasp and until their armies have left Muslim lands."
In the same 'fatwa' he called on Muslim scholars and their leaders and their youths to *"launch an attack on the American soldiers of Satan."*
and concluded:
"We—with God's help—call on every Muslim who believes in God and wishes to be rewarded to comply with God's order to kill Americans and plunder their money whenever and wherever they find it. We also call on Muslims . . . to launch the raid on

Satan's US troops and the devil's supporters allying with them, and to displace those who are behind them."

When asked, in 1998, about obtaining chemical or nuclear weapons he said:

"acquiring such weapons for the defence of Muslims [was] a religious duty."

In an interview aired on Al Jazira (Doha, Qatar) television he stated:

"Our enemy is every American male, whether he is directly fighting us or paying taxes."

In two interviews broadcast on US television in 1997 and 1998 he referred to the terrorists who carried out the earlier attack on the World Trade Center in 1993 as *"role models"*. He went on to exhort his followers *"to take the fighting to America."*

23. From the early 1990s Usama Bin Laden has sought to obtain nuclear and chemical materials for use as weapons of terror.

24. Although US targets are Al Qaida's priority, it also explicitly threatens the United States' allies. References to *"Zionist-Crusader alliance and their collaborators,"* and to *"Satan's US troops and the devil's supporters allying with them"* are references which unquestionably include the United Kingdom.

25. There is a continuing threat. Based on our experience of the way the network has operated in the past, other cells, like those that carried out the terrorist attacks on 11 September, must be assumed to exist.

26. Al Qaida functions both on its own and through a network of other terrorist organisations. These include Egyptian Islamic Jihad and other north African Islamic extremist terrorist groups, and a number of other jihadi groups in other countries including the Sudan, Yemen, Somalia, Pakistan and India. Al Qaida also maintains cells and personnel in a number of other countries to facilitate its activities.

27. Usama Bin Laden heads the Al Qaida network. Below him is a body known as the Shura, which includes representatives of other terrorist groups, such as Egyptian Islamic Jihad leader Ayman Zawahiri and prominent lieutenants of Bin Laden such as Abu Hafs Al-Masri. Egyptian Islamic Jihad has, in effect, merged with Al Qaida.

28. In addition to the Shura, Al Qaida has several groups dealing with military, media, financial and Islamic issues.

29. Mohamed Atef is a member of the group that deals with military and terrorist operations. His duties include principal responsibility for training Al Qaida members.

30. Members of Al Qaida must make a pledge of allegiance to follow the orders of Usama Bin Laden.

31. A great deal of evidence about Usama Bin Laden and Al Qaida has been made available in the US indictment for earlier crimes.

32. Since 1989, Usama Bin Laden has conducted substantial financial and business transactions on behalf of Al Qaida and in pursuit of its goals. These include purchasing land for training camps, purchasing warehouses for the storage of items, including explosives, purchasing communications and electronics equipment, and transporting currency and weapons to members of Al Qaida and associated terrorist groups in countries throughout the world.

33. Since 1989 Usama Bin Laden has provided training camps and guest houses in Afghanistan, Pakistan, the Sudan, Somalia and Kenya for the use of Al Qaida and associated terrorist groups. We know from intelligence that there are currently at least a dozen camps across Afghanistan, of which at least four are used for training terrorists.

34. Since 1989, Usama Bin Laden has established a series of businesses to provide income for Al Qaida, and to provide cover for the procurement of explosives, weapons and chemicals, and for the travel of Al Qaida operatives. The businesses have included a holding company known as 'Wadi Al Aqiq', a construction business known as 'Al Hijra', an agricultural business known as 'Al Themar Al Mubaraka', and investment companies known as 'Ladin International' and 'Taba Investments'.

Usama Bin Laden and previous attacks

35. In 1992 and 1993 Mohamed Atef travelled to Somalia on several occasions for the purpose of organising violence against United States and United Nations troops then stationed in Somalia. On each occasion he reported back to Usama Bin Laden, at his base in the Riyadh district of Khartoum.

36. In the spring of 1993 Atef, Saif al Adel, another senior member

of Al Qaida, and other members began to provide military training to Somali tribes for the purpose of fighting the United Nations forces.

37. On 3 and 4 October 1993 operatives of Al Qaida participated in the attack on US military personnel serving in Somalia as part of the operation 'Restore Hope.' Eighteen US military personnel were killed in the attack.

38. From 1993 members of Al Qaida began to live in Nairobi and set up businesses there, including Asma Ltd, and Tanzanite King. They were regularly visited there by senior members of Al Qaida, in particular by Atef and Abu Ubadiah al Banshiri.

39. Beginning in the latter part of 1993, members of Al Qaida in Kenya began to discuss the possibility of attacking the US Embassy in Nairobi in retaliation for US participation in Operation Restore Hope in Somalia. Ali Mohamed, a US citizen and admitted member of Al Qaida, surveyed the US Embassy as a possible target for a terrorist attack. He took photographs and made sketches, which he presented to Usama Bin Laden while Bin Laden was in Sudan. He also admitted that he had trained terrorists for Al Qaida in Afghanistan in the early 1990s, and that those whom he trained included many involved in the East African bombings in August 1998.

40. In June or July 1998, two Al Qaida operatives, Fahid Mohammed Ali Msalam and Sheik Ahmed Salim Swedan, purchased a Toyota truck and made various alterations to the back of the truck.

41. In early August 1998, operatives of Al Qaida gathered in 43, New Runda Estates, Nairobi to execute the bombing of the US Embassy in Nairobi.

42. On 7 August 1998, Assam, a Saudi national and Al Qaida operative, drove the Toyota truck to the US embassy. There was a large bomb in the back of the truck.

43. Also in the truck was Mohamed Rashed Daoud Al 'Owali, another Saudi. He, by his own confession, was an Al Qaida operative, who from about 1996 had been trained in Al Qaida camps in Afghanistan in explosives, hijacking, kidnapping, assassination, and intelligence techniques. With Usama Bin Laden's express permission, he fought alongside the Taleban in Afghanistan. He had met Usama Bin Laden personally in 1996 and asked for another 'mission.' Usama Bin Laden sent

him to East Africa after extensive specialised training at camps in Afghanistan.

44. As the truck approached the Embassy, Al 'Owali got out and threw a stun grenade at a security guard. Assam drove the truck up to the rear of the embassy. He got out and then detonated the bomb, which demolished a multi-storey secretarial college and severely damaged the US embassy, and the Co-operative bank building. The bomb killed 213 people and injured 4500. Assam was killed in the explosion.

45. Al 'Owali expected the mission to end in his death. He had been willing to die for Al Qaida. But at the last minute he ran away from the bomb truck and survived. He had no money, passport or plan to escape after the mission, because he had expected to die.

46. After a few days, he called a telephone number in Yemen to have money transferred to him in Kenya. The number he rang in Yemen was contacted by Usama Bin Laden's phone on the same day as Al 'Owali was arranging to get the money.

47. Another person arrested in connection with the Nairobi bombing was Mohamed Sadeek Odeh. He admitted to his involvement. He identified the principal participants in the bombing. He named three other persons, all of whom were Al Qaida or Egyptian Islamic Jihad members.

48. In Dar es Salaam the same day, at about the same time, operatives of Al Qaida detonated a bomb at the US embassy, killing 11 people. The Al Qaida operatives involved included Mustafa Mohamed Fadhil and Khaflan Khamis Mohamed. The bomb was carried in a Nissan Atlas truck, which Ahmed Khfaklan Ghailani and Sheikh Ahmed Salim Swedan, two Al Qaida operatives, had purchased in July 1998, in Dar es Salaam.

49. Khaflan Khamis Mohamed was arrested for the bombing. He admitted membership of Al Qaida, and implicated other members of Al Qaida in the bombing.

50. On 7 and 8 August 1998, two other members of Al Qaida disseminated claims of responsibility for the two bombings by sending faxes to media organisations in Paris, Doha in Qatar, and Dubai in the United Arab Emirates.

51. Additional evidence of the involvement of Al Qaida in the East African bombings came from a search conducted in London of

several residences and businesses belonging to Al Qaida and Egyptian Islamic Jihad members. In those searches a number of documents were found including claims of responsibility for the East African bombings in the name of a fictitious group, 'the Islamic Army for the liberation of the Holy Places.'

52. Al 'Owali, the would-be suicide bomber, admitted he was told to make a videotape of himself using the name of the same fictitious group.

53. The faxed claims of responsibility were traced to a telephone number, which had been in contact with Usama Bin Laden's cell phone. The claims disseminated to the press were clearly written by someone familiar with the conspiracy. They stated that the bombings had been carried out by two Saudis in Kenya, and one Egyptian in Dar es Salaam. They were probably sent before the bombings had even taken place. They referred to two Saudis dying in the Nairobi attack. In fact, because Al 'Owali fled at the last minute, only one Saudi died.

54. On 22 December 1998 Usama Bin Laden was asked by *Time* magazine whether he was responsible for the August 1998 attacks. He replied:

"The International Islamic Jihad Front for the jihad against the US and Israel has, by the grace of God, issued a crystal clear fatwa calling on the Islamic nation to carry on Jihad aimed at liberating the holy sites. The nation of Mohammed has responded to this appeal. If instigation for jihad against the Jews and the Americans . . . is considered to be a crime, then let history be a witness that I am a criminal. Our job is to instigate and, by the grace of God, we did that, and certain people responded to this instigation."

He was asked if he knew the attackers:

". . . those who risked their lives to earn the pleasure of God are real men. They managed to rid the Islamic nation of disgrace. We hold them in the highest esteem."

And what the US could expect of him:

". . . any thief or criminal who enters another country to steal should expect to be exposed to murder at any time . . . The US knows that I have attacked it, by the grace of God, for more than ten years now . . . God knows that we have been pleased by the killing of American soldiers [in Somalia in 1993]. *This was achieved by the grace of God and the efforts of the mujahideen . . . Hostility towards America*

is a religious duty and we hope to be rewarded for it by God. I am confident that Muslims will be able to end the legend of the so-called superpower that is America."

55. In December 1999 a terrorist cell linked to Al Qaida was discovered trying to carry out attacks inside the United States. An Algerian, Ahmed Ressam, was stopped at the US-Canadian border and over 100 lbs of bomb making material was found in his car. Ressam admitted he was planning to set off a large bomb at Los Angeles International airport on New Year's Day. He said that he had received terrorist training at Al Qaida camps in Afghanistan and then been instructed to go abroad and kill US civilians and military personnel.

56. On 3 January 2000, a group of Al Qaida members, and other terrorists who had trained in Al Qaida camps in Afghanistan, attempted to attack a US destroyer with a small boat loaded with explosives. Their boat sank, aborting the attack.

57. On 12 October 2000, however, the USS *Cole* was struck by an explosive-laden boat while refuelling in Aden harbour. Seventeen crew were killed, and 40 injured.

58. Several of the perpetrators of the *Cole* attack (mostly Yemenis and Saudis) were trained at Usama Bin Laden's camps in Afghanistan. Al 'Owali has identified the two commanders of the attack on the USS *Cole* as having participated in the planning and preparation for the East African embassy bombings.

59. In the months before the September 11 attacks, propaganda videos were distributed throughout the Middle East and Muslim world by Al Qaida, in which Usama Bin Laden and others were shown encouraging Muslims to attack American and Jewish targets.

60. Similar videos, extolling violence against the United States and other targets, were distributed before the East African embassy attacks in August 1998.

Usama Bin Laden and the 11 September attacks

61. Nineteen men have been identified as the hijackers from the passenger lists of the four planes hijacked on 11 September 2001. At least three of them have already been positively identified as associates of Al Qaida. One has been identified as playing key roles in both the East African embassy attacks and the USS

Cole attack. Investigations continue into the backgrounds of all the hijackers.

62. From intelligence sources, the following facts have been established subsequent to 11 September; for intelligence reasons, the names of associates, though known, are not given.

   • In the run-up to 11 September, Bin Laden was mounting a concerted propaganda campaign amongst like-minded groups of people—including videos and documentation—justifying attacks on Jewish and American targets; and claiming that those who died in the course of them were carrying out God's work.

   • We have learned, subsequent to 11 September, that Bin Laden himself asserted shortly before 11 September that he was preparing a major attack on America.

   • In August and early September close associates of Bin Laden were warned to return to Afghanistan from other parts of the world by 10 September.

   • Immediately prior to 11 September some known associates of Bin Laden were naming the date for action as on or around 11 September.

   • Since 11 September we have learned that one of Bin Laden's closest and most senior associates was responsible for the detailed planning of the attacks.

   • There is evidence of a very specific nature relating to the guilt of Bin Laden and his associates that is too sensitive to release.

63. Usama Bin Laden remains in charge, and the mastermind, of Al Qaida. In Al Qaida, an operation on the scale of the 11 September attacks would have been approved by Usama Bin Laden himself.

64. The modus operandi of 11 September was entirely consistent with previous attacks. Al Qaida's record of atrocities is characterised by meticulous long term planning, a desire to inflict mass casualties, suicide bombers, and multiple simultaneous attacks.

65. The attacks of 11 September 2001 are entirely consistent with the scale and sophistication of the planning which went into the attacks on the East African Embassies and the USS *Cole*. No warnings were given for these three attacks, just as there was none on 11 September.

66. Al Qaida operatives, in evidence given in the East African Embassy bomb trials, have described how the group spends years preparing for an attack. They conduct repeated surveillance, patiently gather materials, and identify and vet operatives, who have the skills to participate in the attack and the willingness to die for their cause.

67. The operatives involved in the 11 September atrocities attended flight schools, used flight simulators to study the controls of larger aircraft and placed potential airports and routes under surveillance.

68. Al Qaida's attacks are characterised by total disregard for innocent lives, including Muslims. In an interview after the East African bombings, Usama Bin Laden insisted that the need to attack the United States excused the killing of other innocent civilians, Muslim and non-Muslim alike.

69. No other organisation has both the motivation and the capability to carry out attacks like those of the 11 September—only the Al Qaida network under Usama Bin Laden.

Conclusion

70. The attacks of the 11 September 2001 were planned and carried out by Al Qaida, an organisation whose head is Usama Bin Laden. That organisation has the will, and the resources, to execute further attacks of similar scale. Both the United States and its close allies are targets for such attacks. The attack could not have occurred without the alliance between the Taleban and Usama Bin Laden, which allowed Bin Laden to operate freely in Afghanistan, promoting, planning and executing terrorist activity.

Selected Bibliography

Aburish, Saïd K. *Arafat*. London: Bloomsbury, 1998.

Aburish, Saïd K. *Saddam Hussein*. New York: Bloomsbury, 2000.

Adams, James. *Secret Armies*. London: Pan Books, 1988.

Adams, James. *The Next World War*. New York: Simon & Schuster, 1998.

Alexander, Yonah, and Michael S. Swetnam. *Usama Bin Laden's al -Qaida: Profile of a Terrorist Network*. Ardsley: Transnational Publishing, 2001.

Algosaibi, Ghazi A. *The Gulf Crisis*. London: Kegan Paul International, 1993.

Arendt, Hannah. *The Origins of Totalitarianism*. Cleveland: The Word Publishing Company, 1969.

Attali, Jacques. *Millennium*. Trans. Leila Conners and Nathan Gardels. New York: Times Books, 1990.

Bamford, James. *The Puzzle Palace*. Middlesex, England: Penguin Books, 1987.

Bennett, Ramon. *Philistine*. Keno: The Shekinah Books, 1995.

Bernstein, Richard, and Ross H. Munro. *The Coming Conflict with China*. New York: Knopf, 1997.

Bodansky, Yossef. *Bin Laden*. Roseville: Prima Publishing, 2001.

Bodansky, Yossef. *Islamic Anti-Semitism As A Political Instrument*. Houston: The Freeman Center for Strategic Studies, 1999.

Bowen, William M., Jr. *Globalism: America's Demise*. Shreveport, La.: Huntington House, 1984.

Bradley, John. *World War III—Strategies, Tactics and Weapons*. New York: Cresent Books, 1982.

Bresler, Fenton. *Interpol*. Toronto: Penguin, 1992.

Brown, Lester R., et al. *State of the World*. New York: W. W. Norton, 1997.

Brown, Rebecca. *Prepare for War*. New Kensington, Pa.: Whitaker House, 1992.

Childers, Erskine, and Brian Urquhart. *Renewing the United Nations System*. Uppsala, Sweden: Dag Hammarskjold Foundation, 1994.

Cockburn, Andrew, and Patrick Cockburn. *Out of the Ashes*. New York: HarperPerennial, 2000.

Coughlin, Con. *A Golden Basin Full of Scorpions*. London: Little, Brown, 1997.

Cuddy, Dennis Laurence. *Now Is the Dawning of the New Age New World Order*. Oklahoma City: Hearthstone Publishing, 1991.

Darwish, Adel, and Gregory Alexander. *Unholy Babylon*. New York: St. Martin's, 1991.

Davidson, Elishua. *Islam, Israel, and the Last Days*. Eugene: Harvest House, 1991.

de Marenches, Count, and David A. Andelman. *The Fourth World War*. New York: William Morrow, 1992.

Ellisen, Stanley A. *Who Owns the Land?*. Sisters, Oreg.: Multnomah, 1991.

Epperson, A. Ralph. *The New World Order*. Tucson: Publius Press, 1990.

Fialka, John J. *War By Other Means*. New York: W. W. Norton, 1997.

Gazit, Shlomo, and Zeev Eytan. *The Middle East Military Balance*. Jerusalem: Jerusalem Post Press, 1992.

Gill, Stephen. *American Hegemony and the Trilateral Commission*. Cambridge, Mass.: Cambridge University Press, 1991.

Gilbert, Martin. *The Arab-Israeli Conflict: Its History in Maps*. Jerusalem: Steimatzky, 1985.

Golitsyn, Anatoliy. *New Lies for Old*. New York: Dodd, Mead and Company, 1984.

Graham, Billy. *Approaching Hoofbeats: The Four Horsemen of the Apocalypse.* Waco: Word, 1983.

Herman, Edward, and Gerry O'Sullivan. *The "Terrorism" Industry.* New York: Pantheon, 1989.

Hindson, Ed. *Approaching Armageddon.* Eugene: Harvest House, 1997.

Hindson, Ed. *The New World Order.* Wheaton: Victor, 1991.

Hunt, Dave. *Global Peace.* Eugene: Harvest House Publishers, 1990.

Kah, Gary H. *En Route to Global Occupation.* Lafayette, La.: Huntington House, 1992.

Kahn, Herman. *Thinking about the Unthinkable in the 1980s.* New York: Simon & Schuster, 1984.

Keegan, John, and Andrew Wheatcroft. *Zones of Conflict: An Atlas of Future Wars.* New York: Simon & Schuster, 1986.

Kidron, Michael, and Ronald Segal. *The New State of the World.* New York: Simon & Schuster, 1991.

Kincaid, Cliff. *Global Bondage.* Lafayette, La.: Huntington House, 1995.

King, Alexander, and Bertrand Schneider. *The First Global Revolution.* New York: Pantheon, 1991.

Kremers, Marion F. *God Intervenes in the Middle East.* Shippensburg, Pa.: Companion Press, 1992.

Lewis, David Allen, and Jim Fletcher. *The Last War.* Greenforest, Ark.: New Leaf Press, 2001.

Lindsay, Hal. *The Final Battle.* Palos Verdes, Calif.: Western Front, 1995.

Livingstone, Neil C. *The Cult of Counterterrorism.* Lexington: Lexington Books, 1990.

McAlvany, Donald, S. *Toward a New World Order.* Oklahoma City: Hearthstone, 1990.

Mesorah Publications. *Ezekiel: A New Commentary Anthologized from Talmudic, Midrashic and Rabbinical Sources.* Brooklyn: Mesorah Publications, 1980.

Miller, Charles W. *Today's Technology in Bible Prophecy.* Lansing, Mich., 1990.

Mordecai, Victor. *Is Fanatic Islam a Global Threat?.* Springfield, Missouri, 1996.

Mylroie, Laurie. *Study of Revenge*. Washington, D.C.: AEI Press, 2000.

Pacepa, Ion. *Red Horizons*. Washington, D.C.: Regnery Gateway, 1987.

Peccei, Aurelio. *One Hundred Pages for the Future*. New York: New American Library, 1981.

Pentecost, Dwight. *Things to Come*. Grand Rapids: Dunham, 1958.

Peters, Joan. *From Time Immemorial: The Origins of the Arab-Israeli Conflict Over Palestine*. New York: Harper & Row, 1984.

Peterson, Jeannie, ed. *The Aftermath:*. New York: Pantheon, 1983.

Pink, Arthur W. *The Antichrist*. Grand Rapids: Kregel, 1988.

Price, Randall. *Jerusalem in Prophecy*. Eugene, Oreg.: Harvest House, 1998.

Ray, James Lee. *Global Politics*. Boston: Houghton Mifflin, 1990.

Reagan, David. *The Master Plan*. Eugene, Oreg.: Harvest House, 1993.

Record, Jeffrey. *Hollow Victory*. New York: Brassey's, 1993.

Robertson, Pat. *The New World Order*. Waco, Tex.: Word, 1991.

Saleem, Musa. *The Muslims and the New World Order*. London: ISDS Books, 1993.

Schmitt, Gary. *Silent Warfare*. New York: Brassey's, 1993.

Schneier, Bruce, and David Banisar. *The Electronic Privacy Papers*. New York: Wiley Computer Publishing, 1997.

Schwartau, Winn. *Information Warfare*. New York: Thunder's Mouth Press, 1994.

Sklar, Holly, ed. *Trilateralism*. Montreal: Black Rose Books, 1980.

Smith, Wilbur M. *Israeli/Arab Conflict and the Bible*. Glendale, Calif.: Regal Books, 1967.

Tinbergen, Jan. *Reshaping the International Order: A Report to the Club of Rome*. Scarborough, Canada: The New American Library of Canada, 1976.

Toffler, Alvin, and Heidi Toffler. *War and Anti-War*. Boston: Little, Brown, 1993.

United States. The Report of The Commission on Global Governance. *Our Global Neighborhood*. New York: Oxford University Press, 1995.

Van Impe, Jack. *2001: On the Edge of Eternity*. Waco, Tex.: Word, 1996.

Walvoord, John F. *The Nations in Prophecy*. Grand Rapids, Mich.: Zondervan, 1976.

Warner, Philip. *The SAS*. London: Sphere Books, 1983.